Private Property

Private Property

THE HISTORY OF AN IDEA

BY

RICHARD SCHLATTER

Professor of History, Rutgers University

NEW YORK / RUSSELL & RUSSELL

FIRST PUBLISHED, 1951, BY
GEORGE ALLEN & UNWIN LTD., LONDON
REISSUED, 1973, BY RUSSELL & RUSSELL
A DIVISION OF ATHENEUM PUBLISHERS, INC.
BY ARRANGEMENT WITH RICHARD SCHLATTER
L. C. CATALOG CARD NO: 72-85007
ISBN 0-8462-1697-3
PRINTED IN THE UNITED STATES OF AMERICA

Preface

☆

This essay was written during the last years of the war while I was teaching American history to young soldiers and sailors in Harvard College. It served the purpose, for me, of demonstrating the essential continuity of Western civilization, and the importance of the traditional concepts of man and society which the Nazis were attempting to destroy.

Since the essay was written, new editions of some of the works cited in the text, and new works relevant to the subject, have appeared. But because this is an essay, rather than an exhaustive work, I have not altered my references except in a few cases where the argument was affected.

It is a pleasure to acknowledge here the courteous co-operation of the staffs of the libraries at Harvard, Rutgers, and Princeton. I am especially indebted to the Rutgers University Research Fund whose generous financial assistance made possible the preparation and publication of the manuscript. My severest and best critics have been Professor and Mrs. Perry Miller, the late Professor F. O. Matthiessen, Professor David Owen, and Mr. Paul Sweezy. My wife may never read this book, but it would not have been written without her help.

Neshanic Station, N.J. RICHARD SCHLATTER

CONTENTS

☆

CHAPTER ONE

☆

Greece

Let us consider what should be our arrangements about property: should the citizens of the perfect state have their possessions in common or not? Aristotle, *Politics*, II, 5.

Opponents of private property, wrote Jean Bodin in the sixteenth century, are foolhardy dreamers. 'In taking away these words of Mine and Thine, they ruine the foundation of all Commonweales, the which were chiefly established to yeeld unto every man that which is his own.' Since Bodin wrote, many men have thought that the protection of private property is in fact the primary task of governments, and that the wholesale abolition of rights of ownership is the essential characteristic of social revolution. But if justice is the rendering to each man of that which is his own, if the determination of mine and thine is the principal object of political wisdom, the political scientist must elucidate the principles of ownership. What reasons can a man give for calling a thing his own? How are we to distinguish valid claims of ownership from those which are unjust? A history of the answers to these questions is a history of the theory of property.

Nearly two hundred years ago, Blackstone observed that the theory of property deserves our attention:

There are very few that will give themselves the trouble to consider the original and foundation of this right [of property]. Pleased as we are with the possession, we seem afraid to look back to the means by which it was acquired, as if fearful of some defect in our title; or at best we are satisfied with the decision of the laws in our favour, without examining the reason or authority upon which these laws have been built. . . . But when law is to be considered not only as a matter of practice, but also as a rational science, it cannot be improper or useless to examine more deeply the rudiments and grounds of these positive constitutions of society. *Commentaries*, Bk. II.

No doubt the eighteenth century preferred rational treatises expounding the *theory* of property to historical essays describing the *theories* of property. But nowadays we are all historians. We know that the institution of property has had its history and that that history has not yet come to an end. We know that 'intellectual production changes its character as material production is changed.' We begin with the knowledge that there must be as many theories of property as there have been systems of property rights. Consequently we abandon the search for the true theory of property and study the theories of past ages. Only thus can we learn how to construct a theory suitable to our own circumstances.

But if each age has, and will have, to manufacture a theory appropriate to its own needs, it is also true that thinking about property has always moved within the framework of certain common forms and general ideas. Men have always wondered if private ownership is natural. 'Natural' is sometimes taken to mean 'primitive,' and philosophers have sought, both in the legends of the Golden Age and in the accounts of anthropologists, to discover what forms of property are natural in the sense that primitive man recognized them. But 'natural' can also mean 'fully developed or perfect,' and philosophers have constructed imaginary Utopias in an attempt to discover what forms of property are natural in the sense that they would be adopted in perfect societies. Other men have thought that no one form of property is natural in any sense of that word, but that all property is conventional. Then the philosophical problem is to investigate the origin and validity of the conventions upon which ownership rests. But whether property is thought to be natural or conventional, the question always arises as to what kind of ownership is most suitable to the nature of men. Most speculation has proceeded upon the assumption that property ought to be equally or unequally divided according to whether men are by nature equal or unequal. In any case, ideas of human nature (and equality) have always been part of the framework of theories of property. Finally, discussions of property often contain some reference to creative work; the notion that a man owns what his labour has created is an ancient one, although it has been popular only in modern times.

As in so much of all our thinking, so in our thinking about property we are still using the counters which were invented by Greek philosophers more than two thousand years ago. The thinkers of Greece asked whether property was natural or conventional. They speculated about the proper relation between human nature, equal or unequal, and the distribution of property. They had, it is true, very little to say about the relation between ownership and work. Perhaps the explanation is that in societies where slaves do all the work and masters do all the owning, that relationship is hard to conceive. But with this exception, the philosophers of Greece built the framework on which all subsequent theories of property have been constructed. Plato examined the legends of the Golden Age and Aristotle studied the customs of the barbarians to learn what primitive property had been; both men tried to describe the perfect form of property; and both speculated about human nature and equality in their relation to property.

Since Plato and Aristotle wrote, no one has been able to think about property without asking, as they asked, whether or not it is natural. But it is also true that few theorists have defined 'natural' in exactly the same way, or have agreed as to precisely which of the many kinds of property are natural and which are not.[1]

Plato described two ideal systems of property: the first for the perfect state of the *Republic*, the second for the more practical state of the *Laws*. Since the *Republic* is more an allegory of the human soul than a political treatise, we cannot say confidently that its theory of property was meant to be a serious contribution to political thought. But whatever Plato himself intended, the *Republic* has been interpreted as a political treatise since the days of Aristotle; whatever Plato in fact was, later men have thought that he was some kind of communist. In the history of the theory of

[1] *Primitivism and Related Ideas in Antiquity*, by Arthur O. Lovejoy and George Boas, Baltimore, 1935, is an exhaustive study of the concepts of nature, and the primitive state of nature, in the ancient world.

property, it is not what Plato meant, but what men thought he meant, that is important.

In the perfect state all property is, apparently, privately owned by the citizens of the lowest class—farmers, artisans, and merchants—which produces all the wealth and which is excluded from all participation in politics. The rulers of the state will regulate buying and selling, will see to it that wealth and poverty, 'the two causes of the deterioration of the arts,' do not creep into the city, and will educate all citizens to act in accordance with the proverb that 'friends have all things in common.'[1] Beyond these general rules Plato gives us no details of the property arrangements of the lowest class in his ideal state.

The rulers, the class of Guardians, have no private property. They live together in barracks; their food and clothes, of the simplest kind, are provided for them by the lowest class; they are forbidden the use of money, gold and silver. These economic arrangements, together with the abolition of the family, make it impossible for any ruler to call anything 'his own.' And the way of life of the Guardians is the ideal; they are the ideal men. Apparently, then, communism was, in Plato's opinion, the best way of arranging the relation between men and things. But since he thought that even under ideal conditions the majority of men would never attain the perfect wisdom of his Guardians, he granted to the lowest class in the perfect state the permission to own property individually, subject to the far-reaching regulations laid down by the rulers.

Plato repeats in the *Laws* that communism is the best scheme for managing property and then goes on to describe a second-best state which will be more suited to satisfy men as they are, not as they could be. The citizens of this, like the Guardians in the *Republic*, form an aristocratic class which monopolizes all political power and is supported by the other members of the state. But the citizens of the *Laws* each own individually an equal portion of the land which is worked by privately-owned slaves. Elaborate rules of inheritance and bequest, and regulations to prevent the

[1] 421, 424, 425. Jowett translation.

number of citizens from increasing or decreasing, assure that the equal division of the land will continue from generation to generation. Trade and manufacture, carried on by foreigners under strict supervision, are forbidden to the citizens, as is the lending of money on interest. If in spite of these regulations a citizen manages to acquire a fortune more than four times as large as his original landed estate, he must turn over the surplus to the state.

Aristotle's ideal state, described in Book VII of the *Politics*, is similar to the state of the *Laws*. The citizens own the land, but the productive work is done by slaves and foreigners. However, Aristotle stipulates that half the land of the state is to be owned by the citizens in common and worked by publicly-owned slaves; the produce of the public land is to be used to supply the common meals, in which all citizens partake, and to provide for the expenses of religion. The remaining half of the land is to be divided equally among the citizens and worked by their privately-owned slaves.[1]

The similarity between the Aristotelian and Platonic ideals of property is striking, but it does not alter the fact that Plato's ideal, after all, was communism while Aristotle was the defender of private property. To make an adequate definition of their ideas about property we must therefore turn to those sections of the *Politics* where Aristotle speaks in detail of the virtues and disadvantages of common and private ownership.

Book II of the *Politics* opens with a discussion of various ideal societies which other Greek thinkers had already proposed. The basic problem, according to Aristotle, is to determine the relation of the parts to the whole, of the individuals to the community.

[1] The picture of property relationships in the ideal state is somewhat vague, but from what Aristotle says elsewhere in the *Politics* we may be sure that interest on capital, and all but the simplest forms of trade are to be forbidden, even to the non-citizens and slaves. There is even no explicit statement that the private estates are divided equally among the citizens, but most commentators agree that it is implied together with rules to preserve the equality from generation to generation. See Ernest Barker, *The Political Thought of Plato and Aristotle*, p. 397, n. 1, London, 1906.

Three alternatives are conceivable: individuals can have (1) all things, or (2) nothing in common, or (3) some things in common and some not. The second is, however, impossible since by definition a community implies that its members have at least some things in common. Thus the first and the third are the real alternatives, and Socrates has said the first is the better. Was Socrates right? Aristotle thinks not and proceeds to give his reasons.

First, Socrates defends communism on the premise 'that the greater the unity of the state the better.' But this is an error since it is obvious 'that a state may at length attain such a degree of unity as to be no longer a state.' A state is a plurality made up of different kinds of individuals: it ceases to exist if all the individuals are exactly alike and are so dissolved in the whole that they cease to be individuals at all. Here Aristotle is using his broad philosophical principle that the general exists only in its particulars, in opposition to the Platonic principle that the particular exists only as a part of the general. If the particulars, the individuals who make up the community, cease to exist, then the general, the community, will also cease to exist. Socrates' idea of communism, says Aristotle, tries to do away with the individual and thus ends by destroying the state altogether.

The same argument is used to prove that the unity which communism is supposed to support is not only undesirable but also impossible. Socrates has said that unity will follow from the fact 'of all men saying "mine" and "not mine" at the same instant of time.' But this, says Aristotle, is ambiguous. When an individual says 'this is mine' he means either that the thing belongs to him alone or that it is the collective property of a group of which he is a member: he cannot mean both things at the same time. Socrates' unity, however, rests upon the assumption that he can mean both things at the same time and is, consequently, impossible. 'That all persons call the same thing mine in the sense in which each does so may be a fine thing, but it is impracticable. . . .' The gist of Aristotle's argument is again that in the nature of things the particular individual really exists; where there are no individuals—no persons who can say 'this is mine and not yours'—there can be no true community.

Up to this point, Aristotle has been arguing not so much against the principle of communism as against the extreme unification of society which Socrates proposed. But his next argument attacks communism directly: it is the by now well-worn argument of incentive. 'That which is common to the greatest number has the least care bestowed upon it. Everyone thinks chiefly of his own, hardly at all of the common interest; and only when he is himself concerned as an individual. For besides other considerations, everybody is more inclined to neglect the duty which he expects another to fulfil; as in families many attendants are often less useful than a few.' In time this became one of the principal justifications for private ownership. But in the *Politics* it appears as a minor point and is not emphasized;[1] when Aristotle constructed his own sketch for a perfect state he paid little heed to his own argument that private property is necessary as an incentive to work: he made half the land of the state public property and stipulated that it should be tilled by public slaves.

So far Aristotle has followed Plato in talking about communism as including the abolition of the family. After some discussion to prove that the community of wives and children is a bad idea,[2] he proceeds in Book II of the *Politics* to discuss common ownership, assuming that the family is left intact.

Three systems of common ownership are possible: (1) the land may be privately owned, but the produce may be thrown into a common stock for consumption; (2) the land may be common, and worked in common, but the produce divided among individuals for their private use; (3) both the land and the produce may be held in common. The first system, Aristotle remarks, has been adopted by some nations, and the second is said to exist among certain barbarians. Apparently he had not heard of the third system being put into practice.

[1] W. D. Ross, *Aristotle*, 2nd ed., London, 1930, p. 246.

[2] The enemies of Plato's scheme always speak of it as 'the community of wives'; it might just as fairly be called 'the community of husbands.'

Having defined the three systems of common property, Aristotle ignores them in his subsequent discussions. He begins by observing that the question of ownership is much easier to deal with when the men who do the work are not the owners. The implication is that where the land is tilled by slaves, whether the land and its produce is owned by the masters in common or privately is not an important question, but if the owners do the work it is important: 'those who labour much and get little will necessarily complain of those who labour little and receive or consume much.' In other words, they will come to think of their labour as giving them a right to property, they will demand an unequal division corresponding with the inequality of their labour, and common use of the produce will cause disputes.

Aristotle's next point is obscure. He gives as an objection to common property that 'there is always a difficulty in men living together and having all human relations in common. . . .' Thus travelling companions always quarrel about trifles and we are most liable to take offence at those servants who are around us all day long. This objection can hardly be applied to all systems of common property; perhaps it refers to the extreme form of communal living practised by the Guardians of the *Republic*.

After these somewhat scattered and fragmentary observations, Aristotle concludes that 'property should be in a certain sense common, but, as a general rule, private; for when everyone has a distinct interest, men will not complain of one another, and they will make more progress, because everyone will be attending to his own business. And yet by reason of goodness, and in respect of use, "Friends," as the proverb says, "will have all things common".' This principle is already practised in some states: for example, the Spartans use one another's slaves, horses, and dogs in common and when they travel they take what provisions they need from the fields they pass through. 'It is clearly better that property should be private, but the use of it common; and the special business of the legislator is to create in men this benevolent disposition.'

Such a system of property will have several advantages. The

first two are psychological: 'how immeasurably greater is the pleasure, when a man feels a thing to be his own; for surely the love of self is a feeling implanted by nature and not given in vain, although selfishness is rightly censured; this, however, is not the mere love of self, but the love of self in excess.' Secondly, 'there is the greatest pleasure in doing a kindness or service to friends or guests or companions, which can only be rendered when a man has private property.' Finally, 'no one, when men have all things in common, will any longer set an example of liberality or do any liberal action; for liberality consists in the use which is made of property.'[1]

These observations are confusing, partly because Aristotle has slurred over here his original distinction between property in land, for production, and property in produce, for consumption: it is difficult to know which of the three possible systems of common ownership he is arguing against at any one moment. Altogether his remarks do not make a well reasoned or complete defence of any single system of private property. They are rather random observations included in a general discussion of Plato's ideal commonwealth with its very special and limited system of communal living for the ruling class.

The discussion of equality which follows the remarks on Plato's communism, in Book II of the *Politics*, is similarly unsystematic and inconsistent. Sometimes Aristotle appears to be quoting someone else's opinion without telling us whether he agrees with it or not; at other times he seems to be stating both sides of the question without coming to any conclusion. Nevertheless, the emphasis upon the rule of equality is unmistakable.[2]

Aristotle begins by observing that some legislators have

[1] Aristotle had already explained in the *Ethics*, 1120*b*, that 'liberality' is a term used relatively to a man's substance: 'there is therefore nothing to prevent the man who gives less from being the more liberal man, if he has less to give.' Thus an individual does not need great wealth in order to be liberal.

[2] See Werner Jaeger, *Aristotle*, ch. x, Oxford, 1934, and Barker, *Political Thought of Plato and Aristotle*, pp. 251–2, for a discussion of the form of the *Politics*; Barker, p. 422, and A. D. Lindsay, Introduction to Everyman edition of *Politics*, p. xiii, discuss Aristotle's insistence on equality.

thought that in making a constitution 'the regulation of property is the chief point of all, that being the question upon which all revolutions turn. This danger was recognized by Phaleas of Chalcedon, who was the first to affirm that the citizens of states ought to have equal possessions.' Plato specified a measure of equality in the *Laws*—a minimum and a maximum in the proportion of one to five. But such schemes ought to provide for the regulation of the population—if the number of citizens increases some of them will have no land and the original equality will be destroyed.

'That the equalization of property,' Aristotle continues, 'exercises an influence on political society was clearly understood even by some of the old legislators.' The laws of Solon and the laws of other Greek states, some of them still in force, attempt to preserve a more or less equal division of the land. But where equality is preserved there ought to be some regulation of the amount of property—men may be equal and yet have too much or too little. 'Clearly, then, the legislator ought not only to aim at the equalization of properties, but at moderation in their amount.'

Here Aristotle appears to be in general agreement with the argument that equality of property is necessary to preserve the community, to prevent revolutions which destroy the state. His own ideal state adopts the principle; the later chapters of the *Politics*, containing advice to existing states as to how to preserve themselves, recommend the limitation of inequality in every possible way.[1]

Equality, then, is for both Plato and Aristotle a fundamental principle of justice governing the distribution of property. If we think only of the ruling class in their ideal states we may say that

[1] For example, Sparta should regulate the inheritance and gift as well as the sale of land to prevent inequality, 1270*a*; the most stable states are those based on a large middle class, for where everyone is either rich or poor, revolution and tyranny follow, 1296*a*, *b*; in democracies, laws of inheritance should be used to decrease inequality, 1309*a*, and proper relief measures should prevent extreme poverty, 1320*a*; in an agricultural democracy, laws should provide that every farmer has some land of his own, 1319*a*.

Plato and Aristotle were absolute equalitarians in the matter of property distribution. And it is permissible to think of the question in this way since, as Professor McIlwain says, 'Plato believed as strongly as Aristotle that the ruling class *is* the state';[1] its members are the only true men—reasonable beings capable of ruling themselves and for whom their own good is the proper and absolute end of all their action. On the other hand, the problem of securing leisure for the good man in a society where productive work was drudgery led both philosophers to assume that slavery was necessary. Making a virtue of necessity they went on to say that some men were natural slaves—beings in human form but without reason, more like animals than men—who could with justice be used as the instruments of another's good. The proper economic function of the rulers is to consume property and that of the slave to produce it. Consequently the rule of equality does not hold as between the two groups. In this sense, equality of goods is an impossibility for both Plato and Aristotle. They remain the foremost theorists of inequality.

Similarly any conclusions as to Plato's communism and Aristotle's defence of private property must depend upon whether attention is focused on the ruling classes alone or on all the inhabitants of the ideal states of the *Republic* and the *Politics*. If we think only of the ruling classes then certainly Plato is the first great theorist of communism and Aristotle of private ownership. But if we think of all the inhabitants then Plato, as has often been pointed out, is not a theorist of communism, and Aristotle defends an economic system in which the majority of men own no private property.

Other Greek thinkers disagreed with the Platonic and Aristotelian theories of property. Indeed, their ideas, developed by the Stoic philosophers of the Hellenistic period, probably had more influence on later thinking about property than those of Plato and Aristotle. But the surviving record of these other Greek thinkers is slight and we must turn to Rome for the next chapter in the history of the theory of ownership. There we may examine

[1] *Growth of Political Thought*, N.Y., 1932, p. 38.

the 'elemental conceptions as to the nature and ground of property which the Roman lawyers took over from the Stoic philosophy' and which the writings of Cicero made 'the possession of every cultivated man.'[1]

But whatever new ideas about property might be developed in the future, men could never escape from the basic concepts which the Greek thinkers had formulated. We are unable to think about property without using the words natural and conventional, primitive and ideal, equal and unequal, common and individual, public and private. As the forms of actual ownership have changed, the theory of property has also changed. But the basic social and economic institutions of Western society have evolved within so limited a frame that Western men have always been able to use the same root concepts in talking about property. Philosophers, whether they lived on the bounty of feudal and royal princes, or capitalist entrepreneurs, have often done no more than elaborate theories which were first written for an audience of slave-owners. Even the more original theorists have usually found it sufficient to redefine the ancient Greek terms. Not until the seventeenth century was there any real revolution in thinking about property—and even then the old terms were used again.

[1] H. S. Holland, 'Property and Personality,' p. 182, in *Property, Its Duties and Rights*, 2nd ed., N.Y., 1922. For a short account of the theories of property and the primitive state of nature as they are found in the writers of the Hellenistic period see Robert von Pöhlmann, *Geschichte der Sozialen Fragen und des Sozialismus in der Antiken Welt*, 3rd ed., 2 vols., Munich, 1925, Bk. I, chaps. 1 and 6.

CHAPTER TWO

Rome

As far as the law of nature is concerned, all men are equal. *Digest*, L, 17, 32.

Things become the private property of individuals in many ways; for the titles by which we acquire ownership in them are some of them titles of natural law, which, as we said, is called the law of nations, while some of them are titles of civil law. *Institutes* of Justinian, II, 1.

The theory of natural law and property developed by the philosophers of the Hellenistic period and carried to Rome, principally by the Stoic school, was incorporated into the Roman Law. Through the medium of the Law it influenced not only medieval thinking but much modern thinking about property as well. What that theory was, before it became a part of the Law, is known to us chiefly through the writings of Cicero and Seneca.

In a passage of his *Republic* Cicero defined natural law:

True law is right reason in agreement with nature; it is of universal application, unchanging and everlasting; it summons to duty by its commands, and averts from wrongdoing by its prohibitions. . . . It is a sin to try to alter this law, nor is it allowable to attempt to repeal any part of it, and it is impossible to abolish it entirely. We cannot be freed from its obligations by senate or people, and we need not look outside ourselves for an expounder and interpreter of it. And there will not be different laws at Rome and at Athens, or different laws now and in the future, but one eternal and unchangeable law will be valid for all nations and all times, and there will be one master and ruler, that is, God, over us all, for he is the author of this law, its promulgator, and its enforcing judge. Whoever is disobedient is fleeing from himself and denying his human nature. . . .[1]

In a later work, the *Laws*, Cicero explained that this supreme

[1] *Republic*, III, 32. Trans. by C. W. Keyes, Loeb Classical Library, Cambridge, Mass., 1943.

'Law which had its origin ages before any written law existed or any state had been established'[1] is the standard by which we judge whether human laws are good or bad.[2] 'Therefore Law is the distinction between things just and unjust, made in agreement with that primal and most ancient of all things, Nature; and in conformity to Nature's standard are framed those human laws which inflict punishment upon the wicked but defend and protect the good.'[3]

Cicero's concept of nature and justice is not unlike that of Plato and Aristotle except that, as Professor McIlwain says, 'his whole theory of the state is far more dependent on law than theirs, a theory of rights in a sense with which the Greeks were unacquainted; and this legalistic character, apparently of Roman and not Greek origin, confirmed by the later Roman jurists, was handed on by them to remain one of the distinguishing marks of Western political thought almost to our own day, if it is not so still.'[4] But when we look at the application of Cicero's law of nature we see that a revolution in thought separates him from Plato and Aristotle. For that law, according to Cicero, applies equally to all men and by it all men are equal. In fact one of the proofs that such a law exists is that all men, when properly taught, acknowledge and obey it.

We are born for Justice and . . . right is based, not upon men's opinions, but upon Nature. This fact will be immediately plain if you once get a clear conception of man's fellowship and union with his fellow-men. For no single thing is so like another, so exactly its counterpart, as all of us are to one another. Nay, if bad habits and false beliefs did not twist the weaker minds and turn them in whatever direction they are inclined, no one would be so like his own self as all men would be like the others. And so, however we may define man, a single definition will apply to all. This is a sufficient proof that there is no difference in kind between man and man; for if there were, one definition could not be applicable to all men; and indeed reason, which alone raises us above the level of the beasts and enables

[1] I, 6. Trans. by C. W. Keyes, Loeb Classical Library, Cambridge, Mass., 1943.

[2] I, 16.

[3] II, 6.

[4] *Growth of Political Thought*, p. 116.

us to draw inferences, to prove and disprove, to discuss and solve problems, and to come to conclusions is certainly common to all of us, and, though varying in what it learns, at least in the capacity to learn it is invariable. . . . In fact, there is no human being of any race who, if he finds a guide, cannot attain to virtue.[1]

Thus over against the idea of the natural inequality of men which justifies the class divisions of Plato's *Republic*, against Aristotle's opinion that some men are natural slaves, Cicero asserts that all men are by the law of nature equal; and one hundred years later Seneca was repeating Cicero's doctrine.[2] The revolutionary character of this assertion has been recognized by the principal modern authorities: 'there is no change in political theory so startling in its completeness as the change from the theory of Aristotle to the later philosophical view represented by Cicero and Seneca'; it is the 'dividing line between the ancient and the modern political theory';[3] 'the idea of the equality of men is the profoundest contribution of the Stoics to political thought' and 'Locke's theory of the rights of man as antecedent to and independent of the state has been implicit in political thought ever since the Stoics and as a result of Rome's translation of Stoic conceptions of equality.'[4]

The causes of this intellectual revolution have been found in the historical circumstances which distinguished the world of the Athenian Empire from the world of Republican and Imperial Rome: the Stoic doctrines of the brotherhood and equality of men were well suited to the later period when the distinction between civilized Greek and savage barbarian had been obliterated (Aristotle's 'natural slaves' were all barbarians), and the whole known world was being rapidly united into one state under one law.[5] Nevertheless, the actual inequality of men was more striking in Rome than it had been in Athens; slavery and an unequal

[1] *Laws*, I, 10.

[2] See *Of Benefits*, Bk. III; for a summary of Seneca's political ideas see R. W. and A. J. Carlyle, *A History of Medieval Political Theory in the West*, Vol. I, 2nd ed., London, 1927, Pt. I, ch. 2.

[3] *Carlyle*, Vol. I, pp. 8, 9.

[4] McIlwain, p. 115.

[5] Carlyle, Vol. I, pp. 7–11; McIlwain, p. 106.

division of property were as essential to the society of Cicero and Seneca as to that of Plato and Aristotle. How could this actual and necessary inequality be defended against the law of nature which proclaimed that all men were equal?

Cicero's answer to this question is ambiguous. The citizens of the good state outlined in his *Republic* own property, and they are some rich and some poor. A fragment of Cicero's *Republic*[1] indicates that Plato's communism was discussed in that work, but Cicero's comments are lost. In another fragment the defenders of democracy are represented as saying that since law, the foundation of the state, gives justice equally to all, all citizens ought to be equal: if not in wealth, at least in rights.[2] Cicero's objection to democracy in general is that it lacks stability and is likely to run into anarchy: he prefers a government where there is a large measure of equality, where all the citizens have some political rights, but where some are given superior powers to maintain the principle of authority and subjection.[3] We may imagine, although we cannot know, that Cicero justified inequality of property on the same grounds. Finally, in an earlier passage of the *Republic* Cicero praises the Stoic ideal of the wise man who prefers knowledge to all earthly goods: 'Only such a man,' he says, 'can really claim all things as his own, by virtue of the decision, not of the Roman people, but of the wise, not by any obligation of the civil law, but by the common law of nature, which forbids that anything shall belong to any man save to him that knows how to employ and use it.' This suggests that Cicero is making a distinction between things owned by the law of the state and things owned by the law of nature, and further, that the law of nature applies to a primitive age when men appropriated what they could use, but no more, from the common stock.[4] If this is what Cicero had in mind, he was anticipating exactly Locke's definition of the limit imposed on acquisition by the law of nature.

In another work, *De Officiis*,[5] Cicero has more to say about

[1] IV, 5. [2] *Republic*, I, 32. [3] *Republic*, I, 45. [4] I, 17.

[5] Translated by Walter Miller, Loeb Classical Library, New York, 1913.

property, but his statements here are also ambiguous. Book II contains a long and bitter condemnation of agrarian laws, property taxes, confiscations, laws to abolish debts, and all legislation which tends to equalize property. Cicero condemns these things in words which the historians of political thought seem to have overlooked, and which anticipate one of the popular dogmas of modern political theory: he says that the state ought not to interfere with private property because the state was founded principally for the purpose of protecting the property of the individual.[1] However, Book I says that there is 'no such thing as private ownership established by nature, but property becomes private either through long occupancy . . . or through conquest . . . or by law, bargain, purchase, or allotment.' The Stoics teach that men have a common right to use the things produced by nature; consequently, we should follow nature by contributing to the common good, and 'while everything assigned as private property by the statutes and the civil law shall be held as prescribed by those laws, everything else shall be regarded in the light of the Greek proverb, "Among friends all things are common".'[2]

Cicero clearly sympathized with the Stoic theory that the institutions of property sanctioned by the civil law were not natural or primitive and that equality was the rule in the golden age when men lived by the law of nature. But his statements are not wholly consistent and we must turn to Seneca, writing a hundred years later, for the fully developed theory of a state of nature where property was common and men were equal.

One of Seneca's *Letters*[3] described a primitive age when men 'enjoyed nature and shared her amongst them.' Nature was the 'communal treasure with possession unchallenged,' 'nobody could have too much or too little under the brotherly rule of share and share alike,' 'the miser had not yet barred anyone from

[1] II, 21, 22.

[2] I, 7 and 16. See also *De Finibus*, III, 20.

[3] No. 90 in *Letters*, trans. by E. P. Barker, 2 vols, Oxford, 1932. This, as well as the other principal texts of antiquity describing the state of nature, is reprinted in Lovejoy and Boas, *Primitivism and Related Ideas in Antiquity*.

the necessities of life by secreting a hoard,' and man obeyed the 'natural standard which defines a man's desires by the satisfaction of his needs.' But into this ideal arrangement came avarice: 'craving to sequestrate and appropriate something to itself, it succeeded only in making everything somebody else's and reduced itself from the immeasurable to the inconsiderable.' 'Avarice dissolved the partnership and impoverished even those whom it made richest, for in their desire for personal possessions they forfeited universal possession.'[1] Seneca quotes the passage from the first book of Virgil's *Georgics* describing a time when

> 'No fences parted fields, nor marks nor bounds
> Distinguish'd acres of litigious grounds;
> But all was common. . . .' (Dryden's translation.)[2]

Here then in Seneca is the full theory of a state of nature where property was common and used equally by all for the satisfaction of needs. Such a theory implied that private property was not natural, and that the conventions which established it were justified only because human nature was now corrupt, so that instruments of social domination were necessary to preserve even a modest amount of law and order. This theory was, in an ambiguous form, woven into the Roman Law. From the Roman Law it was taken over by clerical theorists, combined with the Christian myths of the Garden of Eden and the Fall of Man, and made the standard theory of the medieval Church.

The later Roman lawyers, like the philosophers, believed in the existence of a law of nature according to which all men are free and equal.[3] *'Quod ad ius naturale attinet, omnes homines aequales sunt'*—as far as the law of nature is concerned, all men

[1] Similarly, Cicero in the passage quoted above, p. 22, said that vice destroyed the natural equality of man.

[2] The Golden Age was also described by Ovid, *Metamorphoses*, I, 89 ff., and Tacitus, *Annals*, III, 26.

[3] The theory of property is found chiefly in three texts: the *Institutes* of Gaius, a handbook of law from the second century A.D.; the *Digest*, a collection of extracts from legal books, most of which were written in the third century; and the *Institutes* of Justinian, a student's manual, issued with the *Digest* in A.D. 533 by commissioners of the Emperor Justinian.

are equal—wrote Ulpian, a famous jurist of the third century.[1] The *Institutes* of Justinian reaffirm the opinions of earlier lawyers that slavery is opposed to the law of nature; by that law all men are born free.[2] Many existing institutions, the lawyers agreed, are not derived from the *ius naturale*, but are the conventional creations of the *ius gentium*—the law of nations common to all peoples, or the *ius civile*—the peculiar law of a particular state. For example, slavery, an institution contrary to the natural law, was based on the law of nations.

But though the Roman jurists agreed that slavery was not according to nature, they were not so clearly in agreement about property. Gaius and the earlier writers excerpted in the *Digest* did not always distinguish clearly between the law of nature (*ius naturale*) and the law of nations (*ius gentium*). Describing the ways of alienating property, Gaius writes in his *Institutes* that some are based on 'civil law' and others on 'the law of nature.'[3] But in another work, excerpted in the *Digest*, Gaius says that we acquire ownership by the 'civil law,' or by the 'law of nations' which is based on 'natural reason' and is as old as the human race: 'tradition,' 'accession,' and 'occupation,' modes of acquisition he listed before as 'natural,' are now attributed to the 'law of nations.'[4]

Several other early jurists are quoted in the *Digest* as saying that some things are by the 'law of nature' common, other things private, and that some methods of acquisition belong to the 'law of nations' and are 'natural,' while others belong to the 'civil law.'[5] Thus the conclusion must be that the earlier jurists, who

1 *Digest*, L, 17, 32.

2 I, 2, 2; I, 3, 2.

3 Among the 'natural' ways of acquiring title to property he specifies 'tradition,' the informal delivery of certain objects from one man to another; 'occupation,' the appropriating of something which has previously belonged to no one, and the capture of an enemy's property; the cases in which new land is added by alluvion to a man's estate or a building is erected by anyone on his land (forms of 'accession' in the usual terminology of the Roman Law), and the case where a man gets a title to someone else's materials by converting them into a new product ('specification'). II, 65, 66, 69, 70, 73, 79.

4 XLI, 1, 1; 1, 5, 7; 1, 7, 1; 1, 7, 5; 1, 9, 3.

5 Marcianus, *Digest*, I, 8, 2 and 4; Paulus, *Digest*, XIX, 2, 1 and XVIII, 1, 1; Modestinus, XLI, 1, 53.

did not differentiate the *ius naturale* from the *ius gentium*, thought some kinds of property were natural, although we do not know just what they meant by that, and that some kinds were held by the *ius civile*. They do not appear to contrast the institution of private property with the ideal arrangement of the golden age, although the distinction between 'natural' and 'civil' property might imply such a contrast.

The later jurists quoted in the *Digest*, and those who compiled Justinian's *Institutes*, did attempt to distinguish the law of nations from natural law. They tended to define the *ius gentium* as a conventional law opposed to the *ius naturale*. Moreover they seem to imply that the *ius naturale* was connected with a primitive state of innocence in which conventional institutions such as slavery did not in fact exist.[1] However, the *Digest* has but few quotations concerning property written by these later jurists. Ulpian says that *precarium*, a kind of loan, belongs to the *ius gentium*, but we cannot conclude from this what he thought about other forms of private property.[2] One passage from Florentinus maintains that precious stones and other things found on the seashore are the property of the finder by 'natural law';[3] two others are quoted by the compilers of the *Digest* in such a way as to imply that the young born of captured animals belong to the captor by the 'law of nations.'[4] Finally, Hermogenianus, a jurist of the fourth century, lists private property along with war, national states, and various kinds of commerce as institutions of the *ius gentium*.[5] If, as Carlyle suggests, Hermogenianus is 'contrasting these institutions with others which belong to the *ius naturale*,'[6] then this passage is the only one in the *Digest* which definitely states that private property is not natural.

The *Institutes* of Justinian do not add anything to the theory of property presented in the *Digest* but merely repeat that theory with all its apparent ambiguities. Title 1 of Book II, which con-

[1] Carlyle, Vol. I, pp. 43–4, 51; McIlwain, pp. 129–30.
[2] Quoted in Carlyle, Vol. I, p. 52.
[3] I, 8, 3.
[4] XLI, 1, 2; 1, 6.
[5] I, 1, 5.
[6] Carlyle, Vol. I, p. 53.

tains most of the statements about property, opens by repeating from the *Digest* that some things

> admit of private ownership, while others, it is held, cannot belong to individuals: for some things are by natural law common to all, some are public, some belong to a society or corporation [*universitas*], and some belong to no one. But most things belong to individuals, being acquired by various titles, as will appear from what follows. Thus, the following things are by natural law common to all—the air, running water, the sea, and consequently the seashore.
>
> Things become the private property of individuals in many ways; for the titles by which we acquire ownership in them are some of them titles of natural law, which, as we said, is called the law of nations, while some of them are titles of civil law. It will thus be most convenient to take the older law first: and natural law is clearly the older, having been instituted by nature at the first origin of mankind, whereas civil laws first came into existence when states began to be founded, magistrates to be created, and laws to be written.[1]

This passage is puzzling since it identifies the law of nations with the law of nature, although normally the authors of the *Institutes* were careful to distinguish between the two: they had not said before, as the passage maintains, that the 'natural law is called the law of nations.' Moreover, in making this paraphrase of Gaius, they added to the confusion by writing *ius naturale* where he wrote *ius gentium*.[2]

The remainder of Title 1, Book II, is a description of the various ways of acquiring property by the 'law of nature' or the 'law of nations'[3]—they are used synonymously—copied without significant changes from the passages in the *Digest* examined above. The later Titles of Book II describe ways of acquiring

[1] Translated by J. B. Moyle, Oxford, 1889.

[2] Gaius, *Digest*, XLI, 1, 1; *Institutes*, II, 1, 11.

[3] 'Tradition,' 'occupation,' 'specification,' 'accession,' and *fructuum perceptio* —the title which a man has to the produce which he has gathered from a property he holds in good faith, according to the usual modern classification; see J. B. Moyle, *Imperatoris Iustiniani Institutionum*, 4th ed., Oxford, 1903, 198–209.

property which apparently are neither 'natural' nor derived from the 'law of nations,' but which are created by the civil law. Several passages here indicate that the authors were accustomed to thinking of only two kinds of property—'natural' and 'civil.'[1]

The lawyers, then, adopted the Stoic concepts of natural and conventional. Slavery is a clear example of an institution which, the lawyers and philosophers agreed, is not natural and did not exist in the golden age; it is the conventional creation of positive law. The philosophers added that private property is conventional, or civil, in exactly the same sense as slavery. But here the lawyers were ambiguous: they made contradictory statements, sometimes implying that property is conventional, at other times implying that property is natural. Later writers were thus able to cite the text of the law in support of several widely varying theories of property.

The medieval students of the Roman Law had difficulty in interpreting the ambiguous phrases of the *Digest* and the *Institutes*, but in general they agreed that some property was natural and some civil. A twelfth-century manual, the *Brachylogus Iuris Civili*, followed the *Institutes* in saying that some property arose from the *ius gentium*, and then classifying modes of acquiring property as 'natural' or 'civil.'[2] Two other works, one of the eleventh or twelfth, the second of the fourteenth or fifteenth centuries, agree that some property is according to nature, and some is civil.[3] However, Placentinus, one of the great Romanists of the Bologna school in the twelfth century, influenced perhaps by the theory of the early Christian Fathers, flatly denied that any

[1] II, 4, 2; II, 6. Similarly, modern commentators list all modes of acquisition under one or the other of these two headings and ignore the distinction between *ius naturale* and *ius gentium*; Rudolph Sohm, *The Institutes of Roman Law*, Bk. II, chap. 2, English translation, Oxford, 1892; Moyle, *Imperatoris Iustiniani Institutionum*, p. 198; H. F. Jolowicz, *Historical Introduction to the Study of the Roman Law*, p. 144, Cambridge, 1932.

[2] I, 2; II, 2–9; edited by Edward Böcking, Berlin, 1829.

[3] *Summa Codicis*, edited by Hermann Fitting, Berlin, 1894, VII, 23, 20; *Summa Legum*, edited by Alexander Gal, Weimar, 1926, II, 2 ff.

property was an institution of the natural law. It belonged exclusively, he said, to the *ius gentium* and the *ius civile*.[1]

Another Bologna doctor, Azo, distinguished in the usual way between property which was natural and property which belonged to the civil law or the law of nations; but, he observed, the law of nations is sometimes identical with the law of nature. Moreover, after quoting the passage from Hermogenianus in the *Digest*,[2] he explained that not all property was derived from the *ius gentium*, because theft had been forbidden by the Decalogue.[3] To this Accursius, whose writings were the standard interpretation of Roman Law from the thirteenth century through the later Middle Ages, replied that the *ius gentium* was already in force when the Decalogue was given to Moses.[4] Here the question was whether the Decalogue is a part of the natural law, or a part of that law which came into force only after men fell from innocence. That is a question related to the Christian theory of property and natural law—a theory which had influenced the medieval civilians and probably accounts for the fact that some of them, like Placentinus, went beyond the law, saying that not merely some, but all property, was unnatural. But the Roman theory that some property was natural in origin continued to be used by medieval thinkers, particularly those interested in limiting the power of kings over the goods of their subjects. It was repeated in the middle of the thirteenth century in Bracton's *De Legibus et Consuetudinibus Angliae*, the most famous of English medieval law books.[5] Up through the sixteenth century even those civilians

[1] *Summa 'Cum essem Mantue,'* I, 47, edited by Gustav Pescatore, Greifswald, 1897.

[2] Above, p. 28.

[3] *Select Passages from the Works of Bracton and Azo*, edited by F. W. Maitland for the Seldon Society, London, 1895, pp. 32 ff., 98 ff., and 40–2.

[4] Quoted in Carlyle, Vol. II, p. 48.

[5] In title *De Adquirendo Rerum Dominio*, pp. 42–7, in Vol. II of G. E. Woodbine's edition, New Haven, 1915–42. Bartolus of Sassoferrato, the most famous of fourteenth-century civilians, thought the emperor was bound to respect property and other institutions derived from the *ius naturale* and *ius gentium*. C. N. S. Woolf, *Bartolus of Sassoferrato*, Cambridge, 1913, pp. 22–3, 45–7.

who made the most extravagant claims for the power of the prince did not extend it to cover arbitrary confiscation of the subject's property; and they sometimes defended this qualification on the basis that property was founded in natural law.[1]

Whatever the lawyers of the Roman Empire meant to say, the important fact for the later history of the theory of property is that they linked property to the law of nature. Early Christian thinkers rejected the idea that private property is natural. But that idea, however ambiguously expressed, was embedded in the texts of the Law; and when the texts of that Law came to be studied again, the theory that property was an institution of the law of nature became popular again. The Doctors of the Church adopted it; both the friends and foes of royal absolutism found it useful; and in the eighteenth century it became an official dogma of the middle-class Liberalism. It is scarcely an exaggeration to say that the natural right theory of property is an outgrowth of the Roman lawyers' theory of the natural modes of acquisition.

[1] See the references in McIlwain, pp. 181, 190; Carlyle, Vol. II, Part I, ch. 8, and Vol. V, Part I, chs. 2 and 5, Part II, ch. 2; Georg Meyer, *Das Recht der Expropriation*, Leipzig, 1868, pp. 85–94, 97–119; and below, ch. 5, V.

CHAPTER THREE

☆

Early Christian Theories of Property

If, however, we consider prudently what has been written, 'The faithful possesses the whole world of riches, the infidel not an obol,' do we not convict all those who enjoy things they have acquired legitimately and who do not know how to use them, of possessing the property of another? St. Augustine, *Letter* 153.

Whence does each possess what he does possess? Is it not by human right? For by divine right 'the earth is the Lord's and the fullness thereof'; poor and rich are supported by one and the same earth. But it is by human right he saith, 'This estate is mine, this house is mine, this slave is mine.' By human right, that is, by right of emperors. How so? Because it is through the emperors and princes of this world that God hath distributed human rights to mankind. St. Augustine, in Gratian, *Decretum*, Dist. VIII.

By natural law all things are common to everyone. Gratian, *Decretum*, Dist. VIII.

The early Fathers of the Christian Church did not find in the New Testament a ready-made theory of property, but they did find there an attitude toward wealth and its use with which any Christian theory of property would have to square. Throughout the New Testament there is a distrust of riches and an emphasis on the advantages of poverty which are dramatically presented by the counsel of perfection which Jesus gave to the rich young man: 'If thou wilt be perfect, go and sell that thou hast, and give to the poor,' and his observation that 'it is easier for a camel to go through the eye of a needle, than for a rich man to enter into the kingdom of God.' Moreover, the gospel of love, of the brotherhood of man, of the equal worth of all the children of God, like the Stoic theory of the equality of men, pointed toward some equalitarian or communistic theory of property. Finally there was the story in *The Acts of the Apostles* of the practice of the first Christians in Jerusalem:

And the multitude of them that believed were of one heart and of one soul: neither said any of them that aught of the things which he possessed was his own; but they had all things common. . . . Neither was there any among them that lacked: for as many as were possessors of lands or houses sold them, and brought the prices of the things that were sold and laid them down at the apostles' feet: and the distribution was made unto every man according as he had need.

These and similar passages of the New Testament imply an attitude toward wealth and property which has influenced all subsequent Christian doctrine. It is reflected in some of the earliest surviving records of the Church;[1] it lay behind the arguments of those men of the Middle Ages and the Reformation who, whether spiritual zealots or covetous laymen, wanted to despoil the clergy of their wealth and reduce them to apostolic poverty; it accounts for monasticism, and for both Catholic and Protestant teaching about charity and economic oppression. Finally, the New Testament inspired those socialistic sects whose practices have angered and frightened the main bodies of Christians from the Middle Ages to modern times.[2]

Nevertheless, the New Testament defines a religious attitude toward property rather than a philosophical theory. Consequently when the Fathers of the Church began to work out a rational doctrine, they turned to the pagan philosophers and the lawyers. There they found a theory of property providentially adapted to their purpose: it could be reconciled with the views of the New Testament, and at the same time it justified inequality and private ownership. It has been conjectured that some of the earliest Church groups, influenced by the example of the Church at Jerusalem, may have regarded private property as unlawful for a Christian. But the great organized Church of which the great

1 'Thou . . . shalt share all things with thy brother, and shalt not say that they are thine own; for if you are fellow-sharers in that which is imperishable, how much more in perishable things.' *The Teaching of the Twelve Apostles*, IV, 8, edited and translated by Philip Schaff, 2nd ed., N.Y., 1886.

2 For full discussions of the Christian doctrine of wealth and its uses, see Vernon Bartlett, 'The Biblical and Early Christian Idea of Property,' in *Property, Its Duties and Rights*, 2nd ed., N.Y., 1922, and Ernst Troeltsch, *The Social Teaching of the Christian Churches*, Eng. trans., N.Y., 1931.

Fathers were members did not, any more than Cicero and the lawyers, or any major Christian group from that day to this, want to demolish the existing property arrangements. On the other hand, it was their function to preach the Biblical precepts and examples of perfection. The Roman theory of property not only solved this dilemma: it dovetailed neatly with other Christian myths and doctrines.

The Golden Age of the philosophers, where men were equal according to the precepts of natural law, corresponded to the Garden of Eden and the doctrine of the equality of believers. The conventional institutions which destroy that primitive equality and freedom were, according to the philosophers, introduced, and are now necessary and justifiable, because of the corruption of human nature. The Church explained the origin of that corruption by the myth of the Fall of Man and the doctrine of human depravity.

The Fall of Man provided the social and political theorists of Christendom with a conservative argument more persuasive and more subtle than Aristotle's theory of natural inequality and natural slavery. It accepts the opinion that men were created equal and insists that even now their souls are of equal worth in the eyes of God. But at the same time it insists that since the Fall the natures of men, all of them depraved, make necessary instruments of social domination. The division of property which gives some men a power over the lives of others is one such instrument. Using the subtle doctrine of the Fall, the Fathers proclaim that all men are equal, while at the same time their theory could have 'considerable effect both in defending the actually existing slavery of the ancient world, and in assisting in its revival in the fifteenth century when Europeans came into contact with the negro races.'[1] For fifteen hundred years the doctrine of the Fall of Man has been the chief conservative answer to radical equalitarians. Stripped of its theological trappings it is still current to-day and can be recognized whenever men say 'as long as human nature remains the same. . . .'

[1] Carlyle, Vol. I, p. 124.

But at the same time the Christian theory of the Fall has constantly inspired the thinking of radical equalitarians. It has given multitudes of men the idea that they might create again that perfect and natural society which existed before Adam sinned. Thus in the seventeenth century George Fox could complain that the Quakers had listened to the ministers of England 'and were glad that they would bring them to a perfect man's state, that is, to the state of Adam and Eve before they fell, for they were perfect then; and when we had followed them, some twenty, some thirty, some more, some less years, then they told us again, that they hoped we would not look for perfection while we are upon the earth, on this side of the grave, for we must carry a body of sin about us; and they hoped we would not look for perfection, and would not hold the erroneous doctine of perfection; we have spent our money, and have spent our labour in following after them, and now they have gotten our money they hope we will not look for perfection here. Oh, Deceivers!'[1]

When they accepted the philosophical distinction between nature and convention, the early Fathers also accepted the theory that private property belonged to the sphere, not of the natural, but the conventional. Near the beginning of the third century Clement of Alexandria was demanding that Christians be charitable on the ground that God had made all things common and that each was to use only what he needed. Clement does not question the right of the rich to own property now, nor does he use the word 'nature'; but he does insist that 'use should be common' in accordance with the way God had created the world.[2] But the Fathers of the fourth and fifth centuries were explicit: private property is not according to nature. St. Ambrose follows the words of Cicero's *De Officiis*, saying that by nature all property is common and that the Stoics had taught that all things

[1] No. 222 of the *Epistles*, London, 1698.

[2] *The Instructor*, II, 13, translated by William Wilson, in the *Ante-Nicene Christian Library*, Vol. IV, Edinburgh, 1867; and in the same, Vol. XXII, 1871, *Who is the Rich Man that Shall be Saved?*

were made for the common use of men.[1] The statements of Ambrose are evidence that the Fathers took over their theory of property directly from the philosophic tradition.

Perhaps the most important patristic statements about property are those of St. Augustine. *The City of God* gives one of his many explicit accounts of the Christian theory of the state of nature which was destroyed by sin.[2] We may safely assume that rich and poor would not have existed in that state, but property is not mentioned in this passage and we must turn elsewhere to find St. Augustine's theory of ownership. To the Donatist heretics who complained that their Church property had been unjustly confiscated by the Emperor at the instigation of the orthodox party, Augustine replied: 'since every earthly possession can be rightly retained only on the ground either of divine right, according to which all things belong to the righteous, or of human right, which is in the jurisdiction of the kings of the earth, you are mistaken in calling those things yours which you do not possess as righteous persons, and which you have forfeited by the laws of earthly sovereigns.' The Donatists, influenced perhaps by the legal theory of natural modes of acquisition, apparently claimed that their labour gave them a title to their property. Augustine answered that they pled in vain ' "We have laboured to gather them" seeing that you may read what is written, "The wealth of the sinner is laid up for the just" (Proverbs xiii. 22)'[3]

In one of his homilies on the Gospel of John, Augustine again replies to the Donatists:

Whence does each possess what he does possess? Is it not human right? For by divine right 'the earth is the Lord's and the fullness thereof': poor and rich are supported by one and the same earth. But it is by human right he saith, 'This estate is mine, this house is mine, this slave is mine.' By human right, that is, by right of emperors. How so? Because it is through the emperors and princes of this world

[1] *De Officiis*, I, 28, *Patrologiae Latinae*, edited by J. P. Migne, Paris, 1844–64, Vol. XVI.

[2] XIX, 15.

[3] Letter XCIII, chap. xii, Migne, *Patrologiae Latinae*, Vol. XXXIII, translated by J. G. Cunningham in *A Select Library of the Nicene and Post-Nicene Fathers*, edited by Philip Schaff, Vol. I, Buffalo, 1886.

that God hath distributed human rights to mankind. . . . Take away the right derived from the emperor, and then who dares say, that estate is mine, or that slave mine, or this house mine?'[1]

From these passages it is clear that Augustine regarded property as the conventional creation of the state and the fruit of sin. Elsewhere he advises Christians not to own property individually and asserts that there will be no private property in Paradise, although he also denounces as heresy the opinion that Christians are forbidden to own property in this world of sin.[2]

These passages also suggest another theory of property, a theory which Augustine developed in one of his letters.

If, however, we consider prudently what has been written, 'The faithful possesses the whole world of riches, the infidel not an obol,' do we not convict all those who enjoy things they have acquired legitimately and who do not know how to use them, of possessing the property of another? For that certainly is not the property of another which is possessed rightly, but that is possessed rightly which is possessed justly, and that is possessed justly which is possessed well. Therefore, all that which is badly possessed is the property of another, but he possesses badly who uses badly.[3]

Augustine used this theory for the limited purpose of justifying the confiscation of the Church property of heretics. But later thinkers, particularly John Wycliffe in the fourteenth century, revived it as the theory of Dominion in Grace and greatly extended its practical application. Meanwhile, the general philosophical theory that property was conventional and contrary to

[1] Homily VI, 25, Migne, *Patrologiae Latinae*, Vol. XXXV, translated in *A Library of the Fathers*, Oxford, 1848.

[2] *Expositions on the Book of Psalms*, 131, chap. 5–6; 105, chap. 34, Migne, *Patrologiae Latinae*, Vol. XXXVII, translated as 132 and 106 in *Library of the Fathers*, Oxford, 1857; *Of the Morals of the Catholic Church*, 78, Migne, *Patrologiae Latinae*, Vol. XXXII, translated in *Works of Augustine*, Vol. V, edited by Marcus Dods, Edinburgh, 1872; *De Haeresibus*, 40, Migne, *Patrologiae Latinae*, Vol. XLII.

[3] Letter 153, VI, 26, in Migne, *Patrologiae Latinae*, Vol. XXXIII, translated by Richard McKeon, 'The Development of the Concept of Property,' *Ethics*, April 1938, Vol. XLVIII, number 3. This article gives the best general view of the Augustinian theory of property.

natural law, having been woven into the Augustinian concept of history and society, became the foundation of much medieval thinking about ownership.

For many early Christian thinkers, the philosophic theory of property was reinforced by the example of the Church at Jerusalem described in Acts. That Church became a kind of legendary Golden Age in later centuries and its property arrangements were cited together with those of the *Republic* and the Golden Age of the Roman philosophers as the ideal standard. In the third century St. Cyprian explained that the practice of the Church at Jerusalem was an example of the universal rule according to which the whole human race ought to share equally in the goods of the world.[1] In the year 400 St. Chrysostom was preaching at Constantinople that the communism of Acts was a practical ideal for Christian communities; he gave facts and figures to prove that everyone in the congregation would be rich if wealth were pooled and he said he hoped this could be done in his own lifetime.[2] About the same time Jerome[3] and Augustine[4] were writing that while Christians might own property, the better way was to give all to the common funds of the society.

The views of the Fathers are expertly summarized by A. J. Carlyle in his essay on 'The Theory of Property in Medieval Theology':[5]

> The institution of property represents both the fall of man from his primitive innocence, the greed and avarice which refused to recognize the common ownership of things, and also the method by which the blind greed of human nature may be controlled and regulated. . . . This view is the opposite of that of Locke, that private property is an institution of natural law, and arises out of labour. To the Fathers the only natural condition is that of common ownership and individual use. The world was made for the common benefit of mankind, that

[1] *On Works and Alms*, 20, Migne, *Patrologiae Latinae*, Vol. IV, translated in *A Library of the Fathers*, Vol. III, Oxford, 1840.

[2] *Homily XI on the Acts of the Apostles*, translated in *A Library of the Fathers* (no vol.), Oxford, 1851.

[3] Epistula CXXX, 14.

[4] Epistola CLVII, 4.

[5] In *Property, Its Duties and Rights*, 2nd edit., New York, 1922, pp. 123–39.

all should receive from it what they require. They admit, however, that human nature being what it is, greedy, avaricious, and vicious, it is impossible for men to live normally under the condition of common ownership. This represents the more perfect way of life, and this principle was represented in the organization of the monastic life, as it gradually took shape. For mankind in general, some organization of ownership became necessary, and this was provided by the state and its laws, which have decided the conditions and limitations of ownership. Private property is therefore practically the creation of the state, and is defined, limited, and changed by the state.

The theory of the Fathers that private property was conventional and the result of sin was taken over by the canon lawyers and the scholastic philosophers who systematized the social ideas of the medieval world. The first great compilation of canon law, Gratian's *Decretum* (about 1140), took the theory directly from one of the late Fathers, St. Isidore of Seville (d. 636). The *Etymologies* of St. Isidore was intended to be a kind of encyclopedia of seventh-century learning. Written about a hundred years after the publication of Justinian's *Digest* and *Institutes*, it adopted the lawyers' tripartite division of the law of nature (*ius naturale*), the law of nations (*ius gentium*), and the civil law (*ius civile*); and as examples of the rules of the natural law it includes 'the common possession of all things' and 'the acquisition of those things [birds, wild animals, and fish] which are captured in the air, on the land, or in the sea.'[1] St. Isidore goes on to say that such things as the settling of cities, war, slavery, and treaties between nations are a part of the *ius gentium*.[2] Although he does not mention the acquisition of property in his definition of the *ius civile*[3] we can hardly doubt that he would have followed the lawyers in distinguishing between those modes of acquisition which were natural and those which were civil.[4]

[1] V, 4, in Migne, *Patrologiae Latinae*, Vol. LXXXII.

[2] V, 6.

[3] V, 5.

[4] Carlyle, Vol. I, pp. 143–4, finds a difficulty in the fact that Isidore says all property is common by nature, and then gives some rules of nature for the acquisition and use of private property. But if we assume, as we may in the case of the lawyers, that Isidore was thinking of a state of nature where the goods

St. Isidore's failure to make clear what he meant by saying that according to nature all property was common, but that some could become private, was the cause of much confusion in later times. The canon lawyers and the theologians took from him the theory that all was common by nature. But they passed over the theory of natural modes of acquisition and did not trouble to explain how, even in a state of innocence, a man could take what food he needed without thereby making it his private property. On the other hand, the civilians found in the Roman Law the theory that some modes of acquisition were natural and, as we saw above, they were puzzled as to how to reconcile this with the dogmatic statement of the canon law and the doctors of theology that no private property was natural. Apparently no one resolved the contradiction by interpreting the theory to mean communal ownership of the common stock and private ownership of that which a man appropriated for his use. The seeming contradiction continued to trouble theorists until St. Thomas abolished its premises by asserting that the natural system was private ownership of the common stock and communal use of it.

The famous collection of canon law compiled by Gratian in the middle of the twelfth century opens by quoting from St. Isidore the passages which assign to natural law both the rule that all property is common, and other rules which are applicable only to private property.[1] Gratian made no effort to solve this confusion: in fact he made it worse. He went on to say that natural law was immutable and that all laws made by man contrary to it were null and void.[2] Then in a famous passage he asserted that private property was an institution of human law—proved by quoting St. Augustine's homily on St. John,[3] and that common property was the rule of natural law—proved by references to the practice of the first Christians in Jerusalem, general philo-

of the earth were a common stock available to all, but where each could appropriate what he needed, in ways which would not destroy equality, then the contradiction vanishes.

[1] Distinction I, 6–9, *Corpus Iuris Canonici*, Pars prior, 'Decretum Magistri Gratiani,' edited by Emil Friedberg, Leipzig, 1879.

[2] Distinctions V; VI, 3; VIII, 1; and IX.

[3] Above, p. 38.

sophic tradition, and Plato's *Republic*.[1] This passage did not mention natural modes of acquisition.

Gratian did not explain how, according to these principles, private property could be legitimate. His statements as they stand do not justify abandoning the rules of nature even in a state of sin and corruption. It was the task of later doctors of the canon law to try to harmonize his contradictory and imprecise thoughts. But by his work the theory that according to nature all property was common was made a part of the law of the medieval Church.

One of the earliest commentaries on Gratian, the *Summa Decretorum* (about 1158) of Rufinus, vigorously attacked the problem of explaining how private property was permissible now, although by the immutable law of nature all property is common. The solution is elaborate, but in essence it is merely an assertion that natural law cannot be abrogated, except in the case of the rules about property. Natural law, wrote Rufinus in expounding the theory of Isidore and Gratian, consists of three parts: mandates, prohibitions, and demonstrations. The first two include such things as 'thou shalt love the Lord thy God' and 'thou shalt not kill'; the demonstrations show some things to be fitting and proper, such as 'all property should be held in common.' All three parts of the natural law are general in character and must be added to in any concrete situation. For example, one mandate orders men and women to procreate, but in the interests of decency discreet customs determine that they shall do so only after having performed certain connubial rites. But if men may add to all parts of the natural law they are not at liberty to abrogate, or detract from, all three of its branches. Only the demonstrations, which neither prohibit nor prescribe but merely show what is good, may suffer derogation. Hence it is permissible for men to institute private property and slavery in spite of the demonstrations which recommend common ownership and equal liberty for all. We cannot doubt, moreover, that laws which make

[1] Distinction VIII, Part 1. A similar argument is given in the second part of the *Decretum*, XII, quest. I, ch. 2, where private property is called the result of sin.

men shrink from evil and choose righteousness are parts of the law of nature. The laws and customs which establish private ownership and slavery are certainly necessary to prevent crime and are, consequently, based on natural law, although they run counter to its demonstrations. The law of nature, almost lost by the first man, restored by the law and the Gospels, is now embellished and modified by good customs and written laws which perfect it even when they deviate from some of its general recommendations.[1]

In commenting on Isidore's statement that wild animals are by natural law the property of their captor, Rufinus says shortly that what belongs to nobody is conceded to belong to the first occupier. But, he adds, if anyone expects to find here a long account of the legal doctrines concerning the acquisition of property let him understand that it is near to sacrilege to clutter a treatise on the canons with long and extraneous discussions of the civil law.[2] If, as his modern editor believes, Rufinus was a doctor of Bologna, this passage may refer to the civilian doctors' differences of opinion, reflected in Placentinus and Azo, about natural and civil modes of acquisition. In any case, Rufinus obviously did not approve of canonists discussing a theory of acquisition, derived from the Roman Law, which did not harmonize with the theory of property of the Church.

This pedantic interpretation of Gratian's first Distinction served Rufinus well when he came to comment on the famous passage about property in Distinction VIII. Natural law differs from constituted and customary law, he repeated, in that by natural law all is common property, but by customary and constituted law this is mine, that is yours. However, constituted law is law, and thus this estate is lawfully mine, that is lawfully yours, for that which is held by law is not held unjustly. How can this be reconciled with the doctrine that property is the fruit of sin and injustice? The doctrine, he answers, means merely that possession had its origin in avarice but is now sanctioned by long

[1] *Die Summa Decretorum des Magister Rufinus*, ed. by Heinrich Singer, Paderborn, 1902, pp. 6–7.

[2] P. 9.

usage and constituted law. Only in this limited sense is private property an institution based on sin.[1]

Thus the doctrine that according to nature all property is common had hardly been adopted by the Church before the commentators were hard at work annulling its provisions in order to give a surer foundation to the *status quo*. Many commentators who wrote after Rufinus adopted his distinction of the three kinds of natural law to prove that private property was now legitimate.[2]

The earlier scholastic philosophers, predecessors of St. Thomas, followed much the same path as the canonists in arriving at the conclusion that private property is a natural and good institution. But Alexander of Hales, perhaps the greatest of the scholastics before St. Thomas, was not satisfied with the rough-shod concept of 'demonstrations'—those parts of the natural law which did not perpetually oblige. He rehearsed the old, and then went on to expound a new and a more subtle solution of the problem of how to justify private property while maintaining the principle that by unchangeable natural law all should be common. The science of medicine, he wrote, prescribes wine for men in health and forbids it to the sick: the science itself does not change although there is variety in its application. Similarly, the law of nature prescribes common ownership for men without sin, but private property for men after the Fall: the law does not change but its prescriptions vary with the circumstances. Having changed the

[1] P. 21.

[2] O. Lottin, *Le Droit Naturel chez Saint Thomas et ses prédécesseurs*, Bruges, 1926, ch. I, quotes five twelfth-century glosses on Gratian which follow Rufinus. See also the thirteenth-century *Glossa Ordinaria* of Johannes Teutonicus, Gloss on Distinction I, c. 7, *Decretum Divi Gratiani*, Paris, 1560. Two famous thirteenth-century canonists, Innocent IV and the Cardinal of Ostia (Hostiensis), both taught that property is natural, and referred to the legal doctrine of natural modes of acquisition; Innocent IV, *Apparatus super V libros Decretalium*, Strasbourg, 1478, I, 'De constitutionibus,' and II, 'De voto et voti redemptioni,' and Hostiensis, *Summa Aurea*, Venice, 1573, II, 'De causa possessionis' and 'De causa proprietas.' See Georg Meyer, *Das Recht der Expropriation*, pp. 94–9, for further quotations from the canon lawyers. Hostiensis repeated the popular civilian doctrine that the emperor could confiscate his subjects' property only '*ex justa causa.*'

whole concept of natural law so that it now included both common and private ownership, and having prescribed the latter for men as they now are, Alexander of Hales could make use of the legal concepts of natural modes of acquisition. He went on to say that things which belong to nobody are the property of the occupier.[1]

With Alexander of Hales, the tendency to reject the idea of property as conventional has finally become explicit. Property is still regarded as the result of sin; and Alexander follows the older Christian theorists in maintaining that in times of necessity all should again be used in common. But granted the corruption of human nature, private ownership is natural. The distinction between institutions which are necessary, but conventional and evil, and those which are impractical, but natural and good, has almost disappeared.

Albertus Magnus, the teacher of St. Thomas and one of the first of the great scholastics to read Aristotle's *Politics*, followed Alexander of Hales in rejecting the clumsy concept of 'demonstrations.' He too asserted that communal ownership was natural in a state of innocence, but that private property was the natural way of providing for a man's family and the poor in a state of sin. He held fast to the venerable doctrine that in times of great crisis all property again becomes common. But for him, as for Alexander of Hales, property is natural, and the distinction between nature and convention has ceased to have real meaning.[2]

Thus a hundred years after Gratian had copied from St. Isidore the doctrine, which he in turn had taken from the Roman Law, that property was naturally common, the canon lawyers

[1] *Summa Theologiae*, III, Q. 27, M. 3, Arts. 2 and 3. Nuremberg, 1482.

[2] Lottin, ch. II, p. 38 quotes from unprinted MSS. of Albertus. Albertus may have been directly influenced here by Aristotle, although his *Commentary on the Politics* was probably later and may not have been written until after the unfinished *Commentary* of St. Thomas; see Georg von Hertling, 'Zu Geschichte der aristotelischen Politik im Mittelalter,' *Historische Beiträge zur Philosophie*, Munich, 1914, and Maurice DeWulf, *Histoire de la Philosophie Médiévale*, Vol. II, p. 132, 6th edition, Paris, 1934–6. The *Commentary* of Albertus explains the passages of the *Politics* which speak of property, but it does not criticize or add to them; it is printed in Vol. VIII of the edition of his works edited by A. Borgnet, Paris, 1890–8.

had interpreted the doctrine away with the help of the same texts of the Roman Law. Those texts were indeed ambiguous and it was not difficult for the earlier Christian theorists to read them in a sense which fitted their pessimistic view of this world; it was just as easy for the members of the Church Triumphant in the thirteenth century to read them in a sense that fitted their more optimistic view of the world. The theologians had accomplished the same result by redefining the concept of natural law. The intellectual leaders of the thirteenth century were already thinking about property in terms similar to those of the *Politics*. It is not surprising that they found it easy to appreciate and adopt the Aristotelian arguments in defence of private ownership.

CHAPTER FOUR

☆

St. Thomas and the Later Middle Ages

We might say that for man to be naked is of the natural law, because nature did not give him clothes, but art invented them. In this sense, *the possession of all things in common and universal freedom* are said to be of the natural law, because, namely, the distinction of possessions and slavery were not brought in by nature, but devised by human reason for the benefit of human life. (Thomas Aquinas, *Summa Theologica*, I–II, Q. 94, Art. 5.)

The external goods of laymen . . . are acquired by individuals through their own manufacture, industry, and labour. And individuals as individuals have right, power, and true dominion. . . . And therefore neither prince nor Pope has the dominion or dispensation of such things. (John of Paris, *De Potestate Regia et Papali*, c. vii.)

The recovery of the works of Aristotle in the thirteenth century helped to complete the revolution in the theory of property. In the *Politics* of the Philosopher scholars read that it was natural and good for men to own things privately. That was in flat contradiction to the Fathers and to Gratian's *Decretum*. But the canonists and theologians had already whittled away the ancient Stoic and Christian theory so that for Innocent IV, Alexander of Hales, or Albert the Great it had little meaning; the *Politics* merely provided new arguments and the prestige of authority for the theory that property was natural.

The earlier medieval theory was no longer appropriate for the all-embracing and powerful Church of the thirteenth century. The Augustinian tradition, into which that theory fitted, had been built up in the days when the Roman Empire was collapsing and when the Church was still waging uncertain battle with heathens and heretics. That the institutions of this world, such as property, were not according to nature, were necessary but evil conventions, did not conflict with the actual experience of the Fathers. But the Church of the thirteenth century took another view of a world in which every man was a Christian, where order and civilization, partly at least through the influence of the Church itself, had been recovered and sanctified, and where the Papal Monarchy was the richest and most powerful of worldly authorities. The institutions of the world were now the institutions of the Church, and the Augustinian differentiation of the terrestrial city and the city of God no longer fitted the facts. Thus it was that St. Thomas Aquinas, with the help of Aristotle, came to think that property and the political authority which protected it were not necessary evils but natural and good. If society was not in fact perfect, that was because sinful men did not make proper use of the good institutions under which they lived. For St. Thomas the actual was but a step from the ideal; for St. Augustine, the two were as far apart as heaven and earth. The different attitudes of the two men is well illustrated by a passage from St. Thomas's *Summa Theologica* in which he answers the question 'whether in the state of innocence man would have been master over man?' St. Augustine had answered in the negative.[1] St. Thomas quoted the answer, but rejected it and gave Aristotle as his authority. Government existed in the state of innocence, although it was free from pain and evil, which are the result of sin; it existed because, as Aristotle says, 'man is naturally a social being' and social life requires rulers.[2]

On the particular subject of property St. Thomas has relatively little to say and his discussions of it are ancillary to more general discussions of law and crime. But what he does say is full and clear. His *Treatise on Law*[3] adopts, with important changes of definition, the ancient division of law into natural, civil, and the law of nations, and he ties these into the hierarchy of law which embraces the whole universe. In considering natural law St. Thomas comes face to face with the old problem of defending

[1] *City of God*, XIX, 15.

[2] I, Q. 96, Art. 4, in *The Basic Writings of St. Thomas*, edited by A. C. Pegis, N.Y., 1945.

[3] *Summa Theologica* I–II, Questions 90–108.

private property while holding fast to the principle that by the unchanging law of nature all ownership is common. His solution of the problem is at once subtle and simple:

A thing is said to belong to the natural law in two ways. First, because nature inclines thereto: e.g. that one should not do harm to another. Secondly, because nature did not bring with it the contrary. Thus we might say that for man to be naked is of the natural law, because nature did not give him clothes, but art invented them. In this sense, *the possession of all things in common and universal freedom* are said to be of the natural law, because, namely, the distinction of possessions and slavery were not brought in by nature, but devised by human reason for the benefit of human life. Accordingly, the law of nature was not changed in this respect, except by addition.[1]

In a later passage the same reasoning is used to distinguish between the *ius naturale* and the *ius gentium*: the latter, on which property is based, is an addition made by human reason to the former. A thing may be said to be natural in two ways:

First, according as it is considered absolutely: thus a male by its very nature is commensurate with the female to beget offspring by her. . . . Secondly, a thing is naturally commensurate with another person, not according as it is considered absolutely, but according to something resultant from it, for instance the possession of property. For if a particular piece of land be considered absolutely, it contains no reason why it should belong to one man more than another, but if it be considered in respect of its adaptability to cultivation, and the unmolested use of the land, it has a certain commensuration to be the property of one and not of another man, as the philosopher shows, *Politics*, II.

But these additions made by the law of nations to the natural law are still natural, St. Thomas continues, since 'to consider a thing by comparing it with what results from it, is proper to reason, wherefore this same is natural to man in respect of natural reason which dictates it.'[2]

[1] I–II, Q. 94, Art. 5, *Basic Writings of St. Thomas*.

[2] *Summa Theologica*, II–II, Q. 57, Art. 3, translated by the Dominican Fathers, London, 1918.

According to St. Thomas, then, private property is natural and good. He omits any mention of property as an institution necessitated by sin, or of communism in the state of innocence. The famous words of St. Isidore and the *Decretum* have been, not rejected—for St. Thomas was too great a respecter of authority to contradict so venerable an opinion—but reduced to absurdity by the persuasive logic of the Angelic Doctor. If Gratian had written that by natural law men were naked, we would not suppose that he meant to criticize the wearing of clothes: nor more did he mean to criticize private ownership when he said that property was naturally common. Gratian might just as well have said that by natural law men are born free and without clothes. Having demolished the traditional Stoic and Christian theory, St. Thomas substituted for it the theory of Aristotle.[1] Private property is not opposed to 'nature' in the Stoic sense; it is according to 'nature' in the Aristotelian sense.

St. Thomas likewise followed Aristotle in giving the law-maker the responsibility for distributing and regulating private property for the common good. Later theorists, agreeing with St. Thomas that private ownership was natural, and wanting to defend the property of the individual against the attacks of powerful princes, took over the theory of natural modes of acquisition and asserted that property so acquired was held by a natural right superior to the claims of the state. But St. Thomas does not refer to the legal theory of acquisition and in his concept of the state there was no place for a theory of individual rights. The ruler was bound by natural law to maintain the general system of private ownership and direct it for the common good, but he was not bound to respect as a natural right the property of any one man. In the *Treatise on Law* St. Thomas defends the elaborate property laws of the Old Testament by pointing out

[1] Thomas's incomplete *Commentary on the Politics* covers the whole of the Second Book and his full explanations of the ideas about property there, although they add nothing, show how carefully he had considered them. The *Commentary* is printed in Vol. XXXI of the edition of his works published at Parma, 1862–73.

that they conformed to Aristotle's theory of property. They provided that some property should be public and some private, in accordance with the rules in the *Politics*, II, 2.

> And since many states have been ruined through want of regulations in matter of possessions, as the Philosopher observes (*Politics*, II, 6), therefore, the Law provided a threefold remedy against the irregularity of possessions. The first was that they should be divided equally. . . . A second remedy was that possessions could not be alienated for ever, but after a certain lapse of time should return to their former owner, so as to avoid confusion of possessions. The third remedy aimed at the removal of this confusion, and provided that the dead should be succeeded by their next of kin. . . . As the Philosopher says, the regulation of possessions conduces much to the preservation of a state or nation (*Politics*, II, 4). Consequently, as he himself observes, it was forbidden by the law in some of the pagan states *that anyone should sell his possessions, except to avoid a manifest loss.* For if possessions were to be sold indiscriminately, they might happen to come into the hands of a few, so that it might become necessary for a state or country to become void of inhabitants. Hence the Old Law, in order to remove this danger, ordered things in such a way that, while provision was made for men's needs by allowing the sale of possessions to avail for a certain period, at the same time the said danger was removed by prescribing the return of those possessions after that period had elapsed.[1]

The state, then, while protecting private ownership, ought to regulate it for the common good. We certainly may not conclude from these passages that St. Thomas thought the ruler ought to distribute property equally among the citizens—like every other medieval thinker, St. Thomas thought that an elaborate hierarchy of classes, analogous to the arrangement of living organisms, was the most perfect and natural form of social organization. But we can say that he would not have objected to equality because it violated the natural rights of the individual.

Up to this point St. Thomas has clearly rejected the traditional theory of property. But his great synthesis of Christian doctrine and Aristotelian philosophy would have been incomplete if it

[1] *Summa Theologica*, I–II, Q. 105, Art. 2, *Basic Writings of St. Thomas.*

had excluded the idea that justice required the rich to help the poor, and that in times of need all property should be common. St. Thomas could not support these principles, as had the Fathers and the early scholastic philosophers, by recalling that all property was common before the Fall. But he conceived another subtle distinction which served, logically if less forcefully, the purpose. At the beginning of a section having to do with theft the *Summa Theologica* comments:

Two things are competent to man in respect of exterior things. One is the power to procure and dispense them, and in this regard it is lawful for man to possess property. Moreover, this is necessary to human life for three reasons. First, because every man is more careful to procure what is for himself alone than that which is common to many or to all: since each one would shirk the labour and leave to another that which concerns the community, as happens where there is a great number of servants. Secondly, because human affairs are conducted in more orderly fashion if each man is charged with taking care of some particular things himself, whereas there would be confusion if everyone had to look after any one thing indeterminately. Thirdly, because a more peaceful state is ensured to man if each one is contented with his own. Hence it is to be observed that quarrels arise more frequently where there is no division of the things possessed.

These are the reasons and examples of Aristotle, copied from the Second Book of the *Politics*. But the *Politics* also recommended that the private property of the citizens should be used in common and St. Thomas continues:

The second thing that is competent to man with regard to external things is their use. In this respect man ought to possess external things, not as his own, but as common, so that, to wit, he is ready to communicate them to others in their need. . . . A rich man does not act unlawfully if he anticipates someone in taking possession of something which at first was common property, and gives others a share: but he sins if he excludes others indiscriminately from using it. . . . When Ambrose says: *Let no man call his own that which is common*, he is speaking of ownership as regards use.[1]

[1] II–II, Q. 66, Art. 2, translated by the Dominican Fathers.

In a following passage Thomas maintains that it is no sin to steal in cases of urgent and manifest need since Divine Providence has given men things to support life and that natural arrangement is not abrogated by the institution of particular systems of private ownership. 'It is not theft, properly speaking, to take secretly and use another's property in case of extreme need: because that which he takes for the support of his life becomes his own property by reason of that need.'[1]

In another connection, when he was defending monasticism and the mendicant orders, St. Thomas again adopted the Augustinian attitude towards property. He emphatically condemned the error of those men who denied that a life of voluntary poverty was the most perfect of earthly states, and defended his arguments by referring to Augustine and other early Fathers as well as the New Testament. Moreover, of the three ways of living without private property—joining a community whose income was derived either from endowments or from the manual labour of the members, or simply begging the bare necessities from day to day—Aquinas maintained that the last was the most perfect way since it freed men most completely from worldly concerns. Communal property is better than private property, but 'it is manifest that it belongs to the culmination of perfection, that some men should have no property, private or common.'[2] St. Thomas is careful to make clear that the life of voluntary poverty is a life of perfection for which not everyone is fitted. It is a counsel of perfection addressed only to those who are capable of it. Moreover, common property is always connected with asceticism. St. Thomas does not suggest that there would be any virtue in communal living which was at the same time luxurious. When the accusation was made shortly after his death that monks who owned no property individually, but lived

[1] The same, Art. 7.

[2] *Contra pestiferam Doctrinam Retrahentium Homines a Religionis Ingressu*, c. 15, in *Opuscula Selecta*, Vol. III, Paris, 1881. The same positions are defended in cc. 6–8, *Contra Impugnantes Dei Cultum et Religionem*, *Opuscula Selecta*, Vol. III, and in *Summa Contra Gentiles* III, Part II, chs. 131–5, trans. by the Dominican Fathers, London, n.d.

richly in heavily endowed communities, were not fulfilling their vows, St. Thomas was frequently quoted by the accusers. He was definitely not recommending communal ownership to society at large.

But he nevertheless did not entirely discard the Augustinian theory of property in favour of that of Aristotle. If the theorists who followed St. Thomas no longer thought of private property as an institution contrary to natural law, if it was now natural and good rather than a deviation from a primitive state of perfection, they also learned from him that the most perfect state for men capable of it would be to have common property or even no property at all. St. Thomas had made a synthesis of Aristotle and traditional Christian thought. The traditional doctrine stated that common ownership was natural because it was the primitive and original form of property; St. Thomas said that private ownership was natural because it was the more highly developed, the more perfected form of ownership. But having adopted this new and Aristotelian concept which regarded the perfection—the end toward which it developed—rather than the original and primitive form of a thing, as its natural state, St. Thomas went on to say that common ownership or no ownership at all was the most perfect, the most natural of all forms of property. And where the Fathers, following the Stoic theory, said that sin made it impossible to return to the primitive ideal of common ownership, St. Thomas, following Aristotle, said that sin made it impossible for any but a very few to go forward to the final and perfect end of common ownership. Thus the argument really hinged on the concept of nature. All agreed that private property was necessary now and that common property was the ideal; but they disagreed as to whether private property should or should not be called natural, and in their attitude toward the institutions which had existed in the primitive state of nature. If the philosophical concept of that primitive state had not been so firmly tied to the Christian myth of the Garden of Eden, the Thomists might well have denied the existence of any such state. As it stood they could not deny the Garden of Eden. But they could identify the philosophers' state of nature with the unhappy and bestial condition of Adam and Eve after they had been driven from that garden, and argue that private property developed naturally as men strove to improve their lot.[1]

The Thomist theory of property has been repeated in one form or another from the fifteenth century to the present day by the theologians of the Church. When they use it to demand that the state shall intervene to provide the necessities of life for everyone it seems to be a radical theory; when they use it to defend the rights of property against proposed reforms it appears as a conservative doctrine. To the ruling classes of the Middle Ages it must have appeared, compared with the older Christian idea that property was the result of sin, as a welcome defence of the unequal division of wealth.

If St. Thomas's theory of property had remained the exclusive possession of the theologians its subsequent influence on the modern world would, perhaps, have been slight. But even in the later Middle Ages it was taken over by political theorists and became a weapon in the great political struggles of the day. Combined in various ways with theories of the origins and limitations of political power it turns up, although not often in a prominent place, in most of the great texts of political thought of the fourteenth and fifteenth centuries. Moreover, almost every justification of private property which has been popular in modern times was anticipated by the pamphleteers and political philosophers of those centuries when princes, popes, parliaments, and peasants were waging wars to determine what classes should rule modern society, and what particular form of property should be their instrument of domination.

Of the early works on political theory one of the most important is the *De Regimine Principum* which was begun by

[1] The Thomistic theory, with slight variations, was repeated by Duns Scotus, *Opus Oxoniensis*, III, d. 37, and IV, d. 15, in *Opera Omnia*, Vol. XV, Paris, 1894; and by Antoninus of Florence, whose social theory is described in Carl Ilgner, *Die Volkswirtschaftlichen Anschauungen Antonins von Florenz*, Paderborn, 1904.

St. Thomas himself and completed after his death by his pupil, Ptolemy of Lucca.[1] Book IV which was written by Ptolemy presents an Aristotelian account of the state and society as a natural outgrowth of the family, following closely the arguments of the *Politics*. One chapter is devoted to a discussion of Plato's communism and Ptolemy summarizes the Aristotelian arguments against it. Ordinary men, he added, require private division of property to live in peace as is shown by the example of Abraham and Lot who divided their pastures when their herdsmen quarrelled. Nevertheless, common ownership is more perfect; thus the Platonists and the Apostles who were contemptuous of the goods of this world lived without private property, and Christ's words to the rich young man were a counsel of perfection for those capable of it.[2] In a later chapter Ptolemy paraphrases the *Politic's* arguments against equalizing property and adds that equality violates 'human nature,' 'reason,' and 'the law of nature.' As St. Augustine has shown, men are unequal on account of sin and deserve unequal rewards; according to the Gospel story one man is rightly given five talents, another two, and another one; finally in the Book of Wisdom it is written that God created everything according to number, weight, and measure, which implies inequality.[3]

Twenty-five years earlier another student of St. Thomas, Aegidius Romanus, had written a *De Regimine Principum* which has been called 'one of the ablest and most interesting political treatises of the whole Middle Ages.'[4] Romanus himself was Archbishop of Bourges, head of the Augustinian order, and the author of many well-known works. The *De Regimine* was translated into several languages and has been reprinted more

[1] For the authorship of this work see McIlwain, pp. 325, 331–2.

[2] Bk. IV, ch. 4; the whole work is printed in St. Thomas's *Opuscula Selecta*, Vol. 3, Paris, 1881.

[3] Bk. IV, ch. 9. In ch. 14, Aristotle's statement that inequality of property at Sparta was a source of disorder is repeated without comment, but Ptolemy does not refer at all to the division of property recommended by Aristotle in his sketch of the ideal state.

[4] McIlwain, p. 248.

than once in modern times.[1] It was probably more influential than Ptolemy's work in introducing the Aristotelian theory of property to the political thinkers of the later Middle Ages.

The theory of property which Aegidius proposed was mostly that of St. Thomas elaborated with quotations from Aristotle. He paraphrased Aristotle's objections to Plato's communism,[2] and in his book the Augustian theory that property is unnatural has almost disappeared. He explicitly denies the idea, which he attributes to the Roman lawyers, that private property and the other institutions of society are debased compared to the natural institutions of primitive men: the former are better, and, in the Aristotelian sense, more natural, because they represent a higher development of man's nature.[3]

But on several important points Aegidius went beyond St. Thomas and even Aristotle. St. Thomas made no sharp distinction between the *ius gentium*—the body of reasonable additions to the natural law, including the laws of property—and the enacted law of the state. It was possible for him to say that private property was natural and at the same time to say that in any specific case it had been instituted by human lawgivers. Likewise Aristotle thought that property was natural but that it was the business of the founder of the city to institute it. But Aegidius introduces the important idea that the *ius gentium* is unwritten and is universally recognized by men before they have established political societies. After the Fall men lived, poor and dispersed, in a state of nature. To secure for themselves the necessities of life they came together and made agreements and pacts establishing property rights. These pacts were a part of the *ius gentium* which is a kind of natural law based on contracts between men

[1] On Aegidius and his work see Richard Scholz, *Die Publizistick zur Zeit Philipps des Schönen und Bonifaz' VIII*, Stuttgart, 1903; and Jean Rivière, *Le Problème de l'Eglise et de l'Etat au Temps de Philippe le Bel*, Paris, 1926. I have used the edition of the *De Regimine* printed at Augsburg in 1473; a thirteenth-century French version, *Li Livres du Gouvernement des Rois*, was published by S. P. Molenaer, N.Y., 1899.

[2] Bk. II, Pt. III, chs. 5–6; Bk. III, Pt. I, chs. 9, 11, 16–18.

[3] III, II, ch. 31.

(*quasi ius naturale contractum*). Only later did men agree to set up political authorities with power to enact positive laws.[1] Thus, in the final form of Aegidius's theory, not only is private property in general natural, as Aristotle and St. Thomas had said, but the particular rights of individual owners are rooted in a natural law which is prior in time, and more binding in authority, than any of the laws of the state.

To achieve this result Aegidius made use of the popular medieval theory of the social contract. Property was natural, as Aristotle had said, but historically it had been instituted by contracts. And in that historical process, through which men escaped from the savage state, contracts establishing property preceded those which instituted political authorities. The rulers, according to Aristotle and St. Thomas, are bound to institute some equitable system of private ownership; but the prince of Aegidius is limited to protecting the particular system of private rights already in existence. In this respect the theory of Aegidius was similar to those which in later centuries the middle class used to defend its property from the exactions of absolute monarchs. But for Aegidius himself the theory was useful primarily in defending the property of the Church—a matter of the greatest practical concern during his lifetime. Much of the practical politics and most of the political theory of the later Middle Ages was concerned with the problem of the relation of the secular and the spiritual powers. At the end of the thirteenth century the struggle between the two had crystallized around the question of property: Pope Boniface VIII and Philip the Fair of France were disputing whether or not the king had the right to tax the property of the French clergy. That dispute was settled by the death of Boniface and the removal of the Papacy to Avignon where it remained, under the control of France, from 1309 to 1377. But the larger question of the relation between the two powers, not definitely settled until the Reformation, developed into open warfare again in the second quarter of the

[1] III, II, ch. 24; III, I, ch. 26; Scholz, pp. 70–2. On Aegidius and the history of the social contract, see Gough, *Social Contract*, Oxford, 1936, pp. 41–2.

fourteenth century when Pope John XXII attempted to interfere in the imperial elections and prevent Lewis of Bavaria from becoming Emperor.

In every case the controversy between the Papacy and the secular power was embittered by the fact that it was tied to another great argument about evangelical poverty. From the early days of the Church the Christian distrust of wealth had led some men to claim that the clergy ought to follow the example of the apostles and live in poverty. The monastic orders had been organized on this principle and held their property in common. But by the thirteenth century the common property of some of the orders had grown so large that the individual monks were no longer living the life of poor men. Among the Franciscans, a party arose demanding that the Order return to St. Francis's ideal and abandon all property whether private or common. They could quote St. Thomas to prove that beggary was the most perfect way of life. The matter was settled temporarily when in 1279 the papacy took over the title to all the property of the Franciscans: the friars were legally propertyless, although the Pope permitted them to use their former endowments. But the question was reopened in 1322 when John XXII returned the property to the Order, excommunicated and imprisoned the leaders of the opposition, and condemned as heretical the opinion that the apostles had owned no property.[1]

If the dispute had remained nothing more than a quarrel within the monastic orders it would probably have had little effect on the theory of property. But it was inevitable that the partisans of the secular power would use the argument of evangelical poverty as a weapon to justify royal control over clerical property. As far back as 1245 the sceptical Emperor Frederick II had written: 'God is our witness that our intention has always been to force churchmen to follow in the footsteps of the primitive Church, to live an apostolic life and to be humble

[1] The Pope maintained that there was little ethical difference between owning and enjoying the use of property; he accused the friars of eating more butter and eggs after the Pope took over their property than before.

like Jesus Christ. In our days the Church has become worldly. We therefore propose to do a work of charity in taking away from such men the treasures with which they are filled for their eternal damnation.'[1] Consequently, both sides were driven to invent theories of property which would support their pretensions, and it is to the controversial literature on state and Church that we must turn to trace the development of the theory of property in the later Middle Ages.

Probably the most important book in defence of the claims of Boniface VIII was the *De Ecclesiastica Potestate* of Aegidius Romanus which appeared in 1301.[2] In this work Aegidius developed the theory of property which he had outlined in the *De Regimine* and made it a weapon of the papal power. He admitted that the life of absolute poverty was the most perfect, but he argued that it was a 'work of supererogation.' He cited appropriate texts from the Bible to prove that it was lawful for the Church to own property and that such ownership did not destroy the perfection required of the ordinary clergy.[3]

Having established the right of the Church to own property he turned to the general theory of ownership. Private property did not exist in the savage state of nature after the Fall: the sons of Adam divided the land *ex convencione et pacto*. The process was repeated after the Flood by the sons of Noah and subsequently, as men multiplied, new agreements were made which regulated buying, selling, inheritance, and the like. Only after these agreements or contracts had been made did men set up kingdoms and make laws about property. But those laws do not create property: they do no more than subsume and guarantee the contracts which had been made long before there was any legislative authority. Only in this sense, concludes Aegidius, is it true to say that property is the creation of the human law promulgated by kings and emperors.[4] Aegidius does not mention

[1] Quoted by Eileen Power, 'Pierre DuBois,' *The Social and Political Ideas of Some Great Medieval Thinkers*, ed. F. J. C. Hearnshaw, N.Y., 1923, p. 160.

[2] Edited by Richard Scholz, Weimar, 1929.

[3] II, 1.

[4] II, 12. Aegidius grants that the laws may add something to the original contract such as awarding title by prescription to a *bona fide* possessor after a

St. Augustine by name but there is no doubt that he is referring to, and interpreting away, the passage quoted in Gratian's *Decretum* where Augustine said that property was instituted by princes.[1]

Property may be conventional, as St. Augustine and the Stoics had said: but the conventions on which it is based are, as St. Thomas proved, additions to the law of nature and are themselves really part of that law; Aegidius added that these conventions of natural law may not be abrogated by the positive legislation of princes. Thus by an astonishing and intricate chain of reasoning the old notion that property is conventional—opposed to nature—has been reconciled with the Aristotelian theory that property is natural, and then used to prove that the rights of property are superior to the rights of the state.

The point of the argument, of course, was to prove that Philip the Fair, King of France, had no right to take the property of the clergy without their consent. The rights of ownership are grounded in natural law and in contracts made before there were kings of France. What the king had not given he obviously had no right to take away. With a judicious mixture of Aristotle, St. Thomas, the theory of the social contract, and the legal theory of acquisition, Aegidius defended Boniface against Philip and, incidentally, he developed a modern theory of ownership which contradicted at every point the traditional Augustian idea that property was the conventional creation of the state and 'not according to nature.'

But the claims of Boniface went much further: kings may have no right to take private property without the consent of the owners, but the Pope does, in certain circumstances, have such a right. In defence of this further claim Aegidius imposed upon his philosophical theory of property a theological theory,[2] revolutionary in its implications and famous in the political thought of the later Middle Ages. Essentially the theological theory was a

certain length of time. This is similar to the legal distinction between civil and natural modes of acquisition with which Aegidius was certainly familiar.

[1] Above, p. 37.

[2] In Bk. II, cc. 1–12.

combination of the traditional Augustinian view that the world belongs to God, who has given it to the faithful who worship him, and the theory of feudal dominion. Aegidius quotes St. Augustine to prove that there can be no right where the lordship of God is not recognized, nor just property rights except those granted through God's grace. But men, because they are born in sin and live sinfully, deny God's lordship and are incapable of receiving his grace. If the king grants a castle to a knight and his heirs, the heirs may lose their inheritance either by the rebellion of the knight himself or by their own rebellion; so men have forfeited God's grant both by Adam's sin and their own.

But men who are born in sin and live sinfully can be made capable of receiving God's grace—through the sacraments of the Church. Men can have lawful property if they are regenerated and have their rights blessed and sanctified by the Church. Aegidius explains in some detail that baptism washes away original sin and all the sins committed up to the time of the administration of the sacrament; subsequent sins can be erased from the record from time to time, by eating the consecrated bread and doing penance. From this it follows that ownership depends upon the blessing of the Church. Infidels, and men to whom the sacraments are denied, have no right to any property whatsoever.

Thus far the religious or theological theory and the rational or philosophical theory have proceeded along parallel and distinct lines and appear to have no point of contact. From the religious point of view, according to which all law is either divine or human, property, as the grant of God, is subject to divine law and comes under the jurisdiction of the Pope. From the philosophical point of view, according to which all law is either natural or positive, property is natural and its rights ought not to be violated by any positive laws of the prince. But in the end Aegidius brings the two together again. The practical instrument by which the Church wields its authority over property is excommunication; and excommunication can be looked at from both the theological and philosophical points of view. Theologically, it bars men from receiving God's grace and thus deprives them of their divine rights of ownership; philosophically, it excludes an individual from the community of men and makes it impossible for him to have any part in those pacts and contracts between men which are the foundation of natural ownership.

Aegidius certainly intended that this theory should give the Papacy a large measure of control over the private property of Christians. But he emphatically did not mean that the Pope was in the modern sense of the word the owner of everything. He repeats more than once that the righteous have a just title to their possessions and that the rights of the Church confirm rather than invalidate these titles.[1] His meaning becomes clear when we think of ownership or dominion in the feudal rather than the Roman or modern sense.

According to Roman legal theory all private property had a single owner whose rights were absolute and exclusive against all the world; he could use, dispose of, or even annihilate his property, as he pleased; he enjoyed absolute sovereignty over the property which he owned. Primitive Germanic law, on the other hand, recognized no such theory of ownership. Property belonged to the clan or to the family, and the individual had merely certain limited rights of using it, together with other individuals. He might be granted the exclusive right to pasture sheep in a particular field, but that did not give him the privilege of excluding other individuals who had rights of cutting wood or gathering fruits in the same field. No member of the tribe owned land in the Roman sense.

With the development of feudal institutions the Germanic theory of property replaced the Roman in medieval legal and political theory.[2] In feudal law all property, and the political privileges tied to it, was thought of as having belonged originally to the king. He had granted the use of it, on certain conditions,

[1] II, cc. 10, 12, 21.

[2] Even the civilians found means to reconcile the Roman theory with the actual facts of feudal dominion; see E. Meynial, 'Notes sur la formation de la théorie du domaine divisé,' *Mélanges Fitting*, II, Montpellier, 1908.

to his vassals. 'The theory developed that everything had moved from some one, was held of some one, had at some time been granted by some one. And it continued to be held of him. His interest in the thing granted did not cease with the grant. If he had granted land as lord to a vassal, his rights over the land remained, except for the particular interest he had parted with.'[1] The result was that no one could be said to own the land; everyone from the king down through tenants and sub-tenants to the peasant who tilled it had a certain dominion over it, but no one had an absolute lordship over it. 'The essence of the theory of dominion,' writes Professor McIlwain, 'is a hierarchy of rights and powers all existing in or exercisable over the same objects or persons, and the fundamental relationship of one power to another in this hierarchy is the superiority of the higher to the lower, rather than a complete supremacy in any one over all the others.'[2]

The feudal theory of dominion coincided completely with St. Augustine's theological theory of the origin of human rights. God is the lord and owner of the world. He grants the right to use his property to the righteous on condition that they render homage and fealty to him. And just as in the feudal theory property and political authority were both denoted by 'dominion' —the land-law was identical with the law of the land—so in Augustine's theory property and political authority were aspects of the same thing—that domination of man by man necessitated by Adam's sin.

Aegidius combined the Augustinian and the feudal theory and claimed that God had granted dominion not to the king but to the Pope, who was the supreme feudal overlord in this world. So long as the feudal system lasted the argument between the Papacy and the secular authorities revolved around this question, whether kings derived their temporal authority directly from God or mediately by way of the Pope. But whichever side men took they were not attacking the fundamental principle of private property. Regardless of whether king or Pope was the supreme

[1] McIlwain, p. 181.

[2] P. 355.

temporal authority, they had only a superior dominion in the property of their vassals and not the ownership of it. The king claimed the right to confiscate the property of his subjects only when they refused to render him the homage stipulated in the feudal contract. The Pope claimed that the property of the Church was not granted by the king and consequently owed him no service; but over the property of laymen he claimed the right of expropriation only when they refused to render God homage. Practically the latter, of course, meant whenever men refused to recognize the authority of the Pope. But in theory neither Pope nor king questioned the proprietary rights of men who performed their feudal obligations. The theory of dominion did not conflict with the argument that private property was natural; it merely defined the rights of the various proprietors.

The *De Ecclesiastica Potestate* of Aegidius Romanus has long been recognized as one of the greatest and most influential texts of medieval political theory, and the best of the books on the Papal side of the argument. It should be added that the importance of his theory of property ranks equally high. In the course of the century both the friends and the enemies of Papal power took over his principal ideas about property and adapted them to their own ends.[1]

In defence of Philip the Fair, the best book was the *Tractatus de Potestate Regia et Papali* which appeared about 1303.[2] The author was John of Paris, a member of the Faculty of the University. In the introduction to his treatise John says that he is going to defend a position between the two extremes which either deny the clergy any right whatever to property or give them authority over all property. Clergymen and the Pope are lawful owners, he asserts, not because they are clergymen and have a monopoly of grace, but because they have been granted property by princes.[3] After describing the origin of society and social institutions in Aristotelian terms as natural,[4] and maintain-

[1] See James of Viterbo, *De Regimine Christiano*, edited by H. S. Arquillière, Paris, 1925, I, 1, and II, 7. This work defends the Papal claims and borrows from Aegidius.

[2] Printed in M. Goldast, *Monarchia*, Vol. II, pp. 108–47, Frankfort, 1614.

[3] Pp. 108–9.

[4] Pp. 109–10.

ing that the property of the Church is communal and does not belong to the Pope or any other individual cleric,[1] he goes on to ask what power the Papacy has over the property of laymen. His answer to that question is on the one hand derived from the Roman Law theory of natural acquisition, and on the other is an anticipation of the theory which John Locke and the classical economists popularized in modern times. The goods of laymen, he wrote, are 'acquired by individuals through their own manufacture, industry, and labour. And individuals as individuals have right, power, and true dominion'[2] over such property and may do with it what they will so long as they injure no one else. Neither prince nor Pope has a right of ownership in such property of the individual. In fact, princes were established by men to enact and administer laws for the protection of property. A few pages later John states that human laws guarantee the appropriation which has converted common property to private and which is necessary for peace and as an incentive to make men work; and he quotes from the *Decretum* the famous statement of Augustine that property is rooted in human law.[3] The conclusion is that disputes about property come under the jurisdiction of secular, not ecclesiastical authorities.[4]

John's answer to the theological and religious theory of Aegidius consists in denying that the spiritual authority of the Church is coercive. In one form or another this argument was developed by all the enemies of the extreme Papal claims. Later

[1] Pp. 114–15. [2] P. 116. [3] P. 126.

[4] A similar use of the words of St. Augustine had been made by two anonymous defenders of the king in pamphlets written shortly before the work of John and whose arguments he took over and elaborated: *Quaestio Disputata in Utramque Partem pro et contra Pontificiam Potestatem*, in Goldast, *Monarchia*, II, p. 97; *Rex Pacificus*, in Pierre Dupuy, *Histoire du Différend d'entre le Pape Boniface VIII et Philippe le Bel*, Preuves, pp. 670–1, Paris, 1655. John's general argument was followed in an anonymous gloss on Boniface's famous Bull, *Unam Sanctam*, Rivière, pp. 300–1. An anonymous tract, *Disputatio inter Militum et Clericum* (about 1296) in Simon Schard, *De Iurisdictione, Auctoritate, et Praeeminentia Imperiali*, Basel, 1566, pp. 677–87, claims that property, clerical as well as lay, is under the jurisdiction of princes, but it does not elaborate a theory of property in defence of this claim.

thinkers denied that excommunication excluded men from secular society as well as from the Church. The clergy might threaten men with the torments of Hell, but they had no power to punish them and deprive them of secular rights in this world. The triumph of this idea after the Reformation made it possible for men to claim that their right to own property was independent of the use they made of it. But in the Middle Ages it was of merely negative importance in the history of property theories. It confined the discussion to the rational and philosophical level and denied that the doctrines of the Church have any practical relation to the rights of ownership: infidels have the same property rights as Christians.

Of the defences of the secular power in the later struggle between the Emperor and John XXII perhaps the most famous were written by Marsiglio of Padua and William of Occam. Marsiglio's *Defensor Pacis* (1324), the first book to push to its uttermost limits the theory that the Church has no coercive power whatsoever and that the secular power is supreme in this world, does not describe the origin of the rights of property, although it implies that they were created by the state.[1] But William of Occam, who was a leader of the Franciscan party which supported evangelical poverty as well as a partisan of the emperor, developed an elaborate theory of property to be used in the service of both causes.[2] Discussing law in general he explained that natural law is used in several different senses: according to one of these it directs that all property should be common, provided that men live according to reason; in another sense it directs men, in appropriate circumstances, to institute private ownership.[3] In defending evangelical poverty he emphasized that property is the result of sin and did not exist in the state of innocence.[4] In a tract written to defend the claims of the

[1] See especially I, x, and II, xii, in the edition by Richard Scholz, Hannover, 1932–3; on the question of Marsiglio's authorship, see McIlwain, pp. 297 ff.

[2] I am indebted here to the exposition of Occam's views given by McKeon, 'The Development of the Concept of Property.' *Ethics*, April 1938.

[3] *Dialogus*, III, ii, 3, c. 6, pp. 932–3, in Goldast, *Monarchia* II.

[4] *Opus Nonaginta Dierum*, c. 2, p. 999, Goldast, *Monarchia* II.

King of England against the Pope, he made use of the theory that property is founded in human law and consequently falls under the jurisdiction of the secular power.[1]

But the most interesting of Occam's statements about property comes from the *Dialogus*. There he inquires what rights the emperor has over the property of his subjects. His answer, although he surrounds it with a mass of subtle distinctions and scholastic paraphernalia, is essentially the philosophic theory of Aegidius and John of Paris. The emperor cannot claim all property by either natural or divine law since Gratian proves that by natural law ownership is common, and Augustine says that by divine law everything belongs to God. But private property rests on human law: can the emperor claim the ownership of all things by that law? Augustine, Occam observes, identifies human law with imperial law and comes to the conclusion that the rights of property are dependent upon the emperor's will. But Augustine's identification of human and imperial law is not exact; he confused them with one another because in his day the people had granted the Emperor all their legislative authority, so that for practical purposes the two were the same. But in fact rights established by human law are independent of the imperial authority.[2] Clearly, in this discussion Occam was using the theory according to which men instituted property before they set up political rulers.

On the Papal side the defenders of John XXII usually elaborated again the arguments of Aegidius Romanus.[3] But at

[1] *An Rex Angliae pro Succursu Guerrae Possit Recipere Bona Ecclesiarum*, pp. 440–1 in Richard Scholz, *Unbekannte Kirchenpolitische Streitschriften aus der Zeit Ludwigs des Bayern*, II, Rome, 1914.

[2] *Dialogus*, III, ii, 2, cc. 21–4, pp. 919–21, in Goldast, *Monarchia* II.

[3] The two most popular books were the *Summa de Potestate Ecclesiastica* (about 1325) of Augustinus Triumphatus and the *De Planctu Ecclesiae* (1330–40) of Alvarus Pelagius. Of Augustinus Triumphatus I have seen only the extracts printed in J. C. L. Gieseler, *Text-Book of Church History*, Vol. III, 33–5, New York, 1858; the references to property in Alvarus are scattered but the principal ones are in I, 13, I, 59, and II, 60 in the edition published at Venice in 1560. Two tracts of the period which follow Aegidius's principal arguments, written by Guilielimus de Cremona and Petrus de Lutra, are printed in Richard Scholz, *Unbekannte Kirchenpolitische Streitschriften*, II.

least one papalist made use of the theories which were most popular on the royalist side.[1] Thus all the various theories were used interchangeably by both papalists and imperialists. The subtleties of scholastic logic and the art of quoting Biblical texts made it possible for each writer to arrive at his chosen conclusion from whatever premise he started, although it is fair to add that in every case the theory of property was only incidental to the main argument.

The same theories of the origin and rights of private property were used to defend or attack evangelical poverty and the authority of king and Pope well into the modern era. But in the hands of one fourteenth-century theologian they were formulated in a new fashion. John Wycliffe's theory of dominion in grace was not original: it followed that of Aegidius.[2] But he used it to come to a conclusion entirely opposite to that of Aegidius. He begins by describing God's lordship over the world and explaining how God has granted the earth to men, contingent upon their service, just as the king grants a fief to his vassals. He quotes again the famous Letter 153 of Augustine: 'The righteous man possesses the whole world of riches, the infidel not an obol.'[3] From this Wycliffe draws the conclusion that the only way each of the righteous can possess the whole world is for all of them to hold it in common; common ownership is the more perfect form of ownership. As authorities for this opinion he refers to the New Testament and Plato. Aristotle has objected that no one will trouble to take care of common property, but Wycliffe answers, 'that most men take less care of the common property is sin, and consequently that does not invalidate the principle that all ought to be common.' Common use is 'natural'

[1] Konrad von Megenburg, *De Translacione Romani Imperii* (1354), pp. 314–16 in Scholz, *Unbekannte Kirchenpolitische Streitschriften*, II.

[2] Wycliffe may have taken it mainly from *De Pauperie Salvatore* (about 1350) by Richard Fitzralph, Archbishop of Armagh. It is printed with Wycliffe's *De Dominio Divino*, edited by R. L. Poole, London, 1890.

[3] *De Civili Dominio*, Liber Primus, edited by R. L. Poole, London, 1885, ch. 1. The Preface to this volume and the article on Wycliffe by R. L. Poole in the *Encyclopaedia Britannica*, 11th edition, summarize his theory of dominion.

and akin to the state of innocence. Aristotle's objections are based on the assumption that Plato also recommended community of wives, but Wycliffe does not believe that Socrates wanted that. The superiority of community ownership is a doctrine both Catholic and philosophical, and may, perhaps, be put into practice in some future time.[1]

But since the Fall of Man, he continues, private property has been introduced by human law and agreement; as Augustine says, private property is rooted in sin. These laws and agreements, however, do not invalidate the fact that only the righteous can have tenure. Men still hold their private estates conditionally and must fulfil the terms of God's grant.[2]

Up to this point Wycliffe has followed closely the theological theory of dominion of Aegidius and the papalists. But from here on he adopted the doctrine of their opponents, joining the camp of William of Occam and Marsiglio of Padua. Aegidius had claimed that it was the province of the Church to deprive the unjust of their property; Wycliffe denied that the Church had any power in temporal affairs and claimed that it was the province of the secular government to deprive unrighteous clergymen of their endowments. His arguments were the familiar ones, denying that excommunication touched a man's temporal concerns, claiming that the life of poverty was most suitable for clergymen, and pointing out that no one has property except conditionally, so that to deny the king the right to confiscate the wealth of the clergy would be to deny that God has provided a remedy for clerical abuse.[3]

Although the elements in Wycliffe's theory of property were not new, his formulation of them had considerable influence. His insistence on the virtues of communal ownership gave new

[1] *De Civili Dominio*, I, ch. 14.

[2] Chs. 18, 19, 36; and *De Dominio Divino Libri Tres*, III, i, edited by R. L. Poole, London, 1890.

[3] *De Civili Dominio*, I, chs. 37, 38, 42. Wycliffe's views about the temporal and spiritual authorities, indicating his strong nationalistic feeling, are developed in his *De Officio Regis*, ed. by A. W. Pollard and C. Sayle, London, 1887.

life to this ancient doctrine of the Church at the very time when peasants were revolting and men were reciting

When Adam delved and Eve span
Who was then the gentleman?

Carried to Bohemia by John Hus, Wycliffe's theory encouraged communistic revolts and experiments which were the bogey of property owners for two centuries. On the other hand, Wycliffe's attacks on ecclesiastical wealth helped prepare men's minds for the Reformation and the destruction of the property relations which characterized feudal society; and his defence of the royal power contributed to the formation of the new property system characteristic of modern capitalist society.

Wycliffe's formulation of the common medieval theories of property was probably unique. But other men continued to use them in the traditional fashion. They were repeated in the fifteenth century during the great struggle to convert the papacy into a constitutional monarchy with the General Council as its Parliament,[1] and the works of this period together with many of the fourteenth-century texts mentioned above were printed more than once in the fifteenth and sixteenth centuries, and were

[1] For example in the *Opera Omnia* of Jean Gerson, 5 vols., Antwerp, 1706; in Vol. I, Peter d'Ailly's *De Legitimo Dominio*, cols. 641–6; in Vol. II, Jacob Almain's *Expositio*, cols. 1028–30, and *Quaestio Resumptivo*, cols. 961 ff.; in Vol. III, Gerson's *Liber de Vita*, cols. 29–31, and *Sermo de Dominio Evangelico*, cols. 202–3; in Vol. IV, Gerson's *Sermo ad Regem Franciae pro Justitia*. Nicholas of Cusa, *De Concordantia Catholica* (1433), III, 4, in Schard, *De Iurisdictione*, quotes the famous words of Augustine to prove that the Church would have no property except for the laws of the emperor. The *De Ortu et Authoritate Imperii Romani* (about 1446) of Aeneas Sylvius (later Pius II), also printed in Schard, does not mention property specifically, but asserts that men lived in a bestial state of nature after the Fall, that they first set up social institutions by agreement, and then later set up political authorities to protect their agreements; chs. 1 and 2. One of the partisans of the Conciliar Party in the Church, Antonius de Rosellis, 'Doctor of both Laws,' made an especially ingenious combination of traditional theories to defend the property of the individual against both Pope and Emperor; *Monarchia, sive Tractatus de Potestate Imperatoris et Papae*, printed in Goldast, *Monarchia*, I. According to Goldast it was written in the second quarter of the fifteenth century.

read and quoted during the Reformation and the constitutional struggles of the seventeenth century.

Of the fifteenth-century writers on law and politics none was quoted more often by Englishmen during the seventeenth century —the century in which modern theories of property and government finally triumphed over those of the Middle Ages—than Sir John Fortescue.[1] Fortescue was the fifteenth-century English advocate of the middle class, the class whose rise to power is the essential ingredient in the transition from feudal to capitalist society. He defended that class and the property on which its power was based against feudal magnates, royal despots, peasant radicals, and Lollard socialists.[2] In doing so he combined the various medieval theories of property in the very fashion in which they were going to serve the purposes of bourgeois apologists for the next three or four hundred years.[3] His defence of property is at once a summary of medieval, and an introduction to modern, history.

Fortescue accepts without question the venerable Christian doctrine that property is the result of sin. He refers to the famous words of Gratian's *Decretum* and states that before the Fall of Man all was common by natural law.[4] But his acceptance of that doctrine is entirely formal and he proceeds at once to prove that property is now rooted in natural law. The same law, he explains, which forbad private ownership before sin prescribes it after the Fall. His analogical proof resembles that of Alexander of Hales.[5] The same breath cools the porridge and kindles the flame; the same sun hardens mud into brick and dissolves ice into snow; and similarly the same law of nature prescribes communism in

1 McIlwain, p. 354.

2 For the class basis of Fortescue's theory see M. A. Shepard, 'The Political and Constitutional Theory of Sir John Fortescue,' *Essays in Honor of C. H. McIlwain*, Cambridge, Mass., 1936.

3 Later thinkers did not derive their theories directly from Fortescue since most of his ideas on property were included in the *De Natura Legis Naturae* which was never printed before Lord Clermont's edition of the *Works*, London, 1869. The seventeenth-century lawyers referred only to the constitutional ideas which were based on his theory of property; McIlwain, 354.

4 *De Natura Legis Naturae*, I, 5; I, 20; II, 32.

5 Above, p. 44.

the state of innocence and private property in the state of corruption. The historical proof is that Cain and Abel had property before there was any *jura gentium* or *lex humana*. 'Wherefore it must be of necessity conceded that property in things, especially in things acquired by the sweat of the brow, first accrued to man by the law of nature alone, seeing there was then no human law; and consequently buyings, sellings, lettings, hirings and the like took their origin from the law of nature which is perpetual law.'[1]

Fortescue thus adopted the theory that property was instituted prior to human law—the popular theory used to limit the claims of government. But for other purposes he proved, by quoting the *Digest*, that the 'law of nature' and the 'law of nations' are the same; he identified the 'law of nations' with 'human law' in general; he proved, by quoting St. Thomas, that valid 'human law' is really a part of the natural law from which it is derived by reason;[2] and he adopted throughout the book the theory that human society and its institutions are natural in the Aristotelian sense. In short, Fortescue could use either the Aristotelian or the Stoic concept of 'natural law' to defend property and he could cite medieval authorities to support him in either case.

In defending the rights of inheritance he made use of yet another popular medieval theory. After the Fall God said to Adam:

> 'In the sweat of thy brow thou shalt eat bread'; in which words was granted to man a property in the things he should acquire by his labour. . . . For since the bread which a man gained by labour was his own, and no man could eat bread without the sweat of his own brow, every man who toiled not was prohibited from eating the bread which by his own sweat another man had acquired; wherefore property in the bread so gained accrued only to the man who toiled for it . . . and in this way property capable of descent first took its rise.

By sweating man impairs his body and the bread or property which he gains is the compensation of the loss. 'Property takes the place of the man's bodily integrity . . . and so thenceforth accompanies his blood.' The son inherits his father's property

[1] I, 20.

[2] I, 5, 19, 20.

along with his blood.[1] Fortescue's allegorical interpretation of the Biblical text is in the medieval tradition, and his theory is obviously related to that of John of Paris, and to the Roman lawyers' concept of occupation. But in its insistence on labour as the basis of man's title to property it is indistinguishable from the theories of Locke and the eighteenth-century proponents of natural right.

Finally, Fortescue makes use of the theories of dominion and contract to explain the rights which the prince has over the property of private individuals. Even the most absolute of princes has only a limited dominion, even though no positive human laws define the limitations: Ahab and Jezebel offended against the laws of nature and God when they despoiled Naboth of his vineyard.[2] But some princes are limited by positive laws and may not touch the property of their subjects without their consent. The difference between the two kinds of principalities Fortescue explains in terms of their origin: in England the agreement between king and people forbids the Government to tax subjects without their consent; in France there is no such stipulation in the fundamental law.[3]

Almost everything that had been said about private property in the Middle Ages finds an echo in Fortescue and at the same time his summary sketches most of the ideas on the subject which men propounded in the course of the next three or four centuries. He repeats in formal fashion that property is based on sin, but his essential argument is that property is natural according to almost any definition of that word. Men continued after Fortescue, as they had done before him, to argue about the precise limits of Papal and royal control over the property of individual Christians

[1] II, 32.

[2] *The Governance of England*, ch. IV, edited by Charles Plummer, Oxford, 1885.

[3] *De Laudibus Angliae*, ed. by S. B. Chrimes, Cambridge, 1942, esp. chs. 12, 13, 36. Fortescue does not use the formal theory of contract: he describes the various kinds of constitutions as developing slowly and the agreements between king and people as being embodied in customary law rather than in a formal contract. But the essential idea of an agreement which excludes royal power from some spheres of action is definitely there.

and subjects, but in doing so they were not questioning the basic institution of private ownership. The issue was primarily one of taxation, and even the theorists who attributed the most absolute powers to Pope or king, never imagined that those powers would be used to abolish private property and the class structure connected with it. They all agreed that private property was fixed in the nature of things. The idea that it was the only possible system was so firmly rooted that Thomas Hobbes in the seventeenth century could categorically deny that his sovereign ruler was in any way limited by a law of nature, and yet take it for granted that he would protect the property of his subjects.

Fortescue still used the concept of dominion, but he connected it with the idea of contract which in the course of time replaced it altogether. The idea that society was an organized hierarchy and that the ruler had the power to deprive men of their possessions and privileges when they failed to fulfil their duties died along with the feudal system. The feudal theory of ownership as a conditional right to use property was replaced with the Roman and modern concept of absolute ownership. 'It was the Roman pagan conception of absolute property that triumphed at the close of the Middle Ages. This idea, which is the foundation of modern capitalism, led at the same time to further attempts to depress the peasants into slavery. It has been fraught with a thousand evils, from which even now the world is slowly and with many struggles trying to recover. The 'reception,' as it is called, of the Roman Law in 1495 in Germany may be taken as the date when the Middle Ages came to an end and the Roman ideas of property had conquered the West.'[1] Authorities in Church and state, as Professor Tawney has shown, tried for some time to claim that they had a moral right as heads of the body politic to see that men used their property for the general welfare. In England, Tudor officials attempted to arrest the enclosure movement and Puritan saints would have liked to supervise the whole of economic life. But the attempts failed and the idea

[1] J. N. Figgis, *The Political Aspect of Saint Augustine's City of God*, London, 1921, p. 99.

that a man should be able to do what he would with his own triumphed: the state had no general moral right but only those limited powers granted in the original contract; churchmen might advise men to use their property as stewards of God, but they might not force them to do so. The feudal theory of dominion lingered on as a formal legal doctrine, but with the collapse of the society which it had sought to explain and justify, it ceased to influence the theory of private property. But combined with the idea of common ownership, as the radical religious sects found it in Wycliffe, it did do service as an argument against private property far down into the modern era.

Another important result of the collapse of the concept of dominion was that men began to distinguish between power relationships which depended on property, and those which were derived from the political authority of the state. Following St. Augustine the theorists of dominion assumed that private property and political authority were both instruments of force necessary to discipline and coerce sinful men. The two were denoted by one word, dominion, and were together the means by which some men dominated others. It did not occur to anyone that the two were separable, that the ruling class would not always be the richest class. The function of the state was not merely to protect a man's property, but to protect his dominion—his property plus the political and social privileges which were invariably connected with ownership. In short the function of the state was to preserve the existing class structure. But in modern times the discarding of the idea of dominion made it possible to think of property apart from political authority. Hence arose the liberal belief that it was possible for men to be free and equal politically, that the state might represent impartially the interest of all citizens, while at the same time the unequal division of private property made owners the economic masters of non-owners. Men defended as good the theory that the primary purpose of the state was to protect property, but condemned the theory that the state ought to protect the privileges of a ruling class. The medieval theorist would have been puzzled by the distinction.

CHAPTER FIVE

☆

The Sixteenth Century

'Thou Shalt Not Steal!'

It is a commonplace of intellectual history that each age must find new arguments to justify and defend its interests even though the interests themselves remain the same. Luther and Calvin would have found St. Thomas's theory of property inadequate, even if they had wished to buttress the institutions of property which he had found natural and good. But in fact they did not want to do that. The problems connected with ownership which the Reformation had to solve were in many ways new and demanded new solutions.

The chief theoretical problem which the religious leaders had to deal with arose out of the confiscation of ecclesiastical wealth and the general transfer of property from an old to a new class of owners. During the sixteenth century a large part of the property of Europe was suddenly wrested from one privileged group and handed over to a new one. The Church was expropriated; the lands of feudal magnates, who opposed both capitalism and the new religion, and the ancient demesne lands of the Crown, were transferred by forced sale to the new ruling class. Even in lands where the old religion survived, its property was attacked, and in Catholic Spain and Austria the property of the Church was confiscated by men whose souls were undefiled with heresy. But the brunt of defending the practice of robbing Peter fell upon the Reformers.

On the left wing of the Reformation radical preachers revived the venerable doctrine of Christian communism and argued that there would be plenty for all if everyone worked and private property were abolished altogether. This was the great age of peasant revolts, and the actual attempt of the Anabaptists to establish a communistic economic society in Germany electrified the whole of Europe. Opponents of the Reformation were quick to pin responsibility on the Reformers; and they had a strong argument. The Reformation was an all-out attack on established authority; it denounced the luxurious wealth of the Roman Church as unchristian and unjust; and in confiscating the wealth of that Church it could not avoid suggesting to the mass of men that a redistribution of wealth was both possible and desirable. Moreover, some of the Reformers, in bursts of evangelical piety which they must have regretted later, encouraged the latent Christian tendencies in the direction of equality and community when they spoke of the liberty of the Christian man justified by faith, and the fellowship of true believers united in the reformed Churches. In an Exposition of the Ten Commandments, the Creed, and the Lord's Prayer, Luther wrote that the true Church was the assembly of men who have faith, the body of true believers wherever they may be in the world, and 'I believe that in this community, or Christian Realm, everything is common, each shares the goods of the other, and no one calls anything his own.'[1] All the Reformers who permitted themselves to speak of the religious revolution in terms of social welfare in this world were confronted by the spectre which devils every revolutionary—the left wing wants to push the revolution far beyond its original aims. The matter was especially serious for Luther since the peasants' revolt and the strong Anabaptist movement in Germany actually threatened the success of the Reformation there. The communistic movement called forth his most vitriolic denunciations. He was no lover of the Catholic hierarchy and his words describing it are scurrilous enough, but he did not counsel the assassination of the Pope and his retinue; he did, however, advise good Germans to kill rebellious peasants on sight, and his pamphlets against them are so bloodthirsty that Protestants have been apologizing for them ever since. In other parts of Europe, too, Reformers found it necessary to refute, and to dissociate themselves from the radical sects which appeared

[1] *Works*, Erlangen edition, Vol. XXII, p. 20.

everywhere in the wake of the revolution. A great part of the Reformation theory of property—almost all the Lutheran theory—was constructed as an answer to the Anabaptists. In the Augsburg Confession, the official statement of Lutheran principles, the right of Christians to own property is expressly confirmed; the thirty-eighth Article of Religion of the Elizabethan Church asserted 'the goods of Christians are not common . . . as certain Anabaptists do falsely boast'; nearly a hundred years later English Puritans explained in the Westminster Confession of Faith, under the heading 'The Communion of Saints,' 'nor doth their communion one with another, as Saints, take away, or infringe the title or propriety which each man hath in his goods and possessions.'

The religious radicals were certainly the most important opponents of the system of private property, but the humanists, influenced perhaps by the revival of Plato, also described fanciful Utopias where private property and want do not exist.[1] These sketches were purely speculative, and in no case did their authors intend to undermine the existing economic society. Nevertheless such speculations were potentially dangerous, particularly so when, as in Sir Thomas More's *Utopia*, they were accompanied with a sharp and shrewd description of the actual misery which the economic revolution was causing. Consequently, more than one defender of the established order judged it expedient to refute the Utopian speculations of educated dreamers as well as the practical claims of the Anabaptists.

Besides having to justify the confiscation of property and at the same time protect the institution in general from the attacks of the left wing, the Reformation theory of property also had to take into the account the old problem of how far the prince might go in interfering with the property rights of his subjects.

[1] Sir Thomas More's *Utopia* (1516) was the most famous of these works. Others are listed in the bibliography of *Nova Solyma*, translated by Walter Begley, London, 1902. Two famous ones of the seventeenth century were Campanella's *City of the Sun* (1623) and J. V. Andreae's *Christianopolis* (1619). See also the references in H. C. White, *Social Criticism in Popular Religious Literature of the Sixteenth Century*, New York, 1944, ch. 11.

In those countries where the Reformation succeeded it was the princes who handed over the monastic lands to the new owners; here the Reformers were inclined to ascribe very extensive rights over property to the government. But no sooner had the transfer been made than the new owners began to resent the restrictions imposed by the government on the use of their new property. The story is especially dramatic in England where the new Tudor landlords had scarcely taken possession of the monastic lands, which the king had made available to them, before they began to complain of the royal restrictions on enclosure and depopulation. Everywhere the new class of property-owners wanted a freedom to use their capital in ways which no government had ever permitted before. They wanted to lend it on interest, to buy as cheaply and sell as dearly as possible, and to farm their agricultural estates in the most profitable way, regardless of the interest of the peasant. Thus at the very moment when the princes were being given very large powers with which to confiscate the property of the old regime, they had to be taught that their power to interfere with the rights of the new owners was more limited than that of a feudal monarch. In England the middle class created an absolute government in the sixteenth century for the purpose of destroying the property relationships (and religion) of feudalism, and then it spent the greater part of the next century in replacing that absolutism with a limited government which could not fail to grant the capitalist the particular brand of freedom he wanted. But everywhere in Europe the supporters of absolutism faced the same problem and their theory of property had to make an attempt to solve it.

In those lands where the prince did not adopt the Reformation programme and deal with property in a Protestant fashion, another theory of the relation of ruler and individual owner was necessary. Men who professed the same theological tenets were proponents of divine right in one land and in another were rebelling against a prince who refused to admit that he could do nothing without the advice and consent of his subjects. In France,

Calvinists and Catholics alternated with one another in asserting that the monarchy was absolute or limited; their opinion at any one time was a function of the policy pursued by the king of that moment.

Out of this turmoil was wrought, not any one consistent theory of property, but a mass of hypotheses which could be used by later thinkers constructing the classical bourgeois theory. In the sixteenth century the practical policies of the middle class were too diverse and opportunistic to be justified by any one formal theory. Not until feudalism had been destroyed and the era of confiscation had drawn to a close could theorists construct a formal argument which would sanctify the rights of private owners and leave the individual capitalist free to use his capital as he saw fit. That was the task of the seventeenth and eighteenth centuries.

The Reformation theorists failed to solve their first great problem. They were not able to work out a theory which would justify large-scale confiscation and at the same time mesh with their other ideas about the nature of private ownership and its rights. For a consistent theory they substituted an emotional attitude. They concentrated on the abuses of clerical wealth, which were no doubt sufficiently exasperating, and made them appear so monstrous that outraged, and greedy, laymen felt free to lay their hands on that wealth without bothering to demonstrate their right to do so. In fact, the Reformers merely expressed with new vigour the old medieval hatred and envy of clerical power and wealth. Luther's *Address to the German Nobility* lists all the familiar medieval complaints against the Church—simony, luxurious living beyond the dreams of temporal magnates, the disparity between the monastic professions of poverty and chastity and actual life in the cloisters, and Papal exactions which impoverish all men from emperor to peasant. Luther extended the list by asserting that many of the goods which the Church sold—indulgences, pardons, prayers for souls in Purgatory, and so on—were worthless, and the general implication of Protestant theory was that since the Church of Rome had no monopoly of grace it had no right to charge monopoly prices for that article.

In one passage denouncing monastic wealth Luther did complain that the monks had no right to be rich, since they did not work. 'If a man will be poor, he should not be rich; if he will be rich, let him put his hand to the plough and get wealth himself out of the earth. . . . It is not right that one should work that another may be idle, and live ill that another may live well, as is now the perverse abuse, for St. Paul says: "If any would not work, neither should he eat."'[1] But it was hardly wise for Luther and any other Reformer to push this argument: as the Anabaptists pointed out, there were lay as well as clerical owners who lived well without working.

In England, too, the same general denunciation of the Church's abuse of wealth did service as an emotional justification for seizing the property of the Church of Rome, and for the next hundred years the Puritans used it to attack the Church of England. Miss White has demonstrated in her excellent study of the popular literature of social criticism in sixteenth-century England how the whole tradition of complaint against wealth and oppression was channelled into an attack on the old religion.[2] For a time the leaders of the middle class were able to turn the discontent of the poor against the feudal order. The origin of much of this literature, which Miss White classifies as a part of the Piers Plowman tradition, goes back to the days of Wycliffe and the Lollards. And the theoretical basis of these attacks on the wealth of the Church, although it was mostly unexpressed, is Wycliffe's theory of Dominion in Grace. For an attack on the wickedness of monks does not justify confiscating their lands unless it is assumed that men hold property contingent upon their righteous use of it. But it is not surprising that the idea of Dominion in Grace was not revived as a formal justification of

[1] *Address to the German Nobility*, p. 71, in *The First Principles of the Reformation*, Henry Wace and C. A. Buchheim, London, 1883.

[2] Helen C. White, *Social Criticism in Popular Religious Literature of the Sixteenth Century*, New York, 1944.

the Reformation confiscations: it was a two-edged sword which could wound lay as well as clerical owners.

The problem of confining the attack on property to ecclesiastical property was somewhat easier in the case of the monasteries since here, as the Reformers pointed out time and again, even if the monks had lived according to their profession they would have been making a wrong use of worldly goods. According to the Protestant ethic of work, and the doctrine of the calling, however blamelessly a monk lived, however zealously he performed his religious devotions and contemplated heavenly things, he was still an idler, a man without a legitimate vocation, a parasite. When Simon Fish complained in 1524 that idle priests, 'setting all labour aside,' held a third of the lands of England, he was not demanding that they should be forced to perform those devotions which Catholics had always assumed to be pleasing to God and helpful to men; he had ceased to believe in the efficacy of those devotions and wanted to confiscate the endowments which had made them possible.[1]

Here again the argument took the form of an emotional diatribe rather than a reasonable theory. But behind it lay the assumption that property should be given to owners who would use it, not to free themselves from all economic activity, but to organize a more productive economic system. This was as near as the theorists came to adopting a utilitarian theory of the rights of ownership.

Finally, it was possible for the Reformers to assume that the attack on ecclesiastical property was not an act of expropriation and did not, therefore, conflict with the rights of private ownership. They could assume that the Church was an endowed institution that needed reforming because its officers had spent the common funds, not for the maintenance of true religion, but for the propagation of superstition and for their own private enjoyment. In carrying out his religious duties the prince was not depriving the Church of its property, not expropriating its

[1] *A Supplication for the Beggars*, reprinted in Early English Text Society Extra Series, No. 13, London, 1871.

wealth, but merely ensuring that that property should be used, as its donors had intended, for the spiritual welfare of the people. Here there was no question of expropriation, but rather one of jurisdiction—who had the authority to reform the Church?[1] The defect of this assumption was that neither the left-wing radicals nor the secular authorities were willing to act on it. The religious leaders wanted the property, formerly at the disposal of monastic and Papal authorities, to be used for religious education, including the endowment of a popular, teaching ministry. But the radicals wanted to use it for the abolition of poverty, and the new men of the court wanted it to line their own pockets.

Against the radicals the Reformers defended the right of the secular authority to determine how the property should be used. In answer to the peasants that the expropriated tithes should be given to each parish to pay ministers of its own choosing and to relieve the poor as it saw fit, Luther said flatly that tithes belonged to the state to spend as it pleased; the peasant's demand was a species of rebellion and robbery.[2] In England, too, radical proposals for abolishing poverty were countered by stressing the right of the secular authorities to administer the confiscated properties. But it is proper to add that in the end the Reformers realized they had been the dupes of the new capitalist owners of Church property. In the very pamphlet in which Luther denounced the peasants he also castigated the ruling class for failing to carry through the social as well as the religious

[1] The question did arise as to whether the use of endowments for new purposes, even religious purposes, did not violate the rights of donors, whose wills contained specific directions for the use of their bequests, and deprive them of the prayers which they counted on to comfort them in the next world. As to the prayers, the answer was that they were ineffectual; see the Act for the Dissolution of Chantries, 1547, printed in J. R. Tanner, *English Constitutional Documents*, Cambridge, 1940. In general, as Thomas Starkey pointed out in a letter to Henry VIII, it is the right of the state to alter testaments provided that the general intention of the testator is carried out; *England in the Reign of Henry VIII*, Early English Text Society, Extra Series, No. 32, Pt. 1, p. iv, London, 1878.

[2] *Ermahnung zum Frieden auf die zwölf Artikel der Bauerschaft in Schwaben* (1525), p. 334, in *Werke*, Vol. VII, Braunschweig, 1892.

reformation, and for failing to abolish some of the oppressive practices of the old order. Some of the most pungent denunciations of the capitalist landlords in England came from Latimer and other Reformers who felt that these men had betrayed the Reformation by appropriating monastic lands for their own private purposes. Like many idealists from that day to this, the Reformers were the beloved teachers of the middle class as long as they confined themselves to denouncing medieval superstition and oppression; when they attempted to mould the new order in accordance with their ideals they were looked upon as impractical dreamers whose schemes should be ignored by hard-headed men of the world. In the reign of Queen Mary many of the religious leaders were killed or exiled, while the men they had helped to enrich quietly accepted the old religion—with the proviso that its confiscated property should not be restored.

Meanwhile, the religious leaders had served their masters well by preparing the mass of men to accept the actual expropriation of clerical wealth. They had done this without popularizing any general theory of the limitation of the rights of ownership which might in the future be directed against the new owners. In England the secular authorities themselves were careful to avoid the appearance of violating the rights of ownership: the larger monasteries were not confiscated, but fell to the Crown either because the abbots had been convicted of treason or had, at the persuasion of the king, voluntarily surrendered their properties. In general, the official assumption was that the Church was undergoing, not expropriation, but reformation.

Nevertheless it was expropriation and there were opponents of the Reformation who pointed to the dangers of that policy. A year before Luther's *Address to the German Nobility* stated that it was wrong for monks to live without working, Simon Fish in England had used the same argument to recommend the expropriation of all the richer clergy.[1] Sir Thomas More's reply to Fish touched the sore spot which Reformation theorists of property never succeeded in healing.

[1] *Supplication for the Beggars* (1524).

He layeth unto the charge of the clergy that they live idle all, and that they be all bound to labour and get their living in the sweat of their faces by the precept that God gave to Adam in the first chapter of Genesis. But it is good to look betime what this beggar's proctor meaneth by this commandment of hand labour that he speaketh of. . . . If ye call it a precept as he doth, and then will that it extend unto all the whole kind of man, as a thing by God commanded unto Adam and all his offspring, then, though he say little now, he meaneth to go farther hereafter than he speaketh of yet. . . . Surely likewise as for the beggars he now maketh his bill to the King's Highness against bishops, abbots, priors, prelates, and priests, so would he then within a while after make another bill to the people against merchants, gentlemen, kings, lords, and princes, and complain that they have all, and say that they do nothing for it but live idle, and that they be commanded in Genesis to live by the labour of their hands in the sweat of their faces, as he saith by the clergy now. Wherein if they will think that they shall stand in other case than the clergy doth now, they may peradventure sore deceive themselves. . . . Whoso will advise princes or lay people to take from the clergy their possessions, alleging matters at large, as laying to their charge that they live not as they should nor use not well their possessions, and therefore it were well done to take from them by force and dispose them better—we dare boldly say, who giveth this device, as now doth this beggar's proctor, we would give you counsel to look well what will follow. For he shall not fail, as we said before, if this bill of his were sped, to find you soon after in a new supplication new bald reasons enough that should please the people's ears, wherewith he would labour to have lords' lands and all honest men's goods to be pulled from them by force and distributed among beggars.[1]

In another work More repeated the same argument and went on to warn that the practical problem of making better use of the wealth of the Church was not easily solved: many different men would like to lay hands on it.[2] Again he had gone to the heart of the matter: it was the actual disposition of the confiscated lands which led the more idealistic Reformers to feel that they had been betrayed by the secular rulers. The theorists of the Reformation could

[1] *A Supplication of Souls*, in *Works*, London, 1557, pp. 303–5.

[2] *Apology*, in *Works*, pp. 881–2.

not answer More's arguments without admitting the principle that all ownership was contingent upon right use. But no property owner was willing to grant that that principle should be enforced by any authority in this world. The theoretical problem was left unsolved.

Thinkers had to be content with accepting the facts. Their theoretical activity was employed, not in justifying the expropriations, but in defending the newly acquired rights of the expropriators. They had succeeded in turning the discontent of the poor against the wealth of the Church; they now had to deflect that discontent from the new owners. Having previously poured oil on the fire, they were now called on either to quench it or suffer the penalties of incendiarism.

Luther's remarks about private ownership illustrate the dilemma of Protestant theory. He began by attacking the property of the Church, particularly that of the monasteries, and ended by defending the rights of ownership against radical Anabaptists. Against the Church he argued that it is the duty of a Christian man to acquire property with which to relieve the poor and that it is his duty to acquire that property by work.[1] Both arguments were directed against the monastic ideals of community ownership and voluntary poverty, and against the title of the clergy to those large properties which had been acquired, not by labour, but by the sale of imaginary spiritual goods and by the donations of the superstitious. Both arguments were proved by quotations from St. Paul and in general, as we should expect, Luther's theory of property depended much more heavily upon the authority of Scriptures than had that of his medieval predecessors. The example of Abraham proves that a godly man may acquire great wealth and engage in trade, and is a sufficient argument against philosophers, monks, and Anabaptists.[2] But monks and Anabaptists also quoted the Bible and

[1] *On Christian Liberty* (1520), p. 125, and *Address to the German Nobility* (1525), p. 71, in Wace and Buchheim, *First Principles of the Reformation.*

[2] *Von Kaufhandlung und Wucher* (1524), p. 515, *Werke*, Vol. VII, Braunschweig, 1892; *Exposition of the Book of Genesis* (1535–45), ch. XIII, 2, Latin text in *Werke*, Weimar edition, Vol. LXII, German text in Vol. I of J. G. Walch's edition, Halle, 1740.

Luther found it necessary to interpret in another sense the verses which they cited. The texts recording the communism of the primitive Church at Jerusalem have, he said, been over-emphasized. The practice of that Church is not binding on later Christians and was not compulsory even then: Ananias was condemned for lying, not for holding back his property. The pooling of property was possible during the first fervour of conversion, but many modern Church members are not true Christians and would not work if communism were introduced; the later Churches founded by the Apostles did not follow the example of Jerusalem; in normal times Christians have families and this is not possible without private property. Finally, Anabaptists err in thinking that the Gospels prescribe forms of domestic and civil government; in fact they are concerned exclusively with teaching men how to procure pardon for their sins. They direct us to help the needy, but only when these are deserving and when such help will not injure the giver.[1] A Christian must hold his property as reason teaches, and the laws of this world prescribe, since Christ gives no rules for matters which are distinct from the life of the spirit.[2]

Philosophers, Luther wrote, saw men quarrelling about private possessions and came to the conclusion that they were evil. But it is man, not things which are evil. St. Francis was following these foolish philosophers when he imagined that the Gospels taught men to sell all their property and give it to the poor, rather than to acknowledge their sins and hope for salvation through Christ. 'I do not maintain that St. Francis was simply wicked, but his works show that he was a weak-minded and freakish man, or to say the truth, a fool.' He at least begged for the poor: his followers beg for themselves alone. Even the Pope condemned the Franciscans, although for the wrong reason: he was afraid their doctrine might be used as a weapon against

[1] *A Sermon on St. Stephen's Day*, pp. 2460 ff., Walsh edition, Vol. XIII, Halle, 1743.

[2] *Exposition of St. Matthew*, chs. V, VI, VII, pp. 144 ff., in Vol. XLIII of the Erlangen edition of the German works.

his property. Finally, Luther sums up the argument against poverty and community property by quoting the Bible: riches are good provided that a man does not put his trust in them; Christ had a purse—Judas managed it for him—and so was a property-owner.[1]

Luther's condemnation of monasticism is, from one point of view, a remarkable paradox. He wants to expropriate the monks because they hold the false theory that riches are evil. Medieval reformers attacked the wealth of the Church because they believed that poverty was meritorious and wanted the clergy to enjoy its benefits. The leaders of the Reformation rejected that belief and confiscated the lands of the monks because these insisted on holding to it. The key for understanding the paradox is the Protestant ethic. The monks were condemned, not for owning property, but because they did not use that property in an economically productive fashion. At best they used it to produce prayers. Luther and the other Reformation leaders insisted that it should be used, not to relieve men from the necessity of working, but as a tool for making more goods. The attitude of the Reformation was practically, 'not prayers, but production.' And production, not for consumption, but for more production. The Reformation leaders were agreed that luxurious living was evil and that alms should be limited to those rare creatures, the deserving poor. What was to be done with the surplus created by the laborious and thrifty Christian? The theorists did not answer the question; economic historians record that it was used as capital, the form of property which gave power to the middle class and characterizes modern society.[2]

[1] *Exposition of the Book of Genesis*, ch. XIII, 2.

[2] Luther's economic ethic was much closer to the medieval tradition than that of later leaders, and in general the preachers were always a step behind their congregations in approving new business methods and practices. See Ernst Troeltsch, *The Social Teaching of the Christian Churches*, translated by Olive Wyon, London, 1931, and R. H. Tawney, *Religion and the Rise of Capitalism*, London, 1926. The theory that the Reformation fostered the growth of capitalism must, after the manner of all generalizations, be qualified in concrete instances; but it remains an indispensable tool for describing the course of events in the sixteenth and seventeenth centuries.

With the Peasants' Revolt and the spread of Anabaptism, Luther used the arguments against monastic communism to defend the property of lay owners. Writing 'against the murdering and robbing gangs of peasants,' he said there was no point in citing Genesis to prove that God gave the earth and its fruits to all men: the Old Testament is revised by the New. The New Testament does not make property common; some of the first Christians pooled their own property voluntarily but they did not try to make the goods of Herod and Pilate common too. What fine Christians are these rebels who want to make, not their own, but other men's goods common! There are no more devils in Hell: they have all got into these peasants.[1]

Against the ancient theory that property was common by natural law, Luther gave the classic Reformation argument. Natural law, he wrote, is identical with the Ten Commandments. The other parts of the Law of Moses are merely civil and do not bind us, but the Ten Commandments can never be abrogated. 'Thou shalt not steal' is the foundation of private ownership.[2] This identification of natural law and the Decalogue, characteristic of Reformation theology, is essentially a denial of the whole late medieval tradition. It rejects that optimistic view of the world which led St. Thomas to say that private property and government were institutions derived from the law of nature. The great theorist of the thirteenth century and its stable social hierarchy could argue that the existing economic and political relationships were approximations of the ideal, were conducive to the welfare of all men, and were natural in the sense that they were better than those of the original and primitive state. But that line of argument was not convincing in the sixteenth century, when the old property relationships were being violently severed, and the new ones seemed to offer no improvement for the mass of men. Indeed, the radicals against whom

[1] *Wider die Mörderischen und Räuberischen Rotten der Bauern* (1525), p. 348, in Vol. VII of the *Werke*, Braunschweig edition.

[2] *Wider die Himmlischen Propheten* (1525), pp. 80–1, in Vol. XVIII, *Werke*, Weimer edition.

Luther and the other leaders had to argue maintained that the new society was less interested in the general welfare than the old. Partly for this reason, the Reformation theorists made little use of the Thomistic argument that private ownership was based on right reason and natural law. For the optimistic argument from reason and the good of men, Luther substituted the pessimistic one from the formal command of God.

In fact, for St. Thomas's optimistic belief in the goodness of man and society, the Reformation substituted the pessimistic view of Augustine. Private property and government are not positive blessings, but evils made necessary by man's depravity.[1] To base them on nature and man's reason is to give them a sandy foundation because both these have been perverted by Adam's sin. The only sure foundation of right is God's Word in the Bible. If all men, Luther granted, lived in the spirit of the Gospels, coercion and inequality would no longer be needed in this world. True faith needs no law. But we know that men will never be able to achieve such perfection, and to try to rule them now according to the rules of the New Testament would be to follow the example of a shepherd who puts wolves, lions, eagles, and sheep into one pen.[2] God's government is merciful, but the governments of the world, which are no other than the agents of God's anger against the wicked, and are really forerunners of Hell and eternal death, must be tough, severe, and wrathful.[3] Peasants who demand the abolition of serfdom are attempting to substitute God's kingdom for the kingdom of this world where inequality is an unavoidable evil.[4]

The advantage of basing the rights of property and the authority of princes on the formal basis of God's command is

[1] Zwingli, the Swiss Reformer, agreed that property was sinful, though necessary. See *Elenchus contra catabaptista*, *Opera*, Vol. III, Zurich, 1832, and the reference in R. H. Tawney, *Religion and the Rise of Capitalism*, p. 103.

[2] *Von Weltlicher Obrigkeit* (1523), pp. 251–2, Weimar edition, Vol. XI; *Von Kaufhandlung und Wucher*, p. 525, Vol. VII, Braunschweig edition.

[3] *Ein Sendbrief von dem Harten Buchlein wider die Bauern* (1525), p. 366 in Vol. VII, Braunschweig edition.

[4] *Ermahnung zum Frieden*, pp. 334–5, in Vol. VII, Braunschweig edition.

that it disposes of all radical proposals to interfere with those rights and that authority on the grounds of utility and the common good. God commands men to respect property and obey princes—period. The question of happiness is not involved; men ought not to expect it from institutions made necessary by their own depravity. Men whose reason is debased, wrote Luther, ought not to appeal to natural laws and rights. Christians who assert their natural rights act like heathens, Turks, and Jews. '*Leiden, Leiden, Kreuz, Kreuz, ist der Christen Recht, das und kein andres!*' When mobs of farmers demand their rights as Christians, we may reflect that Christians are not so common that they can be assembled in a heap; 'he is a rare bird, a Christian.'[1] By forbidding an appeal to the principles of natural law, Luther was in fact forbidding men to plead human standards of justice and utility as an excuse for overturning established economic and political institutions. God's commands are to be obeyed regardless of what men, whose reason is depraved, imagine their interests and rights to be, regardless even of how oppressive the existing social arrangements actually are.

Historians of political thought have long recognized that Luther's writings on the state are a source of absolutist theory and of the doctrine of the divine right of kings. Luther had none of that faith in the rational nature of man which led medieval thinkers to assert that men could control and limit their governments and see to it that these did not abuse the power which had been given them for the good of everyone. In the sixteenth century many thinkers rejected the medieval theory of limited government. Nevertheless, very few of these theorists went so far as to say that the state might arbitrarily violate the rights of private owners. Luther certainly assumed that rulers ought to rule righteously. Moreover, though he denied that subjects might appeal to the law of nature against the commands of their princes, and identified the law of nature with the Decalogue when speaking of the validity of private property, he used the broad medieval

[1] *Exposition of Psalm* 101 (1534–5), Vol. LXI, Weimar edition; *Ermahnung zum Frieden*, pp. 321–4, Vol. VII, Braunschweig edition.

concept of natural law when lecturing on the duties of princes. Subjects might not rebel if their princes did not abide by the law of nature; but princes nevertheless ought to abide by that law.[1] We can hardly doubt that, if the necessity had arisen, Luther would have found here a principle limiting the right of the government to interfere with the subject's property.

That necessity did arise shortly after Luther's death. There was civil war in Germany and the Lutherans found themselves in the embarrassing position of refusing to obey the authority of the Emperor. In these circumstances the Lutheran ministers in the city of Magdeburg issued a proclamation stating that rulers have no right to confiscate the property of their subjects, and that although Christians ought not, perhaps, to resist such seizures with force, it is not unlawful for them to do so.[2] Lutheranism apparently permitted an appeal to the law of nature when it was a question of protecting property from the ravages of Catholic rulers; it denied that appeal when it was made by peasants against Lutheran holders of property.

Luther's remarks on the theory of ownership set the foundation on which much of the later thinking on that subject was built. But his theory was fragmentary and needed systematic elaboration. It was Luther's collaborator and disciple, Philip Melanchthon, who assembled what we may call the full Lutheran theory of private property. Those parts of his writings devoted to refuting the theory of monasticism and, especially, the heresy of the Anabaptists would, if put together, make a fair-sized volume in defence of private ownership. The philosopher and scholar of the Reformation, Melanchthon made ingenious use of arguments taken from Aristotle, the Roman Law, the canonists, and the

[1] See Luther, *Von Weltlicher Obrigkeit*; Troeltsch, *Social Teaching of the Christian Churches*; F. X. Arnold, *Zur Frage des Naturrechts bei Martin Luther*, Munich, 1937. Arnold's book is a good example of the degradation of the doctrine of natural law in modern times; he writes as a Catholic with the purpose of persuading Protestants to support those principles of natural law which authorized Hitler to abrogate treaties and fight the Bolsheviks in Spain.

[2] An account of the *Magdeburg Bekenntnis* (1550), is given in J. W. Allen *A History of Political Thought in the Sixteenth Century*, pp. 104–6, London, 1928.

scholastic philosophers. He was more willing than Luther to accept the traditional concept of a reasonable law of nature as a weapon in the war on communist radicals. Nevertheless, at the end of every discussion he returned to the safe ground of revelation and identified the law of nature with the Decalogue. He was willing to argue that private property was reasonable; but he always clinched the argument by quoting, 'Thou shalt not steal.'

From Aristotle he took the theory that property was natural in the sense that it was the creation of a higher and more perfect form of human society, and he paraphrased all the philosopher's arguments against Plato.[1] But commonly he took natural to mean the primitive form, and accepted the traditional Christian doctrine that in the beginning property was common by natural law. The problem was then the old one of accounting for the abrogation of this supposedly immutable law.

In the first edition of his popular summary of Lutheran theology, the *Loci Communes*, Melanchthon wrote that all law is divine, natural, or human. Since the Fall it is doubtful whether man can know the natural law without the help of the Scriptures; certainly the philosophers who depended upon reason alone went astray. The Christian philosopher recognizes three natural laws: honour God; injure no man; use all things in common. But fallen man would not obey these rules. He could only approximate them by establishing an order in which as few men as possible would be injured. Thus since Adam fell, the natural law has consisted of four commands: honour God; injure no man; but let magistrates be appointed to protect the innocent and punish the guilty; and divide property to keep peace among men.[2]

[1] *Philosophiae Moralis Epitome*, p. 73, in Vol. XVI of the *Opera*, *Corpus Reformatorum*, Halle, 1850; *Commentary on Aristotle's Politics*, Bk. II, pp. 429–33, in the same volume.

[2] Pp. 110–17 in the English translation by C. L. Hill, Boston, 1944. This version of the 1521 edition is more pious than critical and must be compared at all points with the Latin text edited by T. Kolde, 4th edition, Erlangen, 1925. Melanchthon rewrote the *Loci Communes* many times; the final form, the German edition of 1555, is in Vol. XXII of the *Opera*, *Corpus Reformatorum*, Braunschweig, 1855.

In the later editions of the *Loci Communes*, and in several other books, Melanchthon repeated variants of this theory.[1] He explained that although the lawyers attribute property to the law of nations (*ius gentium*) instead of the law of nature (*ius naturale*), they agree in principle with the philosophical opinion that private ownership is natural, since they define the *ius gentium* as the rules of natural reason. Whether they are called the *ius naturale* or *ius gentium*, the rules of right reason are the vestiges of that natural law which God implanted in the minds of all men. This law is immutable, but its precepts are divided into superior and inferior, and in those circumstances where a conflict arises between two of them, the lower must give way to the higher. Hence private property, an institution 'congruent with the present imbecility of human nature, is now a law of nature.'[2]

But in spite of the fact that philosophers and lawyers agree that property is natural, the idea still persists among the stupid that natural law makes all things common, and they continue to cite Distinction VIII of Gratian's *Decretum*.[3] Correctly interpreted that Distinction means that property was common before the Fall and should be private afterward. The words of St. Augustine, quoted in the *Decretum*, have been used to prove that property is an invention of human law: in fact, they prove that it is founded in divine law, for St. Augustine says that 'God distributes' rights to men by the laws of princes. But whatever the *Decretum* says, private property is sanctioned by divine law—'Thou shalt not steal'; by the New Testament—St. Paul's words in Romans xiii; and by reason—which proves that men would not eat their bread in the sweat of their faces if all were common.[4]

To Melanchthon, as to many a theologian before him, the words of St. Augustine, asserting that property rights were

[1] *Loci Communes*, 1555 edition, pp. 256–7, 279–80, in Vol. XXII of the *Opera; Philosophiae Moralis Epitome*, pp. 70–3, in Vol. XVI of the *Opera*; *Commentary on Aristotle's Ethics* (1560), pp. 348, 387–8, *Opera*, Vol. XVI; *Prolegomena in Officia Ciceronis* (3rd edition, 1554), pp. 549–60, *Opera*, Vol. XVI.

[2] *Commentary on Aristotle's Ethics*, p. 388.

[3] See above, pp. 41–2.

[4] *Commentary on Aristotle's Politics*, pp. 429–33.

merely human, seemed to need some interpretation. He commented on them several times and devoted one entire essay to explaining them.[1] He concluded that the original division of things had been made by men themselves, and in this sense Augustine's opinion was true. But, he added, once that division had been made, God sanctioned it by the Seventh Commandment. Thus it is also true to say that a man holds his villa by divine right, and in this sense the opinion of Augustine is false. Things are parcelled out to individuals by the authority of magistrates; but God sets his seal on the deed and it is for ever after inviolable.[2]

All these are restatements of the ancient and medieval arguments for private ownership. But in every one of the passages referred to, Melanchthon returned to the surer and more Protestant ground of revelation. After the Fall, he explained, men's minds were so clouded they could scarcely remember the natural law. Consequently God gave Moses the Ten Commandments, 'the epitome and summary of the laws of nature.'[3] 'Thou shalt not steal' is the solid base on which reasonable theories of natural law and property must ultimately rest. Melanchthon, in common with St. Augustine and Luther, was too convinced of the depravity of man and the sinfulness of this world to believe that institutions like private property could be justified on the basis of reason alone. Property is the result of sin. For St. Thomas's concept of a world of imperfect men striving, not without success, to live according to the laws of their own reason and their own nature, the Reformation substituted a picture of a world of depraved men, incapable of obeying the dictates of nature and reason, and whose only law was the formal will of God. This view of the world and man's history is assumed

[1] *Declamatio No. 76*, 'Oratio de sententia in decretis, singulas possidere, ea quae possident, iure humano' (1543), *Opera*, Vol. II.

[2] The same argument is repeated in *Prolegomena in Officia Ciceronis*, Tertium Argumentum and Nonum Argumentum; and in *The Apology for the Augsburg Confession*, Article XVI, 745–6, in Vol. XVI of Luther's *Werke*, Walch edition Halle, 1745.

[3] *Philosophiae Moralis Epitome*, p. 70; *Loci Communes*, 1555 edition, pp. 240–1.

in Melanchthon's attack on the doctrine of evangelical poverty. The scholastic philosophers, he wrote, distinguish between precepts and counsels of the law. They assert that since the Fall men are permitted to own property, but that the more perfect way is to have all in common. The distinction is wrong, Melanchthon replied: God wants all men to work, to acquire property, and to respect the property rights of others. There is no more perfect way.[1] Men had better strive to follow the new laws which God has decreed for the world corrupted. The saints will have all things in common in heaven, but on earth God wills men to have individual properties.[2]

In his introduction to Cicero's *Offices*, Melanchthon devoted a long passage to refuting some popular arguments against private property. His answers were repeated again and again by the conservative Protestant leaders of the sixteenth and seventeenth centuries. Christians are co-heirs of the kingdom, but not of the kingdom of the world. Friends should have all things in common: it is a virtue to share freely, but virtues are voluntary, and are destroyed by being converted into legal obligations. The communism of the Church of Jerusalem is not an example for later Christians to follow; it was a stratagem enabling these early converts to hide their property from persecutors. In 2 Corinthians xiv., xv., Paul recommends equality of giving, but not equality of possessions. 'Owe no man anything' (Romans xiii. 8) does not cancel debts: it requires Christians to acquire property and pay their debts.[3] When Christ told the man to give all his property to the poor, his words applied to that one man only; God also commanded Moses to lead His people out of Egypt and no one supposes that to be a rule for all men to follow. 'Give to him that asketh thee' (Matthew v. 42) means that

[1] *Loci Communes*, 1521 edition, Hill translation, pp. 122–8; the same, 1555 edition, pp. 283–97, in *Opera*, Vol. XXII. Melanchthon also repeats the more familiar Protestant arguments against monasticism and the iniquity of begging instead of working for a living.

[2] *Prolegomena in Officia Ciceronis*, Secundum Argumentum.

[3] Apparently some radical had translated the Latin '*Nemini quicquam debetis*' as 'You owe no man anything.'

we should give, not to everyone who asks, but only to those who have some just claim on our charity. 'Thus is the fanatical delirium of the Anabaptists exploded.'[1]

On the question of the rights which governments had in the property of subjects, Melanchthon was specific where Luther was vague. He too was a supporter of the theory which is loosely called the divine right of kings, and his opinion of how far the authority of a divine monarch could be stretched in matters of property is particularly interesting, for it was adopted by most of the later theorists of absolutism. Kings, Melanchthon wrote, have the right to tax their subjects. The power to tax is limited in some countries by law and in others is left entirely to the discretion of the monarch. God approves both systems. But no king has the right to confiscate property or destroy the established division of things. The private man's title to his goods is protected by the natural law of the philosophers, by the *ius gentium* of the lawyers, by the Decalogue, and in most countries by the law of the land. The king who defies those laws is a tyrant and a sinner. Melanchthon supported his reasoning by a reference to the story of Ahab and Naboth (1 Kings xxi.), a favourite text of Christian political theorists.[2] Later defenders of absolutism often argued that the power to tax could never be legally limited, but they rarely asserted that the right of kings was arbitrary, free from the limitations imposed by natural and divine law.

One further facet of Melanchthon's theory of property deserves comment. He sometimes defended inequality of possessions on political grounds: men had to get and spend different amounts corresponding to their various political responsibilities. This was the typical medieval view, and in feudal society it was usual to connect ownership and political power. Economic inequality

[1] *Prolegomena in Officia Ciceronis*, pp. 549–60. Some of the same arguments are to be found in the *Apology for the Augsburg Confession*, Art. XVI, 526–8, 744–6, which also contains a refutation of Wycliffe's Dominion in Grace; Christians must respect contracts and these protect wicked as well as good owners.

[2] *Philosophiae Moralis Epitome*, pp. 124–7. The same reasoning is to be found in *Loci Communes*, 1555 edition, pp. 618–20.

was the necessary consequence of political inequality. But the political theorists of capitalist society reversed the terms: political inequality is the consequence of economic inequality. Governments are set up to protect the unequal properties which men already hold by right of natural law. Something of this new way of explaining the fact of inequality can be detected in the writings of Melanchthon. He wrote that common ownership had been abolished after the Fall because the 'will' to 'acquire,' 'use,' and 'share' things was no longer the same in all men.[1] He meant, apparently, that communism no longer worked because some men contributed nothing to the common stock and took more than their share from it; thus the original equality was destroyed and the common stock depleted. But, Melanchthon continued, men were still to share in equal fashion after the introduction of private property; consequently, God directed them to make contracts, to exchange one thing for another thing of equal worth.[2] The argument seems to mean, although Melanchthon did not elaborate it, that under the new dispensation equality of right was substituted for real equality. All men have the right to take from the common stock as much as they have contributed to it. But the law now prevents men from taking more than their share; actual inequality is the result since some men work less and contribute less than others. Melanchthon did not say that the state is created to protect this inequality, although he did write that private ownership was the essence of political society.[3] These passages are an anticipation of that classical bourgeois theory which derived private property from the equality of man. Men have equal rights and ought to have the

[1] *Commentary on Aristotle's Ethics*, pp. 387–8; *Prolegomena in Officia Ciceronis*, p. 549.

[2] *Commentary on Aristotle's Ethics*, pp. 387–8; *Loci Communes*, 1521 edition, Hill translation, pp. 115–16; *Loci Communes*, 1555 edition, p. 241. A similar view is expressed by Luther, *Von Kaufhandlung und Wucher*, p. 515, *Werke*, Vol. VII, Braunschweig edition.

[3] *Wider das Gotteslästerliche und Schändliche Buch, so zu Münster in Druck Neulich ist Ausgegangen*, p. 2137, in Vol. XX of Luther's *Werke*, Walch edition, Halle, 1747.

same opportunities to exercise those rights; and the protection of the actual inequality of possessions—which arises because men do not have the same talents, or do not choose to use their talents in an equally productive fashion—is the chief function of government. No doubt Melanchthon himself would have rejected the theory stated in these bald terms. But later Protestant thinkers, some of whom were familiar with the works of Melanchthon, were its enthusiastic proponents.

In the writings of Melanchthon the tendency to substitute the Bible and the positive laws of God for reason and the law of nature is evident. Nevertheless he by no means rejects the former. He often, in fact, reinforces one with the other: property, he argues, is derived from both the law of nature, amended to fit the state of sin, and the Seventh Commandment. But with John Calvin the Bible is promoted to the first rank, and natural law seems, at first sight, to be almost entirely replaced by divine ukases whose reasonableness, if they are reasonable, cannot be fathomed by the corrupt and feeble mind of man. In his principal work, the *Institutes of the Christian Religion*,[1] Calvin rarely supports a point by a reference to natural law. Sometimes he says the law of nature is to be found in the Bible—the only sure source of our knowledge of law. Once he implied that the law of nature was the rule followed by men in a state of innocence, but that it is no longer applicable to men in a state of sin: he condemned the Anabaptists' proposal to abolish property, government, and inequality, as presupposing a perfection which neither they nor any men could ever attain.[2] Thus he apparently implies that natural law is either unknowable, except as it is revealed in the Bible, or was abrogated at the Fall. Either theory is consistent with the Augustinian view of man's depravity. And either theory made it unnecessary and irrelevant to refer to

[1] The Latin edition of 1559 is the definitive and final form of the *Institutes.* An English translation by John Allen, originally published in 1813, has been revised and reprinted by the Presbyterian Board of Education, seventh American edition, Philadelphia, 1936. Another English translation, by Henry Beveridge, was printed by the Calvin Translation Society, Edinburgh, 1845–6.

[2] IV, xx.

natural law in defending an institution based on God's law. 'Thou shalt not steal' gives men a divine right to the property God bestows upon them.[1] They need no other title.

Against the canonists and scholastic philosophers who distinguished precepts from counsels and argued that although it was permissible to own property it was better not to do so, Calvin wrote that God was a Legislator, not a Counsellor, and that he wanted all men to obey his Law. His Law was that a Christian should have a calling and provide for his family.[2]

Other passages of the *Institutes* developed the familiar theory of stewardship which was popular with Protestant moralists of the sixteenth and seventeenth centuries.[3] In its medieval form the theory stated that men held their lands as vassals of God; in the more modern version the vassals became stewards. But in all versions it was the old idea that ownership entailed obligations and was contingent upon the right use of property. It did occasional service in justifying legislation which limited individuals in the use of their property or, as in the case of the monasteries, confiscated the property of the notoriously wicked. It could also protect the good owner since it proclaimed that his property was given him by God. But it was used principally to induce men to recognize some moral responsibility in the use of their property beyond that enjoined by the law. It supplemented, but was not intended to replace, the various philosophical theories; it could be superimposed on any of them without contradiction.

On the vexatious problem of the rights of the state over the property of its subjects, Calvin had little to say, perhaps because it was not a pressing one in Geneva. In general his political theory was a variant of the popular absolutist doctrines of the day. One or two passages in the *Institutes* indicate that he shared the opinion of most supporters of absolutism that the state should respect the property of individuals, even though it ought not to

1 II, viii.

2 II, viii; IV, xiii. The latter passage also explains that Christ's counsel to the rich young man was a particular direction applying to that man only.

3 III, vii and x.

be resisted if it did not. He listed as one of the primary aims of political authority 'that every person may enjoy his property without molestation.'[1] He wrote that princes have the right to take taxes for public purposes and to maintain themselves with suitable splendour. But if they squander the public revenue—which St. Paul says is not their private income but the property of the community—they are tyrants.[2]

Calvin clearly preferred to support his contentions by quoting the Bible and was inclined to dismiss as ill-founded those arguments of his opponents which were based on the concept of natural law. Nevertheless it would be untrue to say that he denied altogether the importance of that concept. In the *Institutes* he carefully distinguishes two classes of truth: the most important can be discovered only in the Bible, but the lesser is discernible by natural reason as well. In searching for the great truths respecting God, salvation, the future life, and the rules of right conduct, the human reason is either totally blind or so feeble as to need the constant help of revelation.[3] Since Calvin thought these the only essential things, it is not surprising that he did not put much faith in reason and the natural law which it revealed. Still, he was convinced that the mind of man was able to perceive the inferior principles pertaining to terrestrial affairs. 'I call those things terrestrial which do not pertain to God and his kingdom, to true righteousness, or to the blessedness of a future life; but which relate entirely to the present life, and are in some sense confined within the limits of it.' In this category are included 'civil policy, domestic economy, all the mechanical arts, and liberal sciences.'

Now . . . it must be confessed that as man is naturally a creature inclined to society, he has also by nature an instinctive propensity to cherish and preserve that society; and therefore we perceive in the minds of all men general impressions of civil probity and order. Hence it is that not a person can be found who does not understand that all associations of men ought to be governed by laws, or who does not conceive in his mind the principles of those laws. Hence

[1] IV, xx. [2] IV, xxii. [3] II, ii.

that perpetual consent of all nations, as well as individuals, to the laws, because the seeds of them are innate in all mankind, without any instructor or legislator. I regard not the dissensions and contests which afterwards arise, when some desire to invert all justice and propriety, to break down the barriers of the laws, and to substitute mere cupidity in the room of justice, as is the case with thieves and robbers. [We cannot] deny the light of truth to the ancient lawyers who have delivered such just principles of civil order and polity.[1]

These passages prove that Calvin did not simply replace reason with divine law, nor did his doctrine necessarily lessen the importance of the concept of a law of nature. By dividing law into two parts, and asserting that one part could be found only in the Bible and that the other was the discovery or invention of human reason, he asserted in fact that men might manage their purely terrestrial affairs in any way they thought reasonable. Men's spiritual duties, and the form of the true Church, are prescribed, in the minutest detail, in the Bible. But in secular affairs, although the Scriptures give general directions, men are left pretty much to their own discretion. The Bible directs them to divide up property among individuals and requires the state to protect the rights of owners; but the detailed theory of how actual individuals acquire rights to things, and how far the state can go in regulating and redistributing those rights, are questions left to the decision of natural reason. If reason is able to demonstrate that there are universal natural principles, natural laws, which supply the answers, Calvinists may appeal to those laws as well as other men.[2] Calvin rejected the conclusions of natural

[1] II, ii.

[2] At the end of the century, Richard Hooker said the Calvinists were subverting all good government by maintaining that 'every man is left to the freedom of his own mind in such things as are either not exacted or prohibited by the Law of God. . . .'; *Laws of Ecclesiastical Polity*, V, lxxi, 4, edited by John Keble, 5th edition, Oxford, 1865. Anyone who had gone this far could easily go on to accept a theory of natural rights which explained how a man had got his property, and forbade the government to interfere with his use of that property, unless it could quote a verse of Scripture. It was easy, of course, to quote the Bible, but it was just as easy to argue that the quotation was not apropos.

reason as irrelevant in a discussion of the great truths of religion. But he in effect handed over civil affairs to the natural man and directed him to regulate them according to natural principles. Consequently, the followers of Calvin, for whom the problems of property and government were pressing, defended their possessions from the attacks of Anabaptists and tyrants with the whole panoply of arguments based on reason and natural law, as well as with texts of Scripture. They not only repeated the old theories of property: they contributed largely to the construction of the new and classical middle-class defence of property, the theory of natural rights.

Everywhere in the sixteenth and seventeenth centuries pamphleteers, preachers, and political propagandists were repeating the theories of property which the leaders of the Reformation had popularized. Influenced directly by the writings of Melanchthon, a number of German jurists instituted the formal study of the law of nature and founded a tradition which lasted for three centuries. Like Melanchthon they defended property, first by quoting the Seventh Commandment, and then by referring to one or another of the various concepts of natural law scattered through his various writings. But being lawyers rather than theologians they put rather less emphasis on the scriptural basis of property and contributed to that secularization of the concept of natural law and the theory of property which was completed in the next century.[1]

In England both conservatives and men whose opinions were otherwise radical refuted Plato, Sir Thomas More, and the Anabaptists by quoting the Seventh Commandment, interpreting away the Biblical texts which seemed to recommend community, asserting that man's depravity made communism unthinkable,

1 The most important were Johannes Oldendorp, *Isagoge Iuris Naturalis, Gentium, et Civilis* (1539); Nicolaus Hemming, *De Lege Naturae Methodus Apodictica* (1562); and Benedict Winkler, *Principiorum Iuris* (1615). Excerpts from all three, including passages on property, are printed in Carl von Kaltenborn, *Die Vorläufer des Hugo Grotius*, Leipzig, 1848. Kaltenborn states that Oldendorp's book is the first modern work devoted principally to the study of the law of nature.

and repeating the reasonable arguments which made private property seem a necessary part of the nature of the world.[1] Here and there a new idea appears as when Sir John Cheke warns the poor that an equal distribution of wealth would not be in their interest, as it would take from them the opportunity of becoming rich.[2] In contrast to the traditional theory, which counselled the poor to be content with their lot, this implies that they should strive to be rich. It is an early example of that way of thinking which led liberal theorists to condemn equality, but fight for equality of opportunity.

Another pamphleteer expressed succinctly the new theory of the ruling class: 'The poor would be rich and so are not content with their present estate, but desire alteration and change, and all such persons are more meet to be commanded than to command in a common wealth. But of the rich and wealthy it is clean otherwise, for they are already that which the poor have desire to be, and therefore content, and consequently friends and furtherers of peace and unity. . . .'[3] Here the assumption is, not that the rulers need property to perform their function, as the theorists of feudalism had assumed, but that men of property should be the rulers: their interest is identical with that of the state, whose purpose is to preserve the present division of things.

A radical English Protestant combined two popular theories of property in an interesting attempt to avoid the pitfall of communism and at the same time convince the rich to abolish poverty.[4] Property, he wrote, is authorized by God to prevent the strong from oppressing the weak. But 'by nature' the earth belongs to all men and individuals can claim only that which they have gained by the sweat of their faces. Crowley saw, as

[1] Many examples can be found in Helen C. White, *Social Criticism in Popular Religious Literature of the Sixteenth Century*, and in my book, *The Social Ideas of Religious Leaders, 1660–88*, Oxford, 1940.

[2] *The Hurt of Sedition* (1549), quoted in White, *Social Criticism*, p. 145.

[3] Francis Thynne, *Newes from the North* (1579), quoted in White, *Social Criticism*, p. 31.

[4] Robert Crowley, *An Information and Petition against the Oppressors of the Poor Commons of this Realm*, quoted in White, *Social Criticism*, pp. 110–12.

many later defenders of nâtural right did not, that the property of the rich was not protected by this theory. Great wealth, he continued, is not held by a natural title, but is given to men by God. They are to use it as his stewards. Crowley did not say the state was God's agent for the distribution of riches, but his argument seems to imply that, and he was certainly anxious to have the political authority force men to act as stewards of God. By combining the theory of stewardship and the theory that men have a natural right to the products of their own labour, he furnished a defence both for property and for social legislation which limited the use a rich man might make of his property.

Much of the earlier Protestant theory of property was directed against the radical left-wing movements of the Reformation. But as the Reformation spread, Protestant groups, especially the Calvinists, in England, Scotland, France, and elsewhere, had to do battle with governments which were either Catholic, or not sufficiently reformed. A large part of the formal political theory of Protestantism was henceforth devoted to attacks on absolutism and to defences of the religious and political rights of true believers. Calvin himself stressed the duty of obedience to authority; but his followers in other lands became the foremost theorists of rebellion. Since the immediate issues were primarily religious and political, many of the most famous texts of this literature—landmarks in the history of the development of limited and representative government—do not discuss property. But some of them do include it as one of the rights of subjects, and as time went on the rights of ownership were stressed more and more. By the seventeeth century it was possible for dissenting sects to condemn religious persecution on the ground that it violated the rights of property.[1]

One of the earliest Protestant attacks on royal power was John Ponet's *Shorte Treatise of Politike Power*.[2] Ponet was an English bishop who fled to the Continent during the reign of

[1] See my *Social Ideas of Religious Leaders*, pp. 237–8.

[2] Published in 1556. A facsimile reproduction with an introduction by W. S. Hudson has been published by the Chicago University Press, 1942.

Queen Mary. The purpose of his book was to prove that monarchs derived their limited powers from the people and could be deposed when they abused those powers; and some of its principal arguments were based on the popular theories of the rights of property. The book opens with a description of the natural law which, in typical Protestant fashion, is identified with the law of God in the Bible. 'This rule is the law of nature, first planted and grafted only in the mind of man, then after for that his mind was through sin defiled, filled with darkness, and encumbered with many doubts, set forth in writing in the Decalogue or Ten Commandments: and after reduced by Christ our saviour into these two words: Thou shalt love thy Lord God above all things, and thy neighbour as thyself.'[1] Here Ponet was stressing the necessity of relying upon revelation. But in another passage he insisted that the law of nature was known to the heathen philosophers and that it was written, not in books, but in the hearts of men who have 'taken, sucked, and drawn it out of nature'; it is not taught, for men are 'not instructed, but seasoned' in it.[2] Wherever he could, Ponet defended his contentions by quoting the Bible; but where a text was lacking, this flexible concept of the law of nature served his purpose well.

To the Anabaptists he made the usual reply that property was necessary since the Fall to force each man to work for his own living, and that it was sanctioned by the Seventh Commandment.[3] But his chief purpose was to defend the subject's property against the ravages of princes. In general he argued that princes derive their authority from the consent of the people, and that it could be taken for granted that the people had set reasonable limits to the exercise of that authority. But where no positive law specifically defined the limitations, the law of God and nature supplied the defect.[4] Kings who tax their subjects unreasonably, who exact forced loans, and who debase the coinage for their own profit, offend against both these laws; and the doctrine that the king is the owner of the subject's property is disproved by the

[1] Pp. 4, 21–2, 107.

[2] P. 107.

[3] Pp. 79–80.

[4] Pp. 106–7.

story of Ahab and Naboth.[1] Finally, Ponet concluded, even if no law restrained the king he ought to respect property for reasons of expediency: subjects will not work and produce if they cannot enjoy the fruits of their labour.[2]

Ponet's arguments are typical of Protestant anti-monarchical theory in the sixteenth century. He still thinks in terms of natural law rather than natural rights. Natural law is the all-embracing hierarchy of rules which limits men and prescribes for them their duties. A man's property is secure, not because he has a natural right to it, but because the law of nature forbids other men, including princes, to take it from him. But when Ponet argues that men gain their property by their labour, and that princes are limited because they have only the authority delegated to them by their subjects, he is not far from the idea of natural right. Other Protestant theorists went further in that direction.

The most famous and influential of Calvinist anti-monarchical treatises was the anonymous *Vindiciae contra Tyrannos*.[3] Written to justify the resistance of the Huguenot party, the *Vindiciae* is an important text in the history of the contract theory of government, and it has been called 'the first work in modern history that constructs a political philosophy on the basis of certain inalienable rights of man.'[4] This judgment is, perhaps, not wholly accurate, but the author of the *Vindiciae* was certainly not far from a theory of natural rights, including the natural right of property. After a reference to the Golden Age described by Seneca, the *Vindiciae* goes on to say that governments were instituted 'when . . . that these words of mine and thine entered into the world, and that differences fell out amongst fellow-citizens, touching the propriety of goods, and wars amongst

[1] Pp. 79–97, 6, 99. [2] Pp. 93–5.

[3] First published in 1579. A seventeenth-century English translation has been reprinted, with an Introduction, by H. J. Laski, London, 1924; my references are to this edition. The authorship is disputed; see Ernest Barker, *Church, State and Study*, London, 1931.

[4] G. P. Gooch, *English Democratic Ideas in the Seventeenth Century*, 2nd edition, Cambridge, 1927, p. 14.

neighbouring people about the rights of their confines. . . .'[1] Kings, 'ordained by God, and established by the people,'[2] are bound by covenants to rule for the good of the people.[3] 'Neither let us imagine that kings were chosen to apply to their own proper use the goods that are gotten by the sweat of their subjects; for every man loves and cherishes his own.'[4]

A special section of the *Vindiciae* answers the question, 'Whether the goods of the people belong to the king?'[5] 'Is it anything probable,' he answers, 'that men should seek a master to give him frankly all that they had long laboured for, and gained with the sweat of their brows? May we not rather imagine, that they chose such a man on whose integrity they relied for the administering of justice equally both to the poor and the rich, and who would not assume all to himself, but rather maintain every one in the fruition of his own goods?' This answer seems to take for granted a large part of the natural rights theory: men acquire property by their labour; they set up governments based on contract; the contract must protect the property of every man since that is the purpose for which it is made;[6] and finally, the arrangement is just because it is based on equality of right and makes no distinction between rich and poor. But in fact the author of the *Vindiciae* did not develop the theory that labour gives a man a natural title to his property, and his contracts are not the same as those of the natural rights school. He still leans heavily on the Bible, and in the section quoted above he adds the story of Ahab and Naboth to his proofs of the inviolability of the rights of property. Nevertheless, the tone of the book is surprisingly secular and demonstrates how ready Calvinism was to

[1] P. 141. A passage on p. 190 says that property was introduced by the 'law of nations.' This suggests the old distinction between the golden age of community and modern times.

[2] P. 143.

[3] Pp. 174–5. For the contract theory of the *Vindiciae*, see J. W. Gough, *The Social Contract*, Oxford, 1936, pp. 52–5.

[4] P. 140.

[5] Pp. 158–60.

[6] If the contracts are not written, they may be deduced from the law of nature; p. 181. Here as elsewhere in the *Vindiciae* the term 'natural' is used vaguely in the sense of 'reasonable.'

rehabilitate and refurbish the idea of natural law for 'terrestrial' purposes.

At the beginning of the next century, Johannes Althusius, perhaps the greatest of Calvinist political theorists, followed the authors of the *Vindiciae* in deriving property both from divine command and the secular law of nature. Althusius was the spokesman of the Calvinists in Holland and Germany. His *Politica Methodice Digesta*[1] systematized the political ideas of earlier anti-monarchical writers and defended the doctrines of popular sovereignty and social contract.[2] The duty of the state, Althusius wrote, is to enforce the second table of the Decalogue, including the Seventh Commandment, which protects private property.[3] He quoted 2 Samuel xxiv. 24, and the famous story of Ahab and Naboth, to prove that rulers have no right to take a subject's property except for reasons of public necessity, and then only provided that the subject is compensated for his loss.[4] But in the same work he wrote that the property of the individual is protected by natural law. According to that law the ruler is not the owner, but the defender of his subjects' goods, and he may take in taxes only the sum required to provide for the public necessities.[5]

Many sixteenth-century Protestant anti-monarchical pamphlets and treatises use the concepts of natural law and contract, but none of the more famous deal so extensively with the theory of property as Ponet's *Treatise* and the *Vindiciae*. They may be said to imply much the same theory, but they are chiefly concerned with political issues more immediately relevant to religion. Not until the seventeenth century can political thinkers be found who opposed royal absolutism mainly, and even only, because it violated the property rights of the individual. Moreover, in France itself the Protestant party soon abandoned the political

[1] First published in 1603. The third edition, 1614, was reprinted with an Introduction by C. J. Friedrich, Cambridge, Mass., 1932.

[2] See Gough, *Social Contract*, pp. 72–7.

[3] c. X.

[4] c. XXXVII, 111 and 115.

[5] c. XXXVII, 107, and 111 which contains a reference to the *Vindiciae*; c. XIII, 2.

theory of the *Vindiciae*. A decade after that book was published, the Huguenot theorists veered sharply in the direction of absolutism and supported monarchy in the person of Henry IV. Henry's enemies, the Catholic *Ligue*, fell heir to the theory of popular rights. The ideas of the *Vindiciae* were adopted, in part, by the Counter-Reformation, and Jesuit writers attacked heretic kings with the arguments previously employed by Protestants against Catholic monarchs. By 1615 the theories of the *Vindiciae* seemed Catholic and James I of England could plausibly surmise that that book had been 'patcht up by some Romanist.'[1]

The assault troops of the Counter-Reformation were the Jesuits, and Jesuit political theory is one of the great sources of later theories of natural rights. The general purpose of the political writings of the Society of Jesus was to safeguard the power of the Papacy, by showing that all royal authority was limited and contingent, and to prove that heretic kings might be deposed, at the Pope's bidding, by their subjects. Consequently, although they insisted that property was founded in the law of nature, and that political authority was derived from the people and limited by the terms of an original contract, the Jesuit authors were not primarily concerned with protecting the property of the individual subject against the claims of the prince. One of the most famous, Francisco Suarez, used the theory of popular rights to defend the authority and property of the Church, and to attack heretic kings, but he asserted that a legitimate, Catholic monarch could tax his lay subjects without their consent. In England particularly, the Jesuit theories were plagiarized by the defenders of middle-class property, but the Jesuits themselves had no such purpose in mind.

The gist of the Jesuit political theory is a combination of the medieval conception of natural law and the popular modern idea of contract. Private property and the state are good and develop naturally out of the original and primitive age of mankind; but

[1] *The Political Works of James I*, edited by C. H. McIlwain, Cambridge, Mass., 1918, p. 264.

each particular society was created by popular agreement and its form is determined by the terms of the original contract. Property in general is an institution of the natural law; but the particular form of the institution in any one place is determined by the particular agreement which set it up. Thus the Jesuit theory of property is much the same as that of St. Thomas, and his *Summa* was frequently quoted as an authority. In his *De Justitia et Jure*,[1] Luis Molina, S.J., wrote that property was common by natural law only in the sense that that law did not prescribe the manner of division. After the Fall men made a division by 'express or tacit consent,' but in different ways. Adam and Noah divided the land among their children; Abraham and Lot made a pact with one another; other men agreed to respect titles acquired by occupation; and some peoples chose kings and gave them the power to make the original division. But however the laws of property were established, they do not violate the law of nature: they merely add to it. The additions made by reason to the law of nature, although they are classified as the *ius gentium*, are really parts of that law. Thus Aristotle was right in calling property natural; Plato, and those theologians who deny this, are wrong. Molina disposed of St. Augustine's theory, that property was the conventional creation of human law, by identifying Augustine's human law with the *ius gentium*. Finally, he repeated the good medieval doctrine that the prince had the jurisdiction, but not the ownership, of his subjects' property.[2] Except for the emphasis upon popular consent, there is nothing in Molina's theory of property which cannot be found in St. Thomas. The same is true of the other famous Jesuit writers. Their theories of politics differ in important ways, but their theory of property is that of St. Thomas coupled with some theory of contract.[3]

[1] First published in 1593–1600. I have used the five-volume edition published in 1759.

[2] The relevant passages are in Tome I, Tractatus I, i and iv, and Tractatus II, xx and xxv.

[3] See, for example, Francisco Suarez, *Tractatus de Legibus* (1612), modern edition, Naples, 1872, Liber II, chs. vii, viii, and xiv. Juan Mariana, *De Rege*

One example of how Jesuit theories of property and political authority were used by later thinkers who thought the Pope was anti-Christ, but who were warm defenders of 'liberty and property,' is the story of Robert Parsons' *Conference about the next Succession to the Crown of England*, published in 1594.[1] Parsons was the leader of the Jesuits in England and his book was written to prove that Englishmen did not have to accept James of Scotland as the successor to Queen Elizabeth. His chief argument was that kings are created and chosen by the people; no man can claim a throne by divine right, or maintain that he is the one legitimate successor to a crown. That argument he supported by the usual theory that government is natural and good, but that particular governments derive their authority from the people. In one chapter Parsons appealed directly to the interests of property owners.[2] The upholders of divine right and legitimacy, he wrote, also maintain that the king is the absolute owner of all the property in the kingdom. This reduces all subjects to slaves, for as Aristotle defined him, a slave is a man whose property belongs to his master. But the theorists who recognize the popular basis of all governments also recognize the rights of individual owners. Parsons quoted the *Institutes* of Justinian to show that

et Regis Institutione (1599), Mainz, 1605, unlike Suarez, denies that the prince may tax without the consent of his subjects; Liber I, chs. viii and ix. Other Jesuits who repeated the theory of St. Thomas are listed by Carl von Kaltenborn, *Die Vorläufer des Hugo Grotius*, Leipzig, 1848, ch. vi. I have found nothing in the works of the great Jesuit champion, Cardinal Bellarmine, which can be called a theory of property, although his political ideas are typical, and may be said to imply the usual theory. His works do demonstrate how the Jesuit writings were a bridge between medieval and modern political thinking: of the medieval theorists quoted above in ch. iv, he refers to Aegidius Romanus, Augustinus Triumphatus, John of Paris, Hostiensis, and several others. The text and notes of Miss Kathleen Murphy's translation of Bellarmine's *De Laicis*, New York, 1928, are a convenient introduction to Jesuit political theory.

[1] The best account of the book is given by C. H. McIlwain in the Introduction and Appendix D of his edition of the *Political Works of James I*. Professor McIlwain says that Parsons took many of his ideas from the *Vindiciae Contra Tyrannos*. The Huguenot theory that kings are 'ordained by God and established by the people' is similar to the Jesuit theory that government is based on natural law and established by popular agreement; the Protestants emphasized the Bible and divine law, the Catholics stuck to natural law.

[2] Part I, ch. 3.

things belong to men by various titles of natural law, and he referred to the opinion of Bartolus of Sassoferrato, and the Biblical story of Ahab and Naboth, to prove that kings do not own the property of their subjects. Parsons, of course, was writing to defend the true faith, but his arguments were soon turned to other uses. Parts of his book were reprinted in England in 1648 and 1654 and the whole was republished in 1681. 'It is hardly too much to say that this book was the chief storehouse of facts and arguments drawn upon by nearly all opponents of the royal claims for a century. . . .'[1] Together with the *Vindiciae Contra Tyrannos*, which appeared eight times in English dress between 1581 and 1689, Parsons' book was one of the principal weapons of the English defenders of middle-class 'property and liberty,' and one of the important sources of the theory of natural rights.

When Parsons argued that the proponents of absolutism had no regard for the rights of property he was, of course, exaggerating. One answer to Parsons asserted that the laws—divine, natural, civil, and common—which made James the sole rightful heir to the throne of England were the very laws which protected the property-rights of his subjects.[2] In fact, no sixteenth-century

[1] McIlwain, Introduction to the *Political Works of James I*, p. li.

[2] Sir Thomas Craig, *Concerning the Right of Succession to the Kingdom of England*, written in Latin about 1603, published in English in 1703. English constitutional lawyers sometimes held that property could be confiscated, not by the King, but by King and Parliament; see J. W. Allen, *History of Political Thought*, pp. 167, 257–8. Even so, Peter Wentworth's *Discourse of the True and Lawful Successor to Her Majesty*, 1598, pp. 46–8, said that if Parliament confiscated the lands of a private man without sufficient cause, God would avenge the injury. An earlier defender of the Tudor monarchy, Christopher St. German, said that property was protected by the 'Law of Reason' and had never in any age been common; *Doctor and Student*, I, ch. 2. This book was first published in Latin, London, 1523; there are many English translations. Another Tudor lawyer, John Perkins, worked out a variant of the old theory that before the Fall property was common. Originally, he wrote, the land belonged to no one and each man took what he needed from the common stock. But after the Fall the law of nature with respect to property was abrogated and, as St. Augustine says, private property was instituted by human law. Perkins stated this theory in the Proemium of his *Profitable Booke Treating of the Lawes of England*, published in law French in 1528. I have used the English edition of 1621. I am indebted for this reference to F. L. Baumer, *Early Tudor Theories of Kingship*, New Haven, 1940, p. 134, n. 2.

defender of absolutism—particularly one who defended the extreme theory of the divine right of kings—could easily deny that kings were limited by the laws of God and nature. The king's power might be absolute, but it was not arbitrary. No one asserted that the capricious wish of the monarch, though contrary to divine and natural law, could ever be a true rule of justice. The theorists of absolutism generally agreed that the subject had no redress if the monarch wronged him; they usually agreed that the king could tax without the consent of the taxpayers; a few followed the civilians and used the Roman Law doctrine, that ownership was indivisible, to prove that since the king admittedly had some rights in the property of the kingdom, he must in fact be its sole owner. But even the adherents of this most radical theory did not draw from it the conclusion that the king might do what he would with his property or arbitrarily deprive his subjects of their customary right to use it.

The most famous English defence of the theory that the kings are the owners of all the property of the realm was King James's *Trew Law of Free Monarchies*.[1] After proving from the Bible that kings are made by God and that rebellion is never justified, James went on to show that the kings of England and Scotland were absolute owners by right of conquest. By the first kings in Scotland 'was the land distributed (which at the first was whole theirs)'; the 'same ground of the kings right over all the land' is found in all 'free monarchies,' specifically in England where the 'Bastard of Normandie' conquered the country and 'set downe the strangers his followers in many of the old possessours roomes. . . .'[2] Speaking to Parliament in 1609, James said: 'Now a father may dispose of his Inheritance to his children, at his pleasure; yea, even disinherite the eldest upon just occasions, and preferre the youngest, according to his liking; make them beggers, or rich at his pleasure. . . . So may the King deale with his Subjects.'[3] Even in this bold statement of monarchical power

[1] Written in 1598. Printed in C. H. McIlwain's edition of the *Political Works of James I.*

[2] Pp. 62–3.

[3] Speech of 1609, p. 308, in McIlwain, *Political Works of James I.*

there is a qualification: the father must have a 'just occasion' for disinheriting the oldest son; and in other passages James made clear that he was not claiming the right to take back the property which he had lent to his subjects. 'The King might have a better colour for his pleasure, without further reason, to take the land from his lieges, as overlord of the whole, and doe with it as pleaseth him, since all that they hold is of him, then, as foolish writers say, the people might unmake the king, and put an other in his roome: But either of them as unlawful, and against the ordinance of God, ought to be odious to thought, much lesse put in practise.'[1] Under the pressure of hostile criticism in England, James hastened to say that benevolent kings like himself would never rule except by the laws of the land and that he had no desire to replace the common law, the fundamental law of England, with the civil law: 'if the fundamentall Lawes of any Kingdome should be altered, who should discerne what is *Meum and Tuum*, or how should a King governe?'[2] In fact, James probably preferred the civil law which gave the king, as absolute owner of the kingdom, the right to tax without consent. But he never held that the world was 'ordained only for kings, and they without controlment to turne it upside down at their pleasure. . . .' Men may not resist tyrants, but God will punish them.[3] In fact, James added, even tyrants never actually turn the world upside down, and the theory of divine right is a better protection for life and property than theories which permit insurrection. The most vicious king maintains some 'order,' but revolution is anarchy.[4]

James's theory of property is the high point of absolutism. Other royalists admitted that the property of the individual was protected by natural law, but he never refers to the law of nature in this connection. He quoted John of Paris to prove that the Pope had no temporal authority, but he did not give John's opinion that the property which men got by labour belonged

[1] *Trew Law*, p. 62.
[2] Speech of 1609, pp. 309–10.
[3] *Trew Law*, pp. 69–70.
[4] *Trew Law*, p. 66.

neither to Pope nor king.[1] Nevertheless, James did recognize that the law of God ordained private property. His theory of property was not an attack on that institution any more than the theories of his enemies. At bottom the quarrel between the opponents and the defenders of absolutism was not about property, but about the control of the state. The Stuarts and the representatives of the property-owners in Parliament came to blows over who was to formulate the policy of the government. The question of taxation was important only because the side which controlled the purse controlled policy. During the Civil Wars Parliaments voted more taxes and confiscated more property than any Stuart had ever dreamed of doing. Thus in 1678, a pamphleteer could plausibly maintain that kings by divine right were in practice better protectors of 'liberty and property' than governments based on popular supremacy.[2] Neither side intended to attack the basic institution of private ownership. But in their efforts to gain control of the taxing power, they developed different philosophical theories of that institution.

In France, where a large body of opinion supported the monarchy because it alone was capable of creating a modern national state, the defenders of absolutism made a similar use of theories of property. Neither they, nor the Huguenot minority, nor the feudal *Ligueurs*, were primarily interested in constructing an independent theory justifying private ownership. All of them accepted that institution; their theories of its origin and rights were hardly more than weapons with which they fought for control of the state power. Nevertheless their ideas contributed to the formation of modern philosophical theories. As in England the royalists upheld taxation without consent, but they generally agreed that the king was limited by the laws of God and nature

[1] *A Remonstrance for the Right of Kings* (1616), p. 202, in McIlwain, *The Political Works of James I*. In this work James berates the Pope for claiming the power of confiscating the property of heretics, but he is careful never to deny that kings may have that power.

[2] John Nalson, *The Common Interest of King and People: Shewing . . . that Absolute, Papal and Presbyterian Popular Supremacy are utterly inconsistent with Prerogative, Property, and Liberty*, London, 1678.

to taking only the amount necessary for the purpose of good government. One lawyer intimated that the king could tax but not confiscate.[1] Another said that all lands belonged to the king, who had granted the use of it to his subjects. But he drew from this theory only the conclusion that the king could tax without consent.[2] One of the first French exponents of divine right, Pierre de Belloy, wrote that God gave kings power that they might 'render to each what belongs to him.'[3] Pierre Grégoire, another divine right theorist, quoted Distinction VIII of the *Decretum* to prove that the rights of property are derived from the authority of the king; consequently the king can tax at will. But, Grégoire added, he is a tyrant if he taxes for any reason other than that of the public necessity.[4] Finally, William Barclay's famous defence of divine right specifically denied that this theory destroyed the institution of property; men hold their land as vassals of the king and he protects their right.[5] In the next century, with the practical triumph of absolutism in France, many royalists, among them Louis XIV himself, proclaimed that the king was the owner of everything in the realm. But they all agreed that the powers of the king, though absolute, were not despotic: private property, protected by laws divine, natural, or fundamental, was recognized throughout the *ancien régime* as a sacred institution.[6]

The French theorists of absolutism upheld private property, but their major concern was the establishment of a strong national monarchy, and it was for that purpose that their theories of

[1] François Grimaudet, reported in W. F. Church, *Constitutional Thought in Sixteenth-Century France*, Cambridge, Mass., 1941, p. 257.

[2] Adam Blackwood, quoted in Church, *Constitutional Thought*, pp. 259–60.

[3] *De l'Authorité du Roi*, n.p. 1587, leaf 17.

[4] *De Republica*, Paris, 1609, Liber III, ch. ii.

[5] *De Regno et Regali Potestate*, Paris, 1600. Barclay's book was an explicit attack on both Huguenot and Catholic theories of the popular origin of government.

[6] Henri Sée, *Les Idées Politiques en France au XVIIe Siècle*, Paris, 1923. An excellent discussion of property and taxation in French royalist theory is Philip Dur's 'Right of Taxation in the Political Theory of the French Religious Wars,' *Journal of Modern History*, December 1945.

property were constructed. They did not foresee the day when owners of property would demand a theory which would give them the right to control taxation, and which would prevent even their own elected representatives from violating the extensive property-rights of the individual. But one man, perhaps the foremost political writer of the century, sensed that the theory of property could not be handled so negligently. Jean Bodin was also a supporter of the monarchy and wanted to see in France a strong national state. Nevertheless, he saw that the best interest of those classes which supported the king would not, in the long run, be well served by a theory which made the king the sole owner of the kingdom and gave him an unlimited right to tax. Consequently, Bodin elaborated a theory which was much closer to that of medieval constitutionalism, and closer to that of middle-class liberalism, than it was to the theories of the extreme royalists.

In the first chapter of the *Republic*[1], Bodin made clear that his book had nothing in common with the *Republic* of Plato or More's Utopia. He did not intend, he wrote, to deal with the 'imaginary forme and Idea of Commonweale, without effect or substance, as have Plato, and Sir Thomas More, Chauncelor of England, vainely imagined.'[2] Further on in the book he suggested that Plato had not taken his communistic scheme seriously.[3] To the arguments for community of property he opposed some of the usual objections. Everyone neglects that which belongs to no one in particular; the experience of the Anabaptists at Munster proves that communism makes for anarchy; since the state is built on the family, and the family on private property, common ownership destroys both institutions.[4] To these arguments Bodin adds that communism is forbidden by divine and natural law. Plato's commonwealth is 'against the law of God and nature, which detests not onley incests, adulteries, and inevitable murders, if all women should be common; but also expressly forbids us to

[1] *Les Six Livres de la République* was first published in 1576, and an expanded Latin version appeared in 1586. My references are to Richard Knolles' English translation of the Latin, London, 1606; I have compared them with the Latin and with a French edition of 1577.

[2] Bk. I, ch. 1.

[3] II, i.

[4] I, ii.

steale, or so much as desire anything that another mans is.'[1] Theft is forbidden by the word of God, and God 'will have every man to enjoy the proprietie of his own goods: and we may not say, that nature hath made all things common, for the law of the mother is not contrarie to the law of the father (as Salomon said), figuring by an Allegorie the commaundments of God, and the law of nature.'[2] That there had ever been a golden age, where men held all in common by some law of nature, Bodin denied. Both before and after the Flood, he wrote, men lived as beasts and robbery went unpunished. Only slowly were men 'reclaimed from that ferocity and barbarity to the refinement of customs and the law-abiding society which we see about us. Thievery, which once incurred only a civil judgment . . . now everywhere in the world is repaid by capital punishment.'[3]

Thus reason and the laws of God and nature all joined to outlaw common ownership. But the climax of his defence of property was the new and up-to-date theory that the state existed chiefly for the purpose of protecting the rights of ownership: if property is destroyed, the state is robbed of its chief reason for being. 'But the greatest inconvenience is, that in taking away these words of Mine, and Thine, they ruine the foundation of all Commonweales, the which were chiefly established to yeeld unto every man that which is his owne, and to forbid theft. . . .'[4] 'Whereby it evidently appeareth this opinion for the communitie of all things to be erroneous, seeing Commonweals to have been to that end founded and appointed by God, to give unto them that which is common, and unto every man in privat, that which unto him in privat belongeth.'[5] Bodin's use of the theory here is a little odd: it is hardly convincing to argue that theft must not be abolished because that would deprive the policeman, whose principal job is to prevent theft, of his function.

[1] I, ii.

[2] VI, iv.

[3] *Method for the Easy Comprehension of History* (1566), translated by Beatrice Reynolds, New York, 1945, pp. 296–8. In Bk. I, ch. vi of the *Republic*, Bodin again denies that the philosophers' golden age ever existed.

[4] *Republic*, VI, iv. Bodin adds here that since men are naturally unequal, equality of goods (and democracy) are unnatural.

[5] I, ii.

But Bodin also used the theory in the more usual way to prove that the state has no right to destroy the institution which is the very reason for its existence.

A prince 'may not remove the bounds which almightie God (of whom he is the living and breathing image) hath prefined unto the everlasting lawes of nature: neither may he take from another man that which is his, without just cause, whether it be by buying, by exchange, by confiscation, by league with friends, or peace with enemies, if it cannot otherwise be concluded than by privat mens losse. . . .'[1] Authority over all belongs to kings, property to private persons.[2] Kings claim, 'for pompe and show,' to be the owners of all things, and some lawyers have misinterpreted the Roman Law in support of that claim; but in fact 'every subject hath the true proprietie of his owne things, and may therefore dispose at his pleasure. . . .'[3] Nor may a king tax without the consent of his subjects. In England taxes must be granted by Parliament: 'other kings have in this point no more power than the kings of England: for that it is not in the power of any prince in the world, at his pleasure to rayse taxes upon the people, no more than to take another mans goods from him; as Philip Commines wisely showed in the Parliament holden at Tours, as we read in his *Commentaries*. . . .'[4]

Bodin did not resolve the problem of how the king could be forced to obey the laws of nature and God, and raise taxes only by consent.[5] In the circumstances of the time he supported the monarchy and taught that all resistance, even to a wicked king,

[1] I, viii.

[2] This maxim of Seneca is quoted again in the *Method for the Easy Comprehension of History*, Miss Reynolds's translation, p. 205.

[3] *Republic*, II, ii; *Method*, p. 205. Bodin adds that some seigneurial, despotic monarchs, whose titles are based on lawful conquest, are absolute proprietors of everything and rule their subjects as a master rules slaves. But such kingdoms exist only in 'Turkey and Muscovy.' It must be admitted, he said, that victors in a lawful war have an absolute right to what they conquer: otherwise there would be no difference between a conqueror, and a robber. Except for inheritance, he did not describe the modes by which private men get natural titles to property; see *Method*, p. 205.

[4] I, viii; VI, ii.

[5] He suggested that in France the Estates General had the authority to grant taxes, III, vii; but he knew that the King actually taxed without their consent.

was unlawful. He did not adopt the theories of contract and limited government which other defenders of property used to make sure that kings were as limited in practice as they were in law. It was the task of later thinkers to construct a theory of property which would show in detail how men acquired those titles which it was the business of the state to guarantee. But at a time when many men still said that the first duty of the state was the protection of the true religion, he was formulating the most characteristic doctrine of modern political theory—the primary purpose of the state is the protection of private property.[1]

In England at the close of the sixteenth century, the concept of natural law which had been somewhat battered by the Reformation, was reinstated in all its glory. Richard Hooker's *Laws of Ecclesiastical Polity*[2] is an elaborate defence of the Church of England and it has little to say about property. But it helped to introduce Continental ideas in England; and its combination of the theory of contract and natural law influenced Locke and the founders of the philosophy of natural rights.[3] The First Book is a lofty and sublime treatise on the hierarchy of reasonable law which binds the whole creation, from God himself to the lowest forms of inanimate things. In the Third Book Hooker quotes St. Thomas to prove that the reason of man is capable of making valid additions to the law of nature.[4] He does not say that the laws of property are such reasonable additions to natural law, but he does say that society begins as a natural association, resting on the assent of the governed, for economic purposes;[5] and private property is not forbidden by divine law.[6]

[1] He also suggested that the Reformation was essentially an attack on the great wealth of the Church. The pretence, he wrote, was religious reform; but if that excuse had not been handy, the attackers would have found another. *Republic*, V, ii.

[2] Edited by John Keble, 5th edition, Oxford, 1865.

[3] A. P. D'Entrèves, *The Medieval Contribution to Political Thought*, Oxford, 1939, and J. W. Gough, *The Social Contract*, Oxford, 1936, discuss the ideas of natural law and contract in Hooker.

[4] III, ix, 2.

[5] I, x. He also says here that 'regiment' is made necessary by the corruption of human nature; but he generally adopts the Thomistic rather than the Augustinian point of view.

[6] Manuscript citation, p. 332, n. 3, in Vol. I of Keble's 5th edition.

Hooker's is still the old concept of natural law under which the institution of property is generally approved, but the individual has no natural right to hold and use his particular property without regard to the society as a whole. Practically this means that the state has a large authority over the property of individuals. Hooker mentions specifically the laws of inheritance as the kind of rules which may be varied according to the principle of expediency;[1] he observes that the monastic confiscations were inexpedient, but he does not say they were unlawful.[2] Some distance remained to be travelled before men could claim that each held his property by natural right, that every property owner ought to be free to divide his property among his heirs in any way he chose, and that all confiscation was a violation of natural right. That distance was travelled in the next century.

[1] I, x, 10.

[2] VII, xxiv, 23–4.

CHAPTER SIX

☆

The Seventeenth Century

The right whereby what is seized belongs to the first one to occupy it, is founded not upon nature but upon an implicit pact and institution of men. Pufendorf, *De Jure Naturae et Gentium*, Bk. IV, ch. iv.

In the constitutional struggles of the seventeenth century, the modern theory of natural law—the theory of individual rights—was eventually perfected. Stripped of the trappings which each particular theorist hung upon it, the bare theory was a simple pattern of *a priori* assumptions which, in the opinion of the men whose interests they served, were as obviously true as the axioms of Euclid. 'Think of men in a state of nature,' the theorists said. Their critics answered that this was absurd since men had never been in such a state; but the proponents parried this with the answer that they were uncovering the abstract principles of political justice, not the data of history. In this state, they went on to assume, men are naturally free and have equal rights. If we consider how men in this state can set up political authorities with just powers to command, we see at once that they can do so only if each individual transfers some of his natural rights to these authorities. Government is the artificial creation of individuals; it enjoys only those rights granted in the contract which created it. This basic theory could be, and was, used to justify the most diverse types of political state: no two writers agreed in defining the exact rights which had been transferred by contract to the government. Nevertheless it was primarily a revolutionary theory serving the middle classes in their battles with royal absolutism.

Its roots were partly medieval. All the separate pieces which made up the pattern—natural law, equality, contract—had been familiar to medieval thinkers. But now the pieces had been modernized and arranged in a new combination. Catholic enemies of Protestant monarchs, particularly the Jesuits, restating the theories of St. Thomas, had contributed something. Protestants rebelling against Catholic princes had been trying to perfect such a theory for a hundred years. Moreover, Protestant theology had influenced the individualistic cast of the new theory. In the Protestant world God gives grace, not to a Church, but to individual Christians who then unite to form a Church; in the new political philosophy, God (or nature) gives rights, not to rulers, but to individuals who then proceed to create rulers.

The new scientific thinking also influenced the political writers. The scientists had been uncovering the laws governing the physical world by observing simple phenomena and applying the logic of mathematics to their observations. It was tempting for the political scientists to assume that there was a natural moral law governing the human world—a 'dictate of right reason,' 'manifest and clear,' having a 'degree of validity even if we should concede that which cannot be conceded without the utmost wickedness, that there is no God,' and 'unchangeable—even in the sense that it cannot be changed by God.'[1] Why should they not uncover the natural law relating to human affairs by applying rational principles to the observation of the simple phenomenon, man—man in a state of nature, abstracted from those accidental circumstances of birth and fortune which differentiate individuals in society? Like the laws of motion, this moral law, demonstrable by reason alone, would have the advantage of being acknowledged by men of every religious faith.

Finally, the economic revolution which destroyed feudalism not only set the problem which the new theory of natural rights was designed to solve, but it also suggested some of the premises of that theory. The new owners of property inevitably protested against the inherited privileges of the old ruling class. They saw

[1] The quotations are from Hugo Grotius, *De Jure Belli ac Pacis*, 1646 edition, translated by F. W. Kelsey and others, Oxford, 1925, pp. 38, 23, 13–14, and 40, respectively. The first edition was published in 1625.

no justice or reason in a system which discriminated against a man, even a rich one, merely because he was low-born. They had played a game whose rules gave special advantages to the well-born competitor, they had won the game in spite of those rules, and then found that the prizes were reserved for those with noble ancestors. Of course they demanded that the rules of the game should be the same for everybody and that prizes should be awarded on the basis of merit alone. Their own experience, in short, led the middle classes to accept as axioms of natural law the idea that all men are born equal and that the equality of their rights should, in some sense, be recognized by the laws of the state.[1] The medieval thinker did not conceive that inequality of legal status was any more objectionable than inequality of wealth. But the theorist of natural right was convinced that, while differences of wealth are justifiable, the law should make no distinction between rich and poor. He insisted that the state should protect property, but he denied that it should give special protection to the privileges which property confers.

Hugo Grotius's *Three Books on the Law of War and Peace*, first published in 1625, was primarily a treatise on international law. But it was also one of the first and most influential of the books expounding the theory of natural rights. Grotius was a citizen of the Netherlands, the land whose middle class had led a successful revolution against absolutism, and whose natural philosophers were leaders in the new science. In religion he was an Arminian—a member of that group which accepted the main tenets of Protestantism, but insisted that God and nature acted, and could not help but act, according to rational principles. The laws of God and the laws of nature were none other than the laws of human reason. Moreover, Grotius was one of the most learned men of his time and he drew upon the classical philosophers, the Roman and canon law, medieval theory, and the writings of both Catholic and Protestant opponents of absolutism in his own day. His theory of property contained elements from

[1] Franz Borkenau, *Der Ubergang vom feudalen zum bürgerlichen Weltbild*, Paris, 1934, presents a thoughtful analysis of the origins of the theory of natural rights.

all these sources; he combined them anew according to the formula of the philosophy of natural rights.

In the Prolegomena to his treatise Grotius defined a law of nature as a 'dictate of right reason' and explicitly rejected the earlier Protestant theory that these laws were set forth in the Bible. Many of the rules of the Old Testament, he said, are positive commands of God and, although they never conflict with the law of nature, are not parts of it; the New Testament, for example, frequently enjoins upon Christians a greater degree of perfection than is required by natural law.[1] Grotius was one of the first Protestant theorists to condemn theft without referring to the Seventh Commandment: he quoted instead the *Digest* to show that it was forbidden by the law of nature.[2]

This rational law of nature is, of course, unchangeable. But its prescriptions vary with the times and Grotius repeated the hoary formula that the common use of things and private ownership are, each in its appropriate setting, equally natural.[3] What does the law of nature prescribe in the modern setting? That question is answered in Book II.[4]

At the creation, and again after the Flood, God gave the world to men to use as a common inheritance. They lived without strife since they were content to consume only those things which the earth freely offered. The only private property was those consumable goods which each man gathered for his immediate use: to steal these was forbidden by the law of nature, but theft was no problem so long as there was enough to supply the simple wants of everyone. This was the golden age of the poets and its basic institution of common ownership survives even to-day where men live simply, as do the American Indians, or are unusually affectionate, as are those ascetic religious groups who follow the example of the first Christians. But most men were not content to 'feed on the spontaneous products of the earth.' Impelled by the vices of avarice and ambition as well as by the

[1] Pp. 26–7. All my references are to the Kelsey translation of the 1646 edition.

[2] P. 39.

[3] P. 39.

[4] Ch. ii.

desire to obtain a 'more refined mode of life,' men strove to create and acquire more and more things, quarrels arose, and the preservation of peace required the institution of private property. At first men were content to divide up moveable goods such as flocks and other personal belongings, but eventually the land was divided as well.

The actual division, Grotius went on to explain, required more than the mere will of the individual. The earth belongs to all in common and no one person can establish a valid right to a portion merely by claiming or taking possession of it. By the law of nature all men have equal rights and they are not, consequently, obliged to respect the special rights and exclusive privileges of private owners. Tom cannot impose on Dick and Harry an obligation to respect as his exclusive property a field which by nature belongs to all three of them. Fortunately for Tom, Dick and Harry may obligate themselves if they choose. 'It is a rule of the law of nature to abide by pacts (for it was necessary that among men there be some method of obligating themselves one to another, and no other natural method can be imagined). . . .'[1] Consequently, private ownership was introduced 'by a kind of agreement, either expressed, as by a division, or implied, as by occupation. In fact, as soon as community ownership was abandoned, and as yet no division had been made, it is to be supposed that all agreed, that whatever each one had taken possession of should be his property.'[2] After the first division of things had been made, occupation remained as the only primary mode of acquisition. It is a natural mode of acquisition only on the presupposition that all men have consented to respect the rights of the occupier, and that by the law of nature they cannot withdraw their consent once it has been given.

Grotius asserted that the compact introducing private ownership preceded the institution of government—'the right to use

[1] P. 14.

[2] Pp. 189–90. Grotius refers the reader to his earlier work, *Mare Liberum* (1609), ch. xv, where the same theory of property is outlined, and to John Selden, 'the glory of England,' whose *Mare Clausum* (1635) repeated, with acknowledgement, the theory of Grotius.

force in obtaining one's own existed before laws were promulgated.'[1] But after the introduction of government, the rules governing the acquisition of property were modified. A sovereign may occupy new territory in several different ways: he may claim only the sovereignty of the land and permit individuals to acquire titles of ownership by occupation, or by such other modes of acquisition as he may deem suitable; or he may occupy both the sovereignty and the ownership of the new territory.[2] The sovereign may also claim the ownership of various things—wild animals, treasure-troves, intestate property—which in the state of nature belong, by agreement, to the first occupier.[3] Finally the sovereign may add to the law of nature by permitting children and insane persons to own property, and by recognizing titles based on prescription alone.[4] But, apart from modifications of this kind, the state must respect the property of the subject; laws, for example, which award shipwrecked goods to the crown are unjust,[5] and on those extraordinary occasions when the king has to take property from his subjects, he must compensate them for their loss.[6]

Grotius's theory of property is, in the main, the theory of the natural rights school. But his particular version of that theory had several serious weaknesses which it was the business of later theorists to remedy. He did not succeed in making property a natural right: he in fact bases private ownership on a suppositious convention subscribed to by the whole human race. Natural law

[1] P. 40. On p. 295, he denies that modes of acquisition are defined by the law of nations, as the Roman lawyers maintained; they are part of the law of nature in that 'state which followed the introduction of property ownership and preceded all civil law.' Grotius, of course, identifies the law of nations with international law.

[2] Pp. 192, 207. Grotius quotes the Senecan maxim—to kings belongs authority over all, to private persons, property—to illustrate the difference between sovereignty and ownership.

[3] Pp. 297 ff. and 269 ff. The latter passage asserts that the children of intestate persons have a natural right to so much of the estate as is necessary for their maintenance. The right to make a will is a natural right which, presumably, the state has no power to deny; pp. 265–6.

[4] Pp. 208, 220 ff.

[5] P. 267.

[6] P. 807.

no doubt obliges men to respect that convention; nevertheless, as he himself confesses,[1] property is, according to his theory, a creation of human law. Here there are two difficulties. The first, common to all contract theories, is that men may deny that such a contract was ever made, or if it was, that it in any way obligated those who were not yet born. Secondly, if the rights of property are created by human authority, why may they not be abrogated by human authority? The usual answer to that question was that a convention may be revoked only if all the parties to it consent—if only one property owner held out, property would be safe. Nevertheless, men may still ask how anyone could reasonably assume that they gave their consent to an unalterable convention which in effect destroys natural equality and grants special privileges to the few.

The answer which Grotius gave to this question reveals another weakness in his theory. In common with all the other theorists of natural right, he maintained that the institution of private property really protected men's natural equality of rights. 'Now property ownership was introduced for the purpose of preserving equality to this end, in fact, that each should enjoy his own.'[2] But what is this 'own' to which each man has an equal right? At one point Grotius came near to defining it as the property which each acquires by his labour,[3] but he later rejected this on the ground that labour has to be applied to things, and all things, before men agree to institute private property, belong to everybody. Hence common property cannot become individual property merely because someone chooses to labour on it.[4] In fact, the 'own' which the laws of property protect is whatever an individual has managed to get hold of, and equality of right, applied to property, means only that every man has an equal right to grab. The institution

[1] P. 39.

[2] P. 322, Bk. II, ch. xii, expounds the usual theory that this equality must be preserved in all exchanges of property; monopolies and other special privileges are forbidden by the law of nature.

[3] P. 189, where he describes how the primitive community of ownership broke down when some men took more from the common store than their labour entitled them to take.

[4] P. 206.

of property was an agreement among men legalizing what each had already grabbed, without any right to do so, and granting, for the future, a formal right of ownership to the first grabber. As a result of this agreement, which, by a remarkable oversight, puts no limit on the amount of property any one person may occupy, everything would soon pass into private ownership, and the equal right to grab would cease to have any practical value.

In short, Grotius's theory, although it makes use of all the familiar phrases, is scarcely a theory of natural right at all. It derives the rights of property not from natural law, but from the agreement of men. It provides no rational explanation of why men should have subscribed to an agreement which took away equality of right, an agreement which legalized and perpetuated the unjust claims of those who had taken more than their share of the common property.

Whether it was that many men read Grotius, or that he set down what was already obvious to his contemporaries, his theory of property was expounded again and again in the course of the century. It was introduced in England by the most learned of authorities: John Selden subscribed to the theory of the 'most excellent Hugo Grotius,' and buttressed it with Hebrew and Arabic references.[1] Other English writers paraphrased either Grotius or Selden and the fundamental concepts of the natural right theory of property were rapidly domiciled in England.[2] Those concepts were readily assimilated by constitutional writers who were already accustomed to think of the common law and Magna Charta as embodiments of the laws of reason and nature.[3]

[1] *Mare Clausum*, London, 1635, I, iv. This work, translated by Marchamont Nedham, 1652, *Of the Dominion, or, Ownership of the Sea*, was written as a refutation of Grotius's book on the freedom of the seas, the *Mare Liberum*.

[2] Richard Cumberland, *De Legibus Naturae*, London, 1672; Samuel Parker, *A Demonstration of the Divine Authority of the Laws of Nature*, London, 1681; Gabriel Towerson, *Explication of the Decalogue*, London, 1676. Towerson and other divines continued the Protestant custom of quoting the Decalogue as a defence of private ownership; see my *Social Ideas of Religious Leaders*, II, i.

[3] C. H. McIlwain, *The High Court of Parliament*, New Haven, 1910, pp. 105–8; J. W. Allen, *English Political Thought*, 1603–60, London, 1938, p. 37, and Pt. VII, ii.

Opponents of the first two Stuarts who complained that royal taxation violated the natural as well as the common law were carrying on a long-established constitutional tradition. John Lilburne, the great champion of the natural rights of Englishmen, discovered those rights in the lawyers' commentaries on the laws of England.[1] The union of this popular tradition of natural right with the learned theories imported from the Continent made possible the achievement of Locke at the end of the century.

It was Lilburne's Leveller party which made the concepts of natural law and natural right the chief weapons of political debate in Cromwell's England. The Levellers were the small property-owners and London shopkeepers. They were also radical Puritans in whose minds the tradition of Protestant individualism had developed to the point where, according to a hostile observer, they reject Scriptural authority when it contradicts what each man knows by the 'light of nature,' and 'they go from the laws and constitutions of kingdoms, and will be governed by rules according to nature and right reason; and though the laws and customs of a kingdom be never so plain and clear against their ways, yet they will not submit, but cry out for natural rights derived from Adam and right reason.'[2] These were the men who in the short space of four years (1646–1650), in the midst of civil war, set forth all the basic demands of middle-class democracy and liberalism. In their hands the concept of natural rights became a weapon of radical equalitarianism.

But the difficulties which beset the Leveller programme were a warning, both to friends and enemies, of the danger of appealing to natural rights without troubling to define the natural right of property. The Levellers insisted that by the law of nature all men are equal and endowed with the same natural rights. From this principle they deduced that all special privileges are usurp-

[1] William Haller and Godfrey Davies, *The Leveller Tracts*, Introduction, pp. 41 ff., New York, 1944; David W. Petegorsky, *Left-Wing Democracy in the English Civil War*, London, 1940, p. 81.

[2] Thomas Edwards, *Gangraena*, Pt. III, p. 20, London, 1646.

ations. By the law of nature, all men have an equal right to vote;[1] they ought all to enjoy the same legal rights; equal economic opportunity must not be restricted by laws establishing monopolies, servile tenures, primogeniture, and the like; and equality in religion demands that no one religious group should be granted the special privileges of a state Church. Obviously the Levellers were demanding that a large measure of that equality decreed by nature ought to be preserved in the social state. Some of their friends and most of their enemies assumed, reasonably enough, that they also wanted equality of goods.

The Leveller leaders let drop occasional remarks which seemed to substantiate this assumption. Richard Overton wrote in 1647 that 'to every individual in nature is given an individual propriety by nature, not to be invaded or usurped by any (as in mine *Arrow against Tyranny* is proved and discovered more at large); for every one as he is himself hath a self propriety—else could not be himself—and on this no second may presume without consent; and by natural birth all men are equal, and alike born to like propriety and freedom. . . .'[2] Undoubtedly Overton meant to say only that every man is the owner of his own person—the principle from which Locke deduced that each man was also the owner of those things with which he had mixed his person in the form of labour. But the words could easily be misread to mean that men ought to have equal amounts of wealth. Actually, the practical programme of the Levellers, demanding the abolition of economic privileges and the parcelling among small owners of the confiscated estates of Royalists and the Church, would have tended to equalize property. Certainly these radical democrats were no lovers of plutocracy. Moreover, some men who started with the assumptions of Lilburne and his

[1] The 1649 platform, *An Agreement of the Free People of England*, denied the vote to wage-earners and paupers—that is, unfree men. This *Agreement* is printed in both the recent collections of Leveller writings: Haller and Davies, *The Leveller Tracts*, and Don M. Wolfe, *Leveller Manifestoes*, N.Y., 1944.

[2] *An Appeal from the Commons to the Free People*, p. 327 of the abridgement printed in A. S. P. Woodhouse, *Puritanism and Liberty*, London, 1938. *An Arrow Against Tyranny* was published in 1646.

party did end by advocating equality of property. In 1648 a group, calling themselves Levellers, maintained that 'men were to enjoy the creatures alike without propriety one more than the other. . . .'[1] Finally, Gerrard Winstanley, the Digger, wanted to achieve economic equality by abolishing private property altogether. When the Levellers repudiated his communism, he called himself the 'true Leveller,' implying that Lilburne and his friends were being false to their own principles. It is hardly surprising that Lilburne's conservative opponents, despite his frequent denials, insisted that his theory of natural right did lead straight to equality of ownership.

To the charge that they were communists, or that they wanted to introduce economic equality, the Levellers made repeated denials. Most of their later petitions and paper-constitutions demanded that Parliament formally bind itself never to abolish or abrogate the right of property. They implied that that was one of the rights guaranteed by the law of nature. They contended that their whole programme was intended to secure owners against the usurpations and oppressions of tyranny. One pamphleteer decried 'parity' as a 'Utopian fiction' whose impossibility was proved by the text, 'the poor ye shall always have with you. . . .'[2] William Walwyn maintained that private ownership could not be equalized or abolished unless every single individual gave his consent;[3] the implication was that property was founded, as Grotius had said, on a universal agreement. But the Leveller party never adopted a well-defined theory of property. Consequently, they were never able to reply satisfactorily to the charges of their opponents.

The inadequacy of Leveller thought on property was dramatically demonstrated in the great debate on the constitution held at Putney in the fall of 1647. There the repre-

[1] *Light Shining in Buckinghamshire*, printed in the *Works of Gerrard Winstanley*, edited by G. H. Sabine, Ithaca, N.Y., 1941; see p. 606 for an account of the left-wing Levellers who probably sponsored this pamphlet.

[2] John Cooke, *Unum Necessarium*, 1648, quoted in Petegorsky, *Left-Wing Democracy in the English Civil War*, pp. 111–12.

[3] *A Manifestation*, p. 279, in Haller and Davies, *Leveller Tracts.*

sentatives of the soldiers and some of the Leveller leaders met with the officers, led by Cromwell and his son-in-law, Henry Ireton, to determine what kind of government England should have. The radicals were determined that all men 'that have not lost their birthrights should have an equal voice in elections.'[1] They supported that demand by the Laws of God and Nature,[2] and by the proposition that since 'the poorest he in England hath a life to live, as the greatest he,'[3] and since 'the chief end of this government is to preserve persons as well as estates,'[4] 'it's clear that every man that is to live under a government ought first by his own consent to put himself under that government.'[5]

Henry Ireton, speaking for the more conservative officers, opposed the Leveller proposal on the grounds that it endangered property. Ireton was certainly the best debater at Putney and his arguments, outlining some of the chief objections to the theory of natural rights, confounded even when they did not convince his opponents. 'All the main thing that I speak for,' he said, 'is because I would have an eye to property. I hope we do not come to contend for victory—but let every man consider with himself that he do not go that way to take away all property.'[6]

> Now I wish we may consider of what right you will challenge that all the people should have a right to elections. Is it by the right of nature? If you will hold forth that as your ground, then I think you must deny all property too, and this is my reason. For thus: by that same right of nature (whatever it be) that you pretend, by which you can say, one man hath an equal right with another to the choosing of him that shall govern him—by the same right of nature, he hath the same right in any goods he sees—meat, drink, clothes—to take and use them for his sustenance. He hath a freedom to the land, the ground, to exercise it, to till it; he hath the freedom to anything that any one doth account himself to have any propriety in. [7]

'The Law of God doth not give me property, nor the Law of

[1] P. 53, in the edition of the Putney Debates by A. S. P. Woodhouse, *Puritanism and Liberty*, London, 1938.

[2] P. 56. [3] P. 53. [4] P. 67.

[5] P. 53. [6] P. 57. [7] P. 59.

Nature, but property is of human constitution.'[1] It rests in the covenants, recorded in law, which men have made with one another. 'For matter of goods, that which does fence me from that [right] which another man may claim by the Law of Nature, of taking my goods, that which makes it mine really and civilly, is the law.'[2] Therefore, Ireton concludes, to alter the suffrage, to tamper with those original conventions, embodied in the fundamental law of England, which limit the vote to property owners, is to destroy the foundation of private property and open the way to anarchy. To abandon the constitution of England for principles of 'absolute natural right' and 'that wild or vast notion of what in every man's conception is just or unjust' is to abandon the sole rule for distinguishing between mine and thine. If it is admitted that the fundamental constitution may be amended, then it must be admitted that the rights of property may be abrogated, for they are part of that constitution. What arguments could deter a Parliament elected by the propertyless majority from abolishing property altogether?[3]

Ireton's theory is, of course, precisely that of Hugo Grotius: the rights of property are derived from an agreement subscribed to by all men; that agreement is guaranteed by the law of nature which requires men to keep the covenants they have made. Grotius, thinking of the guarantee, wrote that property was natural; Ireton, thinking of the agreement, said that it was conventional; but in fact their theories were identical.

Although the Levellers were not convinced by Ireton's argument they were unable to answer it. Colonel Rainborough, their most eloquent representative, tried to argue that property was protected by the Law of God—'Thou shalt not steal.' But Ireton's reply was that the Law of God was a poor substitute for the laws of England: God's law protects property in general, but it does not distinguish, in particular cases, the property of one man from another. A man would find it hard to demonstrate his title to a particular piece of property from divine law.[4] The Levellers had no detailed theory of the natural right of property

[1] P. 69. [2] P. 26. [3] P. 63. [4] Pp. 59–60.

and were, consequently, unable to refute Ireton's contention that by natural law all was common and that private ownership was a convention based on the consent of men. In one of the most effective speeches in the debate, Colonel Rainborough pointed out the sombre consequences of Ireton's theory; but he had no theory to replace it.

Sir, I see that it is impossible to have liberty but all property must be taken away. If it be laid down for a rule, and if you will say it, it must be so. But I would fain know what the soldier hath fought for all this while. He hath fought to enslave himself, to give power to men of riches, men of estates, to make him a perpetual slave. We do find in all presses[1] that go forth none must be pressed that are freehold men. When these gentlemen fall out among themselves they shall press the poor scrubs to come and kill [one another for] them.[2]

Here, in six sentences, Rainborough expressed the central dilemma of the middle-class revolution. Both Ireton, the spokesman of the Right, and Rainborough, the spokesman of the Left, agreed that men were created free and equal, and that their property should be protected. But neither of them knew how to formulate a theory of property consistent with their theories of liberty and equality. Ireton demonstrated that Rainborough's political programme threatened the foundations of private ownership. Rainborough demonstrated that Ireton's programme protected property only at the cost of abandoning equality of political right and liberty for all. Ireton's answer was no more satisfactory to the poor man who had fought for freedom than was the Leveller programme for the rich man who had fought for the rights of property. The common soldier, Ireton said, fought for the right to be ruled by a Parliament of property-owners rather than by the will of the king; and he had reason to do so since he was free to become a property-owner himself.[3] What both Ireton and Rainborough needed was a theory of property which would satisfy both the owners, and the property-less men who had fought for the abolition of privilege. Only

[1] Impressment—the method of conscripting common soldiers and sailors.

[2] P. 71.

[3] P. 73.

such a theory could cement the uneasy alliance between the poor and the middle class which was necessary for the success of the revolution. But no such theory was at hand. Not until the triumph of modern ideas of government in 1688 did an English thinker work out a theory of natural rights calculated to convince both poor and rich.

Because they had no theory of the rights of ownership to divert it, the Levellers' concept of natural right and equality flowed straight in a radical direction—towards the levelling of estates and communism. Ireton repudiated the Leveller theory of natural rights in order to safeguard property. But in the meantime Thomas Hobbes was adding and subtracting the protean phrases of that theory and labouring to prove that, properly articulated, it might provide a sure foundation of the institution of private property.

Hobbes tells us that he began his study of society by examining the origin of the rights of property. 'My first inquiry was to be, from whence it proceeded that any man should call anything rather his *own*, than another man's. And when I found that this proceeded not from nature, but consent (for what nature at first laid forth in common, men did afterwards distribute into several *impropriations*); I was conducted from thence to another inquiry; namely, to what end and upon what impulsives, when all was equally every man's in common, men did rather think it fitting that every man should have his inclosure.'[1]

On the surface Hobbes's description of the state of nature and the origin of property and government resembles that of Grotius and other proponents of natural right: in the natural state men are free and equal, and property is common; to secure peace men institute, by agreement, private ownership and political authority. But Hobbes altered the definitions of the old terms and produced a wholly different theory. Not the least important of these new definitions had to do with the ancient concept of common

[1] *De Cive*, p. vi, *English Works of Thomas Hobbes*, edited by Sir William Molesworth, Vol. II, London, 1841. Hobbes published the Latin version in 1642 and the English translation in 1651.

property in the state of nature. He defined that concept in a rare, and peculiarly Hobbesian, fashion.

The problem of determining how much each individual might take from the common stock had always perplexed those men who attempted to describe the state of nature. From Seneca on they had usually worked out some rules which permitted the individual to consume whatever was necessary to sustain life, and left enough for all other individuals to do the same. Grotius said one man could use the fruits of the earth when everything was common, but that he could not store them up or appropriate a piece of land without the permission of all his fellow-men. In short, whatever the particular rules might be, all the theorists of the state of nature agreed that common ownership implied equality. The various rules were all meant to guarantee that each man would have his share. When the population increased so that there was no longer enough to go round, or when men refused to be content with their share, private property had been instituted.

Hobbes's concept of common ownership was totally different. In the state of nature, he wrote, 'every man has a right to every thing.'[1] 'It is consequent . . . to the same condition, that there by no Propriety, no Dominion, no *Mine* and *Thine* distinct; but onely that to be every mans, that he can get; and for so long, as he can keep it.'[2] Since each has a right to everything, 'one man invadeth with right, and another with right resisteth. . . .'[3] Where private property has not been introduced, each man has a valid claim, not merely to his equal share, but to the whole stock. That this astonishing system of overlapping rights should lead to the war of every man against every man is not surprising.

In order to escape from this unhappy state of nature, Hobbes continued, men agreed to set up a political authority. But since all men had a right to everything, since all rights overlapped, it

[1] *Leviathan*, p. 99 of the 1651 edition reprinted by the Oxford University Press, 1929; *De Cive*, pp. 9–11.

[2] P. 98.

[3] *Elements of Law*, pp. 55–6, edited by Ferdinand Tönnies, Cambridge, 1928.

is impossible to conceive of this political authority as protecting men's natural rights to property. Nor can we believe with Grotius that property is derived from an agreement made by men prior to founding of political authorities: agreements made before there is an enforcing power are of no validity. The only solution was for all men to transfer their rights to a sovereign and let him distribute them again as he saw fit. Thus private property is in fact the creation of the state. The sovereign, to whom all claims to ownership have been transferred, determines what each subject shall call his own. Hobbes repeats again and again that property is the creation of the state. 'Law-makers were before that which you call *own*, or property of goods and lands . . . for without statute-laws, all men have right to all things. . . . You see then that no private man can claim a propriety in any lands, or other goods, from any title from any man but the King, or them that have the sovereign power.'[1]

It follows from this, Hobbes continued, that the rights of property-owners are not valid against the sovereign. The sovereign conferred those rights; he may resume them whenever he judges it good to do so. He can tax and confiscate without violating any rights of his subjects. 'Propriety therefore being derived from the sovereign power, is not to be pretended against the same; especially when by it every subject hath his propriety against every other subject, which when sovereignty ceaseth, he hath not, because in that case they return to war amongst themselves.'[2] It may be 'inconvenient' if the sovereign pleases to enrich himself and his family inordinately, but the inconvenience is slight compared to the advantage of having a settled government, and it is not to be avoided by substituting a sovereign aristocracy or democracy for a sovereign monarch.[3] Hobbes's defence of absolutism is well known and there is no need to

[1] *Dialogue of the Common Law*, p. 29, in *English Works*, edited by Molesworth, Vol. VI, London, 1840. *De Cive*, p. 84, and p. 157, and many passages of the *Leviathan*, repeat the same theory.

[2] *Elements of Law*, p. 109; *Leviathan*, pp. 250–1.

[3] *Elements of Law*, p. 111.

describe it here. It is a thorough absolutism in which the individual owner has no protection against the arbitrary claims of the government.

But the remarkable fact, which is not always noted, is that Hobbes conceived of his political system as the best possible protection for private property, and insisted that in his absolute state the natural equality of men was preserved and their interests equally protected. To prove that the protection of the state is equally beneficial to rich and poor he used the common technique of arguing that all citizens enjoy the same personal security, and then confusing personal security with the opportunity to acquire and hold property. Speaking of taxation he was careful to avoid saying that the rich paid more because they had more property and thus benefited more from the protection of the state: he argued ingeniously that they paid for the personal security of the poor who served them. 'Seeing then the benefit that every one receiveth thereby, is the enjoyment of life, which is equally dear to poor and rich; the debt which a poor man oweth them that defend his life, is the same which a rich man oweth for the defence of his; saving that the rich, who have the service of the poor, may be debtors not onely for their own persons, but for many more.'[1] Thus all men are equal in the benefits they receive from the state. But on a preceding page Hobbes had said that the 'safety of the people,' which the sovereign is obliged by the law of nature to procure, means not 'a bare preservation, but also all other contentments of life, which every man by lawfull industry without danger, or hurt to the Commonwealth, shall acquire to himself.'[2] Thus security of person includes security of the propeaty which the person owns. Since all are alike free to acquire property, the original equality of men—their equality of right—is preserved even though they actually acquire different amounts. Hobbes's sovereign is always careful to protect this equality. He divides property among his citizens so that each

[1] *Leviathan*, pp. 266–7. This implies that the persons of the rich are of no value to the poor—an implication which Hobbes could hardly have accepted.

[2] P. 258.

may 'exercise and have the benefit of his own industry';[1] he leaves to his subjects their natural liberty 'to buy, and sell, and otherwise contract with one another, to choose their own aboad, their own diet, their own trade of life . . .';[2] he determines the legal form in which contracts shall be made,[3] but he does not interfere, by establishing harmful monopolies for example,[4] with the freedom of his subjects to make what mutual agreements they please. Thus Hobbes's sovereign, like the king by divine right, is not restrained by human law—his subjects have no legal redress if he invades their property rights. But he is bound, nevertheless, to follow the law of nature, to secure the safety of his subjects by protecting their goods. If he fails to do so, Hobbes implies, he forfeits his sovereignty.

Hobbes's theory of property, the foundation of his political theory, is ingenious and logical. It enabled him to describe a state which apparently, in accordance with the law of nature, offers equal protection to all its citizens. Such a state may logically claim that each of its citizens owes it an equal debt of loyalty. It is, Hobbes strives to prove, a popular state conferring an equal benefit on all its members. This ideal state also protects the property as well as the persons of its subjects, but this entails no invidious inequality of benefits even though some people have more property than others: the state makes no distinction between rich and poor and it grants the same rights of acquisition to all men. It is not to blame if all men do not make the same use of their opportunities.

Some of these ideas about property and the state were used by later theorists. But as a practical weapon for the political debates of the seventeenth century, Hobbes's theory was no more adequate than those of the Levellers and Ireton. It offered neither

[1] *Elements of Law*, p. 144. At one point Hobbes seems to say that in the original distribution every man should be granted an equal portion; *Leviathan*, p. 119 and pp. 190–1; another passage seems to say that the sovereign guarantees the division made by universal agreement before the institution of sovereignty, *Leviathan*, p. 110.

[2] *Leviathan*, p. 163, *Elements of Law*, p. 143.

[3] *Leviathan*, pp. 192–3.

[4] P. 178; *Elements of Law*, p. 67.

the equality of positive political rights which the radicals demanded, nor the protection of property against royal claims which the conservatives were determined to secure. Ireton agreed with Hobbes that property was created by human law, but he and his supporters were fighting to insure that that law would be maintained and enforced, not by an irresponsible monarch, but by a Parliament of property-owners. Hobbes's theory could not convince the radicals that the protection of unequal property was equalitarian; it offered the owners of property no practical solution for the 'inconvenience' of absolutism. It was not a theory adapted to the needs of those men who were to make the Revolution of 1688 and call it 'Glorious.'

Shortly after Hobbes published the *Leviathan* some empirically minded thinkers reacted against his extreme and abstract rationalism. Adopting that spirit of scientific observation which political arithmeticians were applying to the study of economics, they investigated the historical origins of property rights and their pragmatic, political consequences. James Harrington, whose *Commonwealth of Oceana* was published five years after the *Leviathan*, dismissed Hobbes's structure of formal right with the modern argument that political power was always a function of economic power.[1] From a study of the facts of English history and society he drew the conclusion that the ruling class is that class which holds the 'balance of property.' The system of government is determined by the system of ownership. The problem of the statesman is how to prevent those changes in the distribution of property which overthrow the 'balance' and result in political revolutions. A defender of republicanism and representative government, Harrington hoped that English statesmen in his own day would see the wisdom of perpetuating that wide

[1] Published in 1656. The best modern edition is that of L. B. Liljegren, Lund and Heidelberg, 1924. For the widespread influence of Harrington's thought, see H. F. Russell Smith, *Harrington and His Oceana*, Cambridge, 1914. See also the excellent essay by R. H. Tawney, 'Harrington's Interpretation of His Age,' *Proceedings of the British Academy*, Vol. XXVII, 1941. Henry Neville, *Plato Redivivus*, 2nd edition, London, 1681, is an adaptation of Harrington's theory by one of his friends.

distribution of landed property which the economic revolution had brought about, and which made possible, he thought, the realization of his political ideals. It was not that property ought to rule, or that government ought to protect it; it was that property did rule, and when the pattern of distribution happened to offer the opportunity of setting up a good system of government, men ought to seize that opportunity and try to perpetuate the pattern of ownership which created it. Private property was not an institution to be condemned or justified: it was an historical fact with which men should reckon.

Other Restoration writers, including Thomas Sprat, the historian of the Royal Society, justified property, but followed Harrington in rejecting theories of formal right. They elaborated the argument from utility. Private ownership, they admitted, may well have been instituted by chance, war, or the cunning of the wiser and the violence of the stronger. It should be maintained now because it is useful. It is defensible, not because its rights are derived from the laws of nature or the universal agreement of mankind, but because it is now expedient.[1] The historical method and the appeal to utility are the familiar tools of the modern theorist of property. But in the seventeenth century property-owners were not willing to abandon the surer basis for their claims which a logical system of natural and formal right, appealing to all reasonable men, whether rich or poor, seemed to offer. For another two hundred years theorists tried to prove that private property was inherent in the structure of the universe.

To Samuel Pufendorf, the famous German student of natural law, belongs the honour of having made the next important improvement in the classical, liberal theory of property. A Lutheran, carrying on the study of the laws of nature which Melanchthon had begun and a host of German professors had continued for a century, a thorough-going rationalist who confidently expected to make of political speculation a science as exact as that of mathematics, Pufendorf adopted and adapted all

[1] See my *Social Ideas of Religious Leaders*, pp. 92–5.

the main tenets of the natural rights school.[1] He believed that all men were created equal, that society should preserve their equality of right, that political power was derived from the consent of the people expressed in a contract, and that the contract ordinarily set limits to the political authority. His theory of property was designed to support his liberal political theses, and it was specifically a refutation of the theory upon which Hobbes had built his doctrine of absolutism. Essentially that of Grotius, it was improved and sharpened by the addition of a clearly-defined concept of community ownership in the state of nature.

Pufendorf opened his discussion of property by distinguishing between negative and positive community.[2] Things in positive community 'differ from things owned, only in the respect that the latter belong to one person while the former belong to several in the same manner.'[3] The several who are owners have the right to exclude all other men, and themselves use and enjoy their property jointly. Each has an equal right to his share and an equal obligation to respect the rights of the others. The joint owners in such a system of positive community must, as Aristotle's comments prove, be men of unusual virtue. The members of the Church of Jerusalem, or the inhabitants of the ideal states of More and Campanella, might operate such a community successfully. But it never existed in the state of nature. There never was a Golden Age. Community of property in the state of nature was negative, not positive.

Negative community means simply that nothing belongs to anyone. Things in a state of negative community

are said to be common, according as they are considered before the interposition of any human act, as a result of which they are held to belong in a special way to this man rather than to that. In the same sense such things are said to be nobody's, more in a negative than a

[1] His *De Jure Naturae et Gentium* was first published at Lund in 1672. I have used the translation of the 1688 edition by C. H. and W. A. Oldfather, Oxford, 1934.

[2] His theory is found in Bk. IV, ch. iv, 'On the Origin of Dominion.'

[3] P. 532.

positive sense; that is, that they are not yet assigned to a particular person, not that they cannot be assigned to a particular person. They are furthermore, called 'things that lie open to any and every person.'[1]

This, Pufendorf contends, was the community established by the law of nature. The first men had neither joint rights, as Grotius assumed, nor did each have a right to everything, as Hobbes maintained. Against the theory of Hobbes, Pufendorf raises the objection that it contains an ambiguity. If Hobbes means that a man in a state of nature is free to take whatever reason tells him is necessary for his preservation, Pufendorf agrees: nothing prevented the first men from consuming whatever they wished. But if he means that each man has a right in the sense of a title which others are bound to respect, he is wrong: he himself admits that men in a state of nature are not obligated to respect the rights of others.[2]

Thus Pufendorf disposed of those theories which assumed that men had positive rights to property in the community system of the state of nature. The community of nature is a negative community. The importance of this concept for the development of the natural right theory of property is apparent: it made it possible to dispense with one part of the agreement which previous theorists had assumed was necessary for the institution of private ownership. Since men had no joint or overlapping rights in the state of nature, it was not necessary to assume that those rights must have been extinguished by universal consent, by a convention subscribed to by all men. Pufendorf was one step nearer to a theory of property which would dispense with agreement and convention altogether, and would demonstrate that the right to property was a right of nature. Most of the later theorists of natural right made use of Pufendorf's theory of negative community.

But Pufendorf himself did not succeed in dispensing with conventions altogether. His theory demonstrated that a man in

[1] P. 532.

[2] P. 96.

the state of nature could take what he wanted without violating the rights of others: neither he nor the others had any rights to violate. But having appropriated something, how could one man impose upon the others an obligation to respect his proprietorship? Only by getting their voluntary consent, Pufendorf concluded. Men acquired things by seizing them, but 'for this to produce a moral effect, that is, an obligation on the parts of others to refrain from a thing already seized by someone else, an antecedent pact was required. . . .'[1] 'Assuming an original equal faculty of men over things, it is impossible to conceive how the mere corporal act of one person can prejudice the faculty of others unless the pact intervenes.'[2] 'Therefore, the right whereby what is seized belongs to the first one to occupy it, is founded not upon nature but upon an implicit pact and institution of men.'[3]

Pufendorf goes on to describe how the first men made an agreement, no doubt a tacit one, allowing each man to appropriate the fruits of the earth, but leaving the land in the state of negative community. Gradually men divided the land by agreement and set up general procedures by which individuals could acquire rights to things which were still negatively common.[4] Thus in the course of time most things capable of it were transferred to private ownership. Private property is a conventional creation, the result of agreements between men; but once instituted it is guaranteed by the law of nature, which forbids men to violate contracts, and by the Decalogue. Pufendorf's theory of property made it possible to assume that the natural state, where a large number of things still remained in negative community, and before political authority had been set up, was neither a Golden Age nor a state of war. Men needed no special virtue to respect the property of others so long as they could all get more by simply agreeing with their neighbours to divide up another

[1] P. 547. [2] P. 539. [3] P. 539.

[4] Bk. IV, chs. vi and vii, describe the various Roman Law methods of acquisition as natural in the sense that they may be supposed to have been established by common agreement.

portion of the land still in a state of negative community; nor, on the other hand, were they led inevitably to war since their rights to property were not, as Hobbes assumed, overlapping, but complementary.

From this theory of the origin of property—essentially the theory of Grotius with the addition of the concept of negative and positive community—Pufendorf goes on to construct a typical liberal theory of government.[1] Agreements establishing property are prior in time to those establishing governments; governments were established to protect those prior agreements; the contracts instituting governments bind them to respect the property of the individual. Furthermore, the state is bound to preserve the original equality of nature by recognizing that all men have the same rights to exchange and acquire property: the granting of monopolies and special privileges is a violation of natural law.[2]

Pufendorf's theory of property was more exact than that of Grotius and a more persuasive alternative to that of Hobbes. But it still failed to meet the criticisms to which the Grotian theory was liable. It still bases property on the sands of human agreement instead of the rock of natural law. Critics could still deny the validity, and even the existence, of such an agreement. Pufendorf candidly admitted that there were historical instances of sovereigns who owned all the property in their states,[3] and he intimated that men might at any time agree to give their sovereign full power over their property.[4] What Hobbes falsely applied to all states is true, he confessed, of some.[5] Finally, Pufendorf, like Grotius, cannot explain how it was that all men were persuaded to make agreements about property—and to set up political power to enforce those agreements—which destroyed their original equality. All men, he wrote, are equally indebted to the

[1] In Bks. VII and VIII.

[2] Pp. 368–9, and Bk. V, esp. chs. iii and v. In Bk. IV, ch. x, Pufendorf argues that ownership ceases with death and that the right to make wills is, consequently, not one of the basic rights of ownership, but a privilege granted by the positive law of the state.

[3] P. 1275. [4] P. 1277. [5] P. 1274.

state for protecting their lives, but the benefits of the state's protection of property are unequally distributed.[1] Thus Pufendorf's theory could neither convince the poor that the protection of property was to their interest—that it was the means of perpetuating the original equality of all men—nor justify resistance to the arbitrary depredations of absolute princes. To serve these ends, within the framework of the philosophy of natural right, it would be necessary to show that private ownership was rooted in the law of nature—a law which dispensed equal justice to all, a law which the most powerful government could not violate with impunity. Pufendorf did not prove that property was natural; but he prepared the way for such a proof.

If as Hobbes assumed, natural community meant that each man had a right to appropriate everything, or if, as Grotius assumed, natural community was a positive system of joint ownership, then only the universal agreement of men could establish private ownership. In both cases it would be necessary to extinguish existing rights and this could only be accomplished with the voluntary consent of the holders of these rights. But if natural community is negative community, if in the beginning no one has a right to anything, then an agreement extinguishing rights is unnecessary. Then the problem will be simply to show that new rights may originate naturally, that a man may acquire rights of property which will obligate others without their prior consent. Pufendorf did not discover the solution to this problem, although he came close to it in an incidental passage. One reason for the introduction of private property, he wrote, is that 'most things require labour and cultivation by men to produce them and make them fit for use. But in such cases it was improper that a man who had contributed no labour should have right to things equal to his by whose industry a thing had been raised or ren-

[1] P. 1283. But unlike Grotius, he did attempt to preserve natural equality in the agreements establishing the rights of occupation; those agreements, he said, could not have given a man the right to occupy more than he could use, or to occupy something for no other purpose than to deprive others of its use and subject them to an unjust servitude. P. 566.

dered fit for service.'[1] John Locke substituted 'unnatural' for 'improper' and demonstrated that the laws of nature imposed an obligation on men to respect the property rights of anyone who, by his own labour, had appropriated things from their state of negative community.

[1] Pp. 540–1.

CHAPTER SEVEN

☆

The Natural Right of Property

I shall endeavour to show how men might come to have a property in several parts of that which God gave to mankind in common, and that without any express compact of all the commoners. John Locke, *Of Civil Government*, Bk. II, sec. 24.

John Locke's theory of property became the standard bourgeois theory, the classical liberal theory. Wherever middle-class revolutionaries rebelled against feudal privilege and royal absolutism, they inscribed on their banners the slogan of 'life, liberty, and property.' That 'property' should be included in the sacred trinity of natural rights was, now that Locke had thought the matter through, one of those truths which express so exactly what men want that they seem self-evident. 'It was a discovery almost as simple, and almost as evident when once stated, as Newton's discovery of the law of gravitation.'[1] At first a revolutionary doctrine, popularized by radicals and rebels, its ability to convince men is measured by the success of the liberal revolutions which it justified. The theory that property was a natural right triumphed with the Glorious, the American, and the French Revolutions. With the decline of liberalism, the theory ceased to be a self-evident truth. But the classical liberal theory of property still lives on as a popular tradition.

Locke's two treatises, *Of Civil Government*, were published in London in 1690 as a defence of the Glorious Revolution and the triumph of Parliamentary government in England. They soon became the standard text of liberalism and natural rights. For the most part Locke restated lucidly and persuasively the doctrines of his predecessors concerning natural law, the state of nature, the social contract, and government limited by law and resting on

[1] H. R. Fox Bourne, *Life of John Locke*, London, 1876, Vol. II, p. 173.

the consent of the governed. The new and original part of his work was the theory of property. He demonstrated how individual men could convert the common property of the state of nature into their personal property without securing the consent of their fellow-men. He tried to prove that property is natural, that the right to property is a natural right, and that private ownership is an institution, not of man, but of nature. Political institutions, founded on the artificial agreements and conventions of men, may be remade whenever the contracting parties so will; property institutions, founded on nature, are as unalterable as the structure of the universe. Men have the right to choose their form of government—monarchy, aristocracy, democracy, or any other which their ingenuity might devise; but in matters of property they have not the right of choosing, but the duty of maintaining the law which nature had dictated. Adam and his sons came to an agreement about political rights; they were born with property rights. If these are not precisely Locke's conclusions, they are those which his readers thought were his. Locke himself was not always a Lockean.

Locke's new theory of property was a direct answer to the critics of Grotius and Pufendorf. The arguments of those critics had been clearly stated by Sir Robert Filmer, the most popular exponent of the divine right theory of government, and the target of Locke's essays.[1] The proponents of natural rights, Filmer wrote, imagine a state of nature in which all men were free and equal and in which all property was common. The only just way out of this unhappy state of primitive communism was for all men to assent to an unequal division of the common property. But how, Filmer asked, can we assume that such an agreement was ever made, that no individual in the world refused to give up his equal right to everything? Even if we swallow this absurd and hypothetical agreement of which history has preserved no record, we are not bound by the actions of our ancestors. Consequently, any individual is now at liberty to resume

[1] Filmer died in 1653, but his books were frequently reprinted in the second half of the century.

the community of nature and assert his equal right to the property of all his neighbours. Finally, even though we assume that the agreement is still binding, individuals may still withdraw their consent and, renouncing their conventional rights, resume these natural, communal rights with which Grotius and Selden have endowed them.[1] The divine right theory, which vests all property in the monarch and directs him to use it for the good of his subjects is, Filmer concludes, not only a more reasonable, but also a safer theory of property. The philosophers of natural right had not been able to derive property from the law of nature, and Filmer had good reason to assert that the man who held his estate from the king had greater security of possession than the man whose title was based on the consent of all men. If the rights of property were to be secure against the attacks of levellers as well as kings, they could not be founded on conventional agreements. 'I shall endeavour to show,' Locke wrote, 'how men might come to have a property in several parts of that which God gave to mankind in common, and that without any express compact of all the commoners.'[2]

Following the traditional natural law theory, Locke maintained, with proofs from 'natural reason' and 'revelation' that the earth had been given to mankind in common. Following Pufendorf he assumed that this was a negative rather than a positive community of ownership: things belong to no one and each shares the common right to take what he needs without getting the consent of the others.[3] 'If such a consent as that was necessary, man had starved, notwithstanding the plenty God had given

[1] *Observations Concerning the Original of Government*, London, 1684, esp. pp. 200, 234–5. Some of these ideas are repeated in *Patriarcha*, 1680, Filmer's most famous work, and in the *Free-holders Grand Inquest*, 1679. All of these were written before 1653.

[2] *Of Civil Government*, II, 24, Everyman edition.

[3] Locke was acquainted with Pufendorf's work, but does not refer to it. It is possible, of course, that he worked out the theory of negative community independently. Some of the sources of Locke's ideas about property are given in two doctoral theses, Casimir J. Czajkowski, *The Theory of Private Property in John Locke's Political Philosophy*, Notre Dame, 1941, and Paschal Larkin, *Property in the Eighteenth Century*, Cork University Press, 1930.

him.'[1] The problem, then, was to show how it came about that when one man took a portion of the common stock, the rest of mankind was obliged to respect that portion as his private property. Pufendorf could not see how that obligation could exist unless mankind had agreed to assume it. Locke discovered that it was imposed by the law of nature, and bound all men fast long before mere human conventions had been thought of.

Though the earth and all inferior creatures be common to all men, yet every man has a 'property' in his own 'person.' This nobody has any right to but himself. The 'labour' of his body and 'work' of his hands, we may say, are properly his. Whatsoever, then, he removes out of the state that Nature hath provided and left it in, he hath mixed his labour with it, and joined to it something that is his own, and thereby makes it his property. It being by him removed from the common state Nature placed it in, it hath by this labour something annexed to it that excludes the common right of other men. For this 'labour' being the unquestionable property of the labourer, no man but he can have a right to what that is once joined to, at least where there is enough, and as good left in common for others.

As much land as a man tills, plants, improves, cultivates, and can use the product of, so much is his property. He by his labour does, as it were, enclose it from the common. Nor will it invalidate his right to say everybody else has an equal title to it, and therefore he cannot appropriate, he cannot enclose, without the consent of all his fellow-commoners, all mankind. God, when He gave the world in common to all mankind, commanded man also to labour, and the penury of his condition required it of him. . . . He that, in obedience to this command of God, subdued, tilled, and sowed any part of it, thereby annexed to it something that was his property, which another had no title to, nor could without injury take from him.

And thus . . . supposing the world, given as it was to children of men in common, we see how labour could make men distinct titles to several parcels of it for their private uses, wherein there could be no doubt of right, no room for quarrel.

Nor is it so strange as, perhaps, before consideration, it may appear, that the property of labour should be able to overbalance the com-

[1] This and the following quotations are taken from Bk. II, ch. v, 'Of Property.'

munity of land, for it is labour indeed that puts the difference of value on everything; and let any one consider what the difference is between an acre of land planted with tobacco or sugar, sown with wheat or barley, and an acre of the same land lying in common without any husbandry upon it, and he will find that the improvement of labour makes the far greater part of the value. . . . If we will rightly estimate things as they come to our use, and cast up the several expenses about them—what in them is purely owing to Nature and what to labour—we shall find that in most of them ninety-nine hundredths are wholly to be put on the account of labour.

From all which it is evident, that though the things of Nature are given in common, man (by being master of himself, and proprietor of his own person, and the actions or labour of it) had still in himself the great foundation of property; and that which made up the great part of what he applied to the support or comfort of his being, when invention and arts had improved the conveniences of life, was perfectly his own, and did not belong in common to others. Thus labour, in the beginning, gave a right to property.

This, in his own words, is Locke's celebrated theory of the natural origin of private property. Its similarity to the Roman Law doctrine of 'occupation' and to the maxim, frequently repeated by medieval and Renaissance writers, that the king has no right to take what the subject has acquired by the sweat of his brow, is apparent. But it was Locke who first stated the theory in its developed form as a part of the philosophy of natural right and he alone was recognized as its discoverer, or inventor, by its professors.[1] And it was fitting that the theory should have been discovered just as the middle class, whose theory it was, achieved its first revolutionary triumph. For it was a theory which grew out of the everyday experience of the middle class. In the ancient and medieval worlds where labour was done by slaves, serfs, and peasants, and its products were the property of masters and feudal magnates, Locke's ideas about property would have been irrelevant. But to the large group of independent producers in the eighteenth century, men without masters or lords, who brought

[1] Otto Gierke, *Natural Law and the Theory of Society*, translated by Ernest Barker, Cambridge, 1934, pp. 103–4.

to market the things which they owned and had made, and whose fortunes were acquired by their own industry, the Lockean theory of property seemed self-evident. By the law of nature things belonged to the man who made them. Feudal customs and royal laws establishing privileged economic groups in effect deprived the unprivileged of that which belonged to them by natural right. Just laws secured to each man the fruits of his labour.

Before 1690 no one understood that a man had a natural right to property created by his labour; after 1690 the idea came to be an axiom of social science. That date might be taken to mark the year when the middle classes rose to power: the year in which their experience, dressed up in philosophical language by John Locke, was presented to the world as the eternal truth of things.

That the Lockean theory of property was in fact ambiguous, that it might easily be used to condemn much property that the middle class regarded as legitimate, and that it would not account for the origin of actual property rights even if the privileged orders and their property were liquidated, is obvious enough now. But that all this was equally obvious to John Locke himself is a surprising fact. However, his text leaves no doubt that he was aware of the radical implications of his theory and that he did not intend it as a justification of existing property rights, however much he desired to see these secured and protected.

Everywhere in his discussion of property and labour, Locke makes clear that he is speaking of the state of nature and not of civilized societies. Filmer ridiculed the idea that primitive men made an agreement dividing up the common stock. Locke answered that men in the state of nature had no need of such an agreement, that they 'might come' to have private property merely by mixing their labour with what was formerly common. But the property acquired by labour in the state of nature was not the property of developed societies. It included only those things which the single individual could produce by his own labour; it was limited to the amount that that individual could use; it was further limited, in the case of land, by the rule that the appropriator must leave enough for the requirements of others. 'The same law of Nature that does by this means give us property, does also bound that property too. . . . As much as anyone can make use of to any advantage of life before it spoils, so much he may by his labour fix a property in. Whatever is beyond this is more than his share, and belongs to others.' The land which he 'cultivates' and 'can use the product of' is his 'where there is enough, and as good left in common for others.'

The assumptions that in the state of nature there was a superfluity of natural resources, and that appropriation was limited so that the natural equality of men was preserved, were traditional elements in the natural law philosophy. Locke repeated them and accepted the conclusion that the natural way of acquiring property, by labour, was equalitarian.

> The measure of property Nature well set, by the extent of men's labour and the conveniency of life. No man's labour could subdue or appropriate all, nor could his enjoyment consume more than a small part; so that it was impossible for any man, this way, to entrench upon the right of another or acquire to himself a property to the prejudice of his neighbour, who would still have room for as good and as large a possession (after the other had taken out his) as before it was appropriated. Which measure did confine every man's possession to a very moderate proportion, and such as he might appropriate to himself without injury to anybody in the first ages of the world. . . . And thus, I think, it is very easy to conceive, without any difficulty, how labour could at first begin a title of property in the common things of Nature, and how the spending it upon our uses bounded it.

All this was an effective answer to Sir Robert Filmer. The necessary forms of private property could be created without the unanimous consent of all mankind. Property could be natural. But in fact, Locke added, it is now conventional. Modern property rights were created by men and are valid only because men have agreed to respect them. Locke's remarks about the conventions which gave birth to modern forms of property are fragmentary, but he apparently assumed that there were two such conventions. The first was when men agreed to use money.

I dare boldly affirm, that the same rule of propriety—viz., that every man should have as much as he could make use of, would hold still in the world, without straitening anybody, since there is land enough in the world to suffice double the inhabitants, had not the invention of money, and the tacit agreement of men to put a value on it, introduced (by consent) larger possessions and a right to them. . . . [Money is a] lasting thing that men might keep without spoiling, and that, by mutual consent, men would take in exchange for the truly useful but perishable supports of life. And as different degrees of industry were apt to give men possessions in different proportions, so this invention of money gave them the opportunity to continue and enlarge them.

The second convention was made up of the positive laws which men consented to after they had instituted political societies, and the treaties made between those societies. 'The several communities settled the bounds of their distinct territories, and, by laws, within themselves, regulated the properties of the private men of their society, and so, by compact and agreement, settled the property which labour and industry began.'[1]

Thus in the end Locke returned to the old theory that property was the conventional creation of men.[2] He did not, as did his successors, assert that property in the modern world was or should be distributed among men in accordance with the law of nature.[3] Nevertheless the modern theory of the natural right of

[1] Other passages in Bk. II, ch. v, repeat that property is now conventional. See especially section 38: Men 'settled themselves together, and built cities, and then, by consent, they came in time to set out the bounds of their distinct territories and agree on limits between them and their neighbours, and by laws within themselves settled the properties of those of the same society.' Locke also refers to inheritance as a natural right of children in the state of nature (Bk. I, sections 88–94): but in the social state, although minors still have a natural right to inherit enough to maintain them, 'law and custom' determine the division of the inheritance (Bk. II, sections 65–73).

[2] David G. Ritchie, *Darwin and Hegel*, ch. vi, London, 1893; Leslie Stephen, *English Thought in the Eighteenth Century*, Vol. II, pp. 141–2, 3rd edition, London, 1902. But G. H. Sabine, *History of Political Theory*, ch. xxvi, does not refer to the conventional element in Locke's theory of property.

[3] He followed the usual tradition, maintaining that the present distribution, though conventional, was inviolable since it was based on voluntary agreements protected by the law of nature. Bk. II, 195–6.

property came from Locke. Later writers did not distinguish between property rights in the state of nature and property rights in society.[1] From Locke's day to our own, the Lockean theory of property has been thought of as the natural right theory of property, the theory that the product of labour belongs to the labourer; and it has been used to explain and defend both the unequal distribution and the complex rights of property in modern societies.

But if Locke was misinterpreted he was himself largely responsible. In the chapter on property as a natural right he was careful to add that most modern property is conventional. But in the following chapters he certainly implied that, in comparison with the conventional rights which rulers derive from the contract of government, the rights of ownership are always natural. His purpose in writing was to protect the solid citizen from the depredations of arbitrary government. His method was to show that all just governments derive their power from the consent of the governed and that the governed are possessed of certain inalienable, natural rights which governments are in duty bound to protect and respect. The reader of Locke's essay gets the impression that property is one of these inalienable rights. The discussion of property comes before the sketch of the origin of governments. In Book I, section 22, life and liberty are proved to be inalienable natural rights; in Book II these are fused with the concept of property. Property is defined as 'life, liberty and estate.'[2] Thus the conventional rights of ownership are joined with the natural rights of life and liberty; property rights and natural rights have been inextricably intertwined in the reader's mind. Furthermore, by linking property with life and liberty, Locke suggested that the possessions of the richest man in England were not different in kind from the acorns gathered by the poor Indian—both were acquired in accordance with the

[1] An exception is Locke's intimate friend, James Tyrrell. His *Brief Disquisition of the Laws of Nature*, 1701, follows Locke faithfully and describes property in society as a creation of the law. He defends it on the grounds of utility.

[2] Sections 87, 123, and 173.

natural right of every man to get his living, to appropriate from the common stock whatever he needed for 'the support or comfort of his being.' The Indian was prohibited by natural law from taking more than he could use; the Englishman had agreed with his fellow-citizens to annul that prohibition by establishing a monetary system and a code of positive law. Locke began by saying that the natural right of property was the equal right of every man to acquire by labour the necessities of life; in the end he implied that it was the right of each man to keep what he had, however he had acquired it and whether he could use it or not. He began by saying that modern property rights had been instituted by law; he ended by asserting that they were superior to all law. Government, having been instituted for the preservation of life, liberty, and property, is bound to hold them all inviolate.

The logical obscurities of the Lockean theory and the futility of attempting to use it as a justification of modern property relations have been clearly exposed in the last hundred years. But in its hey-day it seemed clear, distinct, and true. Wherever property was widely distributed among groups of independent artisans and farmers, the idea that labour was the basis of ownership was readily accepted. Wherever property was monopolized by the inheritors of feudal privilege, the idea that labour ought to be the basis of ownership served as an argument for abolishing monopoly and privilege. Wherever arbitrary governments were to be replaced with representative institutions responsive to the interests of property owners, 'life, liberty, and property,' and its corollary, 'no taxation without consent,' were the revolutionary battle cries. So long as middle-class thinkers were the undisputed expositors of truth, the natural right of property was a standard and accepted theory. Locke proclaimed it for the English; the Declaration of the Rights of Man made it the official theory of the French; Jefferson omitted property from the partial list of natural rights in the Declaration of Independence, but it was included in a number of State Bills of Rights, notably those of Virginia and Massachusetts. Finally, it was the accepted theory of classical, or middle-class, economic theory: 'The property which every man has in his own labour,' Adam Smith wrote, 'as it is the original foundation of all other property, so it is the most sacred and inviolable.'

Other theories of property were not entirely forgotten. For the larger and more spectacular confiscations of ecclesiastical and feudal property it was still convenient to argue that the law could abolish what it had created. Men who placed their hopes of reformation in enlightened despotism were likely to grant the despots full power over the property of their subjects. Conservatives, frightened by the 'excesses' of the French Revolution, and radical theorists frightened by the excessive individualism of the natural rights philosophy, expounded rival theories: neither Burke nor Rousseau accepted the natural right theory of property. But the Lockean theory was accepted by most thinking people and remained the orthodox doctrine until, in the nineteenth century, the socialists appropriated it and the utilitarians found a substitute for it.

CHAPTER EIGHT

☆

The Classical Theory in the Eighteenth Century

. . . the springs of property were bent
And wound so high they cracked the government.
Dryden, *Absalom and Achitophel*, Part I, lines 499–500.

a. England

But who advances next, with cheerful grace,
Joy in her eye, and plenty on her face?
A wheaten garland does her head adorn:
O Property! O goddess, English-born!
Ambrose Philips, 1714.

The doctrine of property revealed to John Locke suffered the fate of more famous revelations: it was more welcome to foreigners than to his own countrymen. By 1800 few Englishmen believed that property was a natural right, for by 1800 the circumstances which had fostered that belief had disappeared. Locke's doctrine was intended to protect the property of the individual from the arbitrary demands of royal governments. But in eighteenth-century England the principal owners of property were the government; they scarcely needed protection from themselves. Moreover, in England the Revolution had not distributed the land to peasant farmers; the great landlords of the eighteenth century shied from a theory which bestowed the title to land upon the man who ploughed it. The Revolution which Locke had justified was ended and English proprietors did not want another.

They preferred the formal legal theory which vested all property in the Crown. The services which the Crown had once exacted of landholders as a condition of their tenure had been abolished or forgotten, so that the holders of Crown grants were in fact absolute owners. The powers of the Crown were now wielded by an omnipotent Parliament of landowners who were enclosing the commons of England by Private Bills. The legal theory of royal dominion justified the arbitrary, though Parliamentary, acts of these improving landlords; the natural rights theory, a weapon of defence against arbitrary government, would have justified the resistance of the small men whose rights of common were being forcibly extinguished. Thus it happened that the natural rights theory was appropriated by the minority of radicals who applauded the revolutions in America and France and demanded a more equitable distribution of wealth at home, while the philosophical theories of Hume, Paley, Bentham, and Burke became the standard conservative defence.

Nevertheless, before the French Revolution stimulated a reaction against the philosophy of natural rights, Locke was not without honour in his own country. If the Lockean theory did not altogether square with the facts of English property, it was less askew there than across the Channel. 'It is probable, at least,' Professor Tawney writes, 'that in the England of 1550 to 1750 a larger proportion of the existing property consisted of land and tools used by their owners than either in contemporary France, where feudal dues absorbed a considerable proportion of the peasants' income, or than in the England of 1800 to 1850, where the new capitalist manufacturers made hundreds per cent. . . .'[1] Thus it was possible for a popular book on natural rights to repeat the Lockean theory of property and assume without question that most English property was the fruit of the owners' industry.[2] The absence of feudal privileges, and the comparative freedom of the English owner to use and dispose of his property, were taken to mean that England had returned to the system of nature.[3] Feudal property, the theorists implied, is natural property encumbered with restrictions and dues created by the law for the

[1] *The Acquisitive Society*, Left Book Club edition, 1937, p. 59.

[2] Thomas Wollaston, *The Religion of Nature Delineated*, 1722, and six editions from 1724 to 1738.

[3] Sir John Dalrymple, *An Essay Towards a General History of Feudal Property in Great Britain*, 1757. This work was admired by Thomas Jefferson.

benefit of privileged classes: if the legal encumbrances are removed, as they had been in England, natural property remains. So long as no one objected that capitalist property was not natural, the theory was useful.

In the middle of the century Thomas Rutherforth, Regius Professor of Divinity at Cambridge, tried to combine the new theory of natural right with the old theory of convention. Labour, he agreed, belongs to the labourer; but the materials worked on belong to all men in common and can never become the property of one man without the assent of the community.[1] Thus property is based on both occupancy and consent; it is partly natural and partly conventional. Such a reconciliation of opposites had great practical advantages: it could be used to prove that property in general, and in some of its specific forms, is inherent in the nature of things, while other forms, which patently violate the natural order, have an equally solid foundation in the voluntary agreements of men. In this interpretation, which was probably more faithful to Locke than the simple theory of natural rights, the Lockean theory was repeated again and again in eighteenth-century England. Its most famous exponent was Sir William Blackstone.

The Second Book of Blackstone's famous *Commentaries on the Laws of England* opens with a discussion of the origin of property.[2]

There is nothing which so generally strikes the imagination, and engages the affections of mankind, as the right of property; or that sole and despotic dominion which one man claims and exercises over the external things of the world, in total exclusion of the right of any other individual in the universe. And yet there are very few that will give themselves the trouble to consider the original and foundation

[1] *Institutes of Natural Law* (1754), American edition, Philadelphia, 1799, Vol. I, ch. iii.

[2] The *Commentaries* were first published between 1765 and 1769. I have used the twelfth edition, edited by Edward Christian, Professor of the Laws of England at Cambridge, London, 1794. The pagination of this edition follows that of the earlier ones. D. J. Boorstin, *The Mysterious Science of the Law*, Cambridge, Mass., 1941, has an excellent chapter on Blackstone's theory of property. I have appropriated most of it in the following pages.

of this right. Pleased as we are with the possession, we seem afraid to look back to the means by which it was acquired, as if fearful of some defect in our title; or at best we rest satisfied with the decision of the laws in our favour, without examining the reason or authority upon which those laws have been built. . . . These inquiries, it must be owned, would be useless and even troublesome in common life. It is well if the mass of mankind will obey the laws when made, without scrutinizing too nicely into the reasons of making them. But when law is to be considered not only as a matter of practice, but also as a rational science, it cannot be improper or useless to examine more deeply the rudiments and grounds of these positive constitutions of society.[1]

This peroration is followed by a somewhat confused statement of the Lockean theory.[2] We learn from the Book of Genesis that God gave the earth in common to all men. The traditions of the Golden Age and the practice of primitive peoples prove that for a long time men had no private property.

Not that this communion of goods seems ever to have been applicable even in the earliest ages, to aught but the *substance* of the thing; nor could it be extended to the *use* of it. For, by the law of nature and reason, he, who first began to use it, acquired therein a kind of transient property, that lasted so long as he was using it, and no longer: or, to speak with greater precision, the *right* of possession continued for the same time only that the *act* of possession lasted. . . . A doctrine well illustrated by Cicero, who compares the world to a great theatre, which is common to the public, and yet the place which any man has taken is for the time his own. But when mankind increased in number, craft, and ambition, it became necessary to entertain conceptions of more permanent dominion; and to appropriate to individuals not the immediate *use* only, but the very *substance* of the thing to be used.[3]

[1] II, pp. 2–3.

[2] II, pp. 3–9.

[3] Here property is a remedy for sin; elsewhere Blackstone regards it as a progressive institution. The contradiction is common to most treatises on the natural law. The philosophers could not decide whether the state of nature was a golden age from which men fell, or a barbarous age from which men have advanced. The former leads to the view that property is a necessary evil, the latter to the view that it is a positive good. The latter generally prevailed in the eighteenth century, when the middle class was in an optimistic mood.

Rights of ownership, as distinguished from temporary rights of possession and use, were first acquired in moveables, 'principally because few of them could be fit for use, till improved and meliorated by the bodily labour of the occupant: which bodily labour, bestowed upon any subject which before lay in common to all men, is universally allowed to give the fairest and most reasonable title to an exclusive property therein.' Later, when men began to plough and plant, the land itself was appropriated. 'And, as we before observed that occupancy gave the right to the temporary *use* of the soil, so it is agreed upon all hands that occupancy gave also the original right to the permanent property in the *substance* of the earth itself; which excludes every one else but the owner from the use of it.' Blackstone knew that the older writers on natural law had not agreed that occupancy was a sufficient title, but he brushed aside their objections as philosophical quibbles repugnant to common sense.

There is indeed some difference of opinion among the writers on natural law, concerning the reason why occupancy would convey this right, and invest one with this absolute property: Grotius and Pufendorf insisting that this right of occupancy is founded on a tacit and implied assent of all mankind, that the first occupant should become the owner; and . . . Mr. Locke, and others, holding that there is no such implied assent, neither is it necessary that there should be; for that the very act of occupancy, alone, being a degree of bodily labour, is, from a principle of natural justice, without any consent or compact, sufficient of itself to gain a title. A dispute that savours too much of nice and scholastic refinement![1]

The lawyer is satisfied with the common-sense Roman doctrine of occupation as a natural mode of acquisition.

Blackstone's version of the natural rights theory is slipshod, but it incorporates the substance of the Lockean doctrine: property is acquired under the law of nature, before civil states

[1] The editor of the twelfth edition, Edward Christian, was not satisfied with this rough argument. In a note to this passage he explained the right of the first occupant was established by the 'reason and sentiments' which 'nature herself has written upon the hearts of all mankind'—the technical, philosophical definition of 'common sense.'

are established. Quibblers may argue whether personal labour is the only natural mode of acquisition, but it 'is universally allowed to give the fairest and most reasonable title.' Blackstone apparently accepted the belief that private property is an institution of the natural law.[1]

But in the same work he wrote:

All property is derived from society, being one of those civil rights which are conferred upon individuals, in exchange for that degree of natural freedom which every man must sacrifice when he enters into social communities. If therefore a member of any national community violates the fundamental contract of his association, by transgressing the municipal law, . . . the state may very justly resume that portion of property, or any portion of it, which the laws have before assigned him.[2]

The right of inheritance, or descent to the children and relations of the deceased . . . is certainly a wise and effectual, but clearly a political, establishment; since the permanent right of property, vested in the ancestor himself, was no *natural*, but merely a *civil*, right.[3]

These passages indicate that Blackstone also accepted the belief that property was conventional. He stands convicted of contradicting himself and confusing his readers.[4] Nevertheless he did make an attempt to reconcile the two ideas of natural property and civil property. When all his statements are put together and the more blatant inconsistencies disregarded, a kind of commonsense theory of property emerges. Private ownership began as an institution of the law of nature; civil societies were organized to secure the rights of property which had already been created; but civil societies were also empowered to abridge or extend these natural rights.

[1] Other passages of the *Commentaries* could be quoted; see especially II, ch. 26, where some of the modes of acquisition recognized by the common law are spoken of as 'natural' in the sense of 'Mr. Locke.'

[2] Bk. I, p. 299.

[3] Bk. II, p. 11. Similar statements are found in II, p. 411, and IV, p. 9.

[4] 'Some of the most obscure—one might say mystical—passages in the *Commentaries* are the descriptions of the right of property.' Boorstin, *Mysterious Science of the Law*, p. 167.

The original of private property is probably founded in nature, as will be more fully explained in the second book of the ensuing commentaries; but certainly the modifications of it under which we at present find it, the method of conserving it in the present owner, and of translating it from man to man, are entirely derived from society, and are some of those civil advantages in exchange for which every individual has resigned a part of his natural liberty.[1]

Thus the right to make a will is a civil extension of the rights of property, for

there is no foundation in nature or in natural law, why a set of words upon parchment should convey the dominion of land; why the son should have a right to exclude his fellow-creatures from a determinate spot of land because his father had done so before him; or why the occupier of a particular field or of a jewel, when lying on his death-bed and no longer able to maintain possession, should be entitled to tell the rest of the world which of them should enjoy it after him.[2]

Thus Blackstone describes the property structure of England as having two foundations—the law of nature and the law of England. But the distinction between the two disappears in the end. For one of Blackstone's major premises is that the laws of England are in fact part of the law of nature. His *Commentaries* carry on the classical and medieval tradition of a law of nature 'coeval with mankind, and dictated by God himself, . . . binding over all the globe, in all countries, and at all times: no human laws are of any validity, if contrary to this; and such of them as are valid derive all their force, and all their authority, mediately

[1] I, p. 138. See also II, p. 400.

[2] II, p. 2. See also II, pp. 10–14. The transfer of property is described as a 'social advantage' conferred by the laws of England, in IV, p. 382. Other quotations describing how the laws of England have limited or extended the natural right of property are given in Boorstin, *Mysterious Science of the Law*, ch. ix. The editor of the Twelfth Edition, II, p. 11, n. 3, insisted in opposition to Blackstone that inheritance was a natural right because it was universally recognized by all men. He did not attempt to reconcile this with the various laws of inheritance of different nations and ages. Locke's successors were not in agreement as to whether the rights of willing or inheriting were included in the right of property. The question was a major dilemma for the exponents of natural right.

or immediately, from this original.'[1] That the laws of England were, for the most part, valid declarations of natural law, Blackstone did not doubt.[2] In the end, then, English property rights are partly natural, partly civil, and yet wholly natural.

The mysterious ambiguity of Blackstone's theory hangs on the concept of 'natural.' He used the word in two different senses and for two different purposes. First, property is a natural right of the individual in the classical Lockean sense. This is a theory useful primarily as a means of protecting the individual from the state. It protects the property owner against any curtailment of his rights in the name of the general welfare. 'So great, moreover, is the regard of the law for private property, that it will not authorize the least violation of it; no, not even for the general good of the whole community.'[3] This conception of 'natural' disposes of the claims of all those, whether paternal autocrats or levelling democrats, who want to redistribute property in accordance with some ideal rule of justice. The property structure is natural, the state is artificial: hence the latter cannot alter the former. The weakness of this theory was that most property had not been acquired 'naturally,' in this first sense of the word.

But property is natural in a second sense. As defined by St. Thomas, the natural law did not confer inalienable rights upon the individual; it directed human legislators to establish and

[1] I, p. 41. Following the traditional theory Blackstone writes that there are a 'number of indifferent points' which positive law alone is competent to settle. I, p. 42.

[2] Blackstone refused to discuss what would happen if Parliament enacted a law contrary to natural justice; see W. M. Geldart, 'Some Aspects of the Law of Property in England,' in *Property, Its Duties and Rights*, New York, 1922, p. 210. He did criticize the legal doctrine that all land is derived, 'or supposed to be derived,' from the king, as 'in reality a mere fiction' and a corruption of the ancient constitution, introduced by 'Norman lawyers' and 'monkish historians'; II, pp. 50–2 and p. 60. Apparently he thought this doctrine repugnant to the law of nature, which had been embodied in the ancient common law of England. All the chapters on feudalism suggest an opposition between feudal and natural property.

[3] I, p. 139. Blackstone cites cases where 'the law of the land has postponed even public necessity to the sacred and inviolable rights of private property.' I, p. 140.

maintain the social institutions requisite for the proper development of mankind. In the traditional interpretation of this natural law, private property was one of the necessary institutions, but it was not anterior in time or superior in right to government. The sovereign might not abolish private ownership, but one of his principal duties was to regulate it in the common interest. His laws determined the rights of property. If his laws were wise, the rights were natural since they served the natural and good ends of human life. Thus it was that Blackstone could say that the rights of property created by the laws of England 'in order to maintain peace and harmony' and promote 'the great ends of civil society' were in reality natural. In this definition of natural property there was no room for a conflict between private rights and the general welfare: the one existed for the sake of the other. Consequently, 'the public good is in nothing more essentially interested than in the protection of every individual's private rights, as modelled by the municipal law.'[1] This second conception of natural property is also a convenient argument against any reformation of the structure of property. The welfare of Englishmen cannot be promoted by violating these rights which the venerable constitution of England, the distillation of centuries of experience, has established. They are the rights which nature herself has prescribed for the common good. The laws of England are declarations of the law of nature: legal property is natural property. The weakness of this theory was that many English property rights, in spite of Blackstone's confident rationalizations, were not obviously fitted by nature to secure 'peace and harmony.'

Nevertheless, by a judicious use of the ambiguous term 'natural,' Blackstone was able to eat his cake and have it too. Private property is a formal right of the individual, secure from the attacks of society even when it clearly conflicts with the public interest. The end—the common good, can never justify the means—the violation of individual rights. On the other hand, property is the creation of human law and is bestowed on parti-

[1] I, p. 139.

cular owners without regard to the primitive rights of acquisition which all men enjoyed in the state of natural liberty. Here the end—social advantage, does justify the means—the abridgement of individual rights. All property enjoys the prestige conferred by the adjective 'natural.' Moreover, since Blackstone blurs together the meanings of that word, all property comes to be both a formal, natural right of the individual, and a social right sanctified by the law of nature as beneficial to the community. The conclusion was not remarkable at a time when many Englishmen thought the true interest of the individual never conflicted with that of the community.

Blackstone's theory was an ingenious and supple defence of property. But it was intended to defend only those forms of property suitable for a business civilization. Feudal property, Blackstone asserted, was a corruption of nature. The feudal doctrine which derived all property from the king was a fiction, fostered by 'monkish historians' and 'Norman lawyers.' It was historically false and was used to injure the common good. It was a corruption of the ancient English constitution, the most perfect textbook of the law of nature. It gave the sovereign an excuse for limiting that 'sole and despotic dominion' which the right of nature gives to every owner.[1] It gave rise to restrictions on the alienation of property, contrary to the general welfare, since 'experience hath shown that property best answers the purposes of civil life, especially in commercial countries, when its transfers and circulation are totally free and unfettered.'[2] Practically, the most pernicious consequences of the feudal doctrine were embodied in the system of military tenures. The abolition of those tenures, Blackstone wrote, was a greater boon to property owners than Magna Charta itself.[3]

[1] I, p. 448; III, p. 138.

[2] II, p. 288.

[3] II, p. 77. Military tenures were abolished during the Cromwellian revolution; the abolition was legalized by a statute at the Restoration. By this act the theory that property was contingent upon the performance of services to the community was virtually killed. 'What your Majesty's exchequer suffers by this act,' said the Speaker of the House to Charles II, 'you will be sure to find it hereafter in the exchequer of your people's hearts.' *Commentaries*, 12th edition, II, p. 77, n. 8.

That the Lockean formulas were woven into the text of the *Commentaries* is a good evidence of their popularity. Another witness is the *Encyclopaedia Britannica* of 1778–83 which taught that every Briton was endowed from birth with the 'three great and primary rights of personal security, personal liberty, and private property.'[1] At the end of the century the Lockean theory, with Blackstone's revisions, was being taught to future Prime Ministers at Edinburgh.[2] Dugald Stewart, the liberal professor of moral philosophy, based property on the 'natural sentiments of mankind, which led them to consider industry as entitled to reward, and in particular, the labourer as entitled to the fruit of his own labour. These, I think, may be fairly stated as *moral axioms*, to which the mind yields its assent, as immediately and necessarily as it does to any axiom in mathematics or metaphysics.'[3] Labour is the only natural foundation of ownership as distinguished from the temporary rights of possession which belong to the first occupant. The natural right of property is not created by society; it effectively limits the powers of the 'political union.'[4]

It must not, however, be inferred from this, that in a civilized society there is anything in that species of property which is acquired by labour to which individuals owe a more sacred regard, than they do to every other species of property created or recognized by positive laws. Among these last there are *many* which have derived their

[1] Article 'Liberty.' The article does not attribute these rights to 'man,' but to Englishmen, and avoids calling them natural rights. Perhaps the author was trying to avoid the entanglements of the word 'natural' now that it had been appropriated by the rebels in America. A few years earlier the Stamp Act had been opposed in Parliament because it violated the natural right of property, and its corollary, no taxation without consent; Lecky, *History of England in the Eighteenth Century*, 2nd edition, London, 1883, Vol. III, p. 338.

[2] Palmerston and Russell were both students of Stewart.

[3] 'On the Right of Property,' in *The Philosophy of the Active and Moral Powers of Man, Collected Works*, edited by Sir William Hamilton, London, 1855, Vol. VII, p. 261.

[4] Pp. 262–4. In these passages Stewart was refuting the theory of property in Lord Kames' *Historical Law Tracts*. I have not seen that work, but apparently it stated that permanent property was wholly civil and that savages recognized no property right except that of actual possession.

origin from a principle no less obligatory than our natural sense of *justice*; a clear perception in the mind of the legislator (sanctioned perhaps by the concurrent experience of different ages and nations) of general utility; and to *all* of them, while they exist, the reverence of the subject is due on the same principle which binds him to respect and maintain the social order.[1]

Some property, then, is a natural right in the Lockean sense, while other forms of ownership are protected by the natural order which obliges men to respect the common good. Philosophers who base all rights on only one of these principles 'have weakened the foundations on which property rests.'[2]

To those radicals who demanded a redistribution in accordance with natural right, Stewart's pupils could urge the claims of 'general utility'; against those who based their demands on the common good, the argument of 'natural justice' sufficed. If any one objected that the two arguments were inconsistent, Stewart could answer that 'general utility' and 'natural justice' are 'two principles which, when properly understood, are, I believe, always in harmony with each other.'[3] Inspired with these arguments, 'men capable of reflection' could be trusted to respect the rights of property. Fortunately, Stewart added, 'it is also beautifully ordered that . . . the same effect is accomplished in the multitude by *habit and the association of idea*; in consequence of which all the inequalities of fortune are sanctioned by mere prescription; and long possession is conceived to found a *right of property* as complete as what, by the law of nature, an individual has in the fruits of his own industry.'[4]

Stewart was judging from experience when he said that those writers who derived all rights of property from a single principle weakened the foundations of ownership. The natural rights tradition was revolutionary and equalitarian, and men who accepted the Lockean theory were sometimes led to attack all concentrations of property, capitalist as well as feudal. They agreed that right and utility always went hand in hand; but they interpreted this to mean that it could never be useful to modify

[1] P. 270. [2] P. 273. [3] P. 271. [4] The same.

the rights of nature by positive laws. Civil rights which abridged the natural rights of acquisition were neither useful nor just. In the circumstances of the time the civil rights most frequently attacked were those of the large landowners. The agrarian radicals attacked the English system of landed property as a violation of natural right.

The most notable agrarian attacks were those of Thomas Spence, William Ogilvie, and Tom Paine.[1] Ogilvie, a professor of classics at Aberdeen, was the most able theorist, but the root ideas were common to all three. They agreed with Locke that the earth had been given to men in common and that labour was the foundation of private ownership. In the state of nature, Locke had continued, land may be appropriated by labour, because where land is plentiful, the appropriation of one does not deprive the others of their common right, and ninety-nine per cent of the value of such appropriations is the result of labour. But where all the land has already been appropriated and there is a large landless population, these reasons no longer hold; here, Locke implied, titles of ownership must be the creation of positive law. The agrarians disagreed with that conclusion. They insisted that ownership could be harmonized with natural right even in the social state.

A man's right to acquire land by cultivating it, Ogilvie argued, is always limited by the equal right of his neighbours: where the supply is limited, each can claim an equal share, but no more. The total number of acres, divided by the total number of inhabitants, gives the number of acres which an individual could occupy by right of nature. Labour confers a just property, but 'it cannot supersede the natural right of occupancy,' or equal access to the land.[2] Spence and Paine vary this argument by asserting that the land itself always remains common, since it cannot be the product of labour; men can acquire by labour only

[1] Spence, *The Real Rights of Man*, 1775; Ogilvie, *Essay on the Right of Property in Land*, 1782; Paine, *Agrarian Justice*, 1796. All are reprinted by Max Beer, *The Pioneers of Land Reform*, London, 1920. Paine's pamphlet was addressed to the people and government of France.

[2] Natural right is discussed in Part I, section 1, of Ogilvie's pamphlet.

the fruits of that labour. 'There could be no such thing as landed property originally. Man did not make the earth, and though he had a natural right to *occupy* it, he had no right to *locate as his property* in perpetuity any part of it. . . .'[1] But whether man could appropriate only a small piece of ground or none at all, the agrarians agreed that present owners had no right to their monopoly of all the land. They agreed that the natural right of a man to enjoy the fruits of his labour was nullified if all the things to be worked on belonged to somebody else. A natural system of land rights must recognize that the land belongs, whether in equal shares or in commonalty, to all the people.

The practical proposals of these radicals were anticipations of Henry George's single tax scheme. Since it was impossible and unpractical to give everyone a piece of land, landholders, they argued, should pay a ground-rent, or tax, for the privilege of using the land. Spence proposed that the existing owners should be expropriated and that each parish should lease its lands to individual farmers; the rents would make taxes unnecessary. Ogilvie wanted to shift the whole burden of taxation to the shoulders of the present landowners.[2] Paine proposed that the state should collect ground-rents, or inheritance taxes, from the present owners of land, and give the proceeds to the landless poor.[3] All these schemes were intended to abolish private rents, and to create a class of independent farmer-owners whose taxes would help the landless labourer. They implied that private rents

[1] *Agrarian Justice*, in Beer, p. 184.

[2] By 'landowner' Ogilvie meant the large owner who received rent for his land. He was to be required to pay over most of his rents to the state. Ogilvie saw that this would lead to the destruction of landlordism. His praises of the small farmer might have been written by Jefferson: 'Of two nations equal in extent of territory and in number of citizens, that may be accounted the happiest in which the number of independent cultivators is the greatest.' Pt. I, section ii.

[3] Paine tried, without success, to distinguish between the land in its uncultivated state, which belonged in common to all, and the improvements which belonged to the improvers. He protested that a redistribution of the land by agrarian laws would be unjust to the latter. But his ground-rents and taxes would accomplish the same end. Perhaps he was influenced here by the French decree making it a capital offence to propose agrarian laws.

were monopolistic infringements of the natural right of property. Their aim was equalitarian. They were agrarian schemes because land was the most important form of property at the time. But practical experience was pushing Paine to demand a more equal division of all kinds of property.

The failure of the French Revolution to abolish all property qualifications for voting was, he saw, a violation of the principle of political equality. Apparently the protection of unequal property was liable to conflict with the equal protection of life and liberty. The pamphlets of 1795[1] indicate that Paine was attempting to whittle away the anti-equalitarian implications of the natural right of property, so that political equality might be preserved. If labour gives a natural title, it follows that some differences of wealth are inevitable since industry and talents differ.[2] But *Agrarian Justice* argued that land should be excluded from the list of things which might be acquired, in unequal amounts, as private property. It went on to suggest that other kinds of property, when accumulated in large amounts, had no foundation in the law of nature.

Personal property is the *effect of society*; and it is as impossible for an individual to acquire personal property without the aid of society, as it is for him to make land originally. Separate an individual from society, and give him an island or a continent to possess, and he cannot acquire personal property. He cannot be rich. So inseparably are the means connected with the end, in all cases, that where the former do not exist the latter cannot be obtained. All accumulation, therefore, of personal property, beyond what a man's own hands produce, is derived to him by living in society; and he owes on every

1 *First Principles of Government*, and Paine's speech of July 7, 1795, written for the Convention, of which he was a member, as well as *Agrarian Justice*, were all attacks on the property qualifications of the French Constitution of 1795. Forty years before, Francis Hutcheson's *System of Moral Philosophy*, London, 1755, had argued that the natural right of acquisition resulted in an unequal division of property injurious to the public interest; he advocated restricting it by positive law. See Vol. I, pp. 319 ff., and Vol. II, pp. 248 ff.

2 *Agrarian Justice*, and *First Principles of Government*, in *Complete Writings of Thomas Paine*, edited by Philip S. Foner, N.Y., 1945, Vol. I, p. 606, and Vol. II, p. 580.

principle of justice, of gratitude, and of civilization, a part of that accumulation back again to society from whence the whole came. . . . If we examine the case minutely, it will be found that the accumulation of personal property is, in many instances, the effect of paying too little for the labour that produced it. . . .[1]

Natural property, then, is limited to those things, the land excluded, which a man can produce without the help of his neighbours. The property produced co-operatively by the labour of many is social. It can, without any violation of natural right, be taken from its legal owners by taxation and distributed to the poorer members of society.[2] By narrowing the definition of natural property, Paine succeeded in diminishing the inequality connected with that institution: natural property must be unequally divided, but most property is not natural. A whole-hearted reliance on the Lockean theory, interpreted in this fashion, led to conclusions as repugnant to the new capitalist as to the old aristocrat. Property remains a right of man, but 'not of the most essential kind. The protection of a man's person is more sacred than the protection of property.'[3] Paine did not work out the theory of social production, but his statements are straws in the wind. They show what could happen when a determined equalitarian set out to interpret the natural right of property.

In the English controversies occasioned by the revolutions in France and America, the radical supporters of the rebels made full use of the theory of natural rights. But because the immediate

[1] P. 620, in *Complete Writings*, Vol. I.

[2] Hints of the same theory can be found in *Common Sense*, p. 5, and *Rights of Man*, p. 434, both in Vol. I of the *Complete Writings*. The latter asserts that there ought to be a ceiling on fortunes 'beyond the probable acquisition to which industry can extend.' Another passage in the *Rights of Man*, p. 276, and an unsigned paper of Paine's found among Jefferson's papers, *Complete Writings*, II, pp. 1298–9, make a distinction between those rights which an individual is competent to exercise by himself and those, including the acquisition of property, which can be exercised only in co-operation with others. These latter are deposited in the common stock, then 'every man is a proprietor in society, and draws on the capital as a matter of right.'

[3] *First Principles of Government*, p. 581, in *Complete Writings*, Vol. II.

issues were primarily political, the theory of property was not argued at length. That property was a natural right in some sense no one doubted, but the purpose of the radical pamphlets was to defend representative government, universal suffrage, republicanism, or some other political measure.[1] The most famous, Paine's *Rights of Man*, dealt with property only incidentally. But Paine's great adversary, Edmund Burke, was quick to recognize the economic equalitarianism implicit in the philosophy of natural rights. His defence of the English political structure was a theory of property as well as a theory of politics.

The end of Burke's arguments was conservation. His method was to appeal to tradition and to reject abstract principles. For the abstract rights of man he substituted the traditional rights of Englishmen. The concept of natural rights, he argued, is false and dangerous.

> Our constitution is a prescriptive constitution; it is a constitution whose sole authority is that it has existed time out of mind. . . . Prescription is the most solid of all titles, not only to property, but, which is to secure that property, to government. It is a presumption in favour of any settled scheme of government against any untried project, that a nation has long existed and flourished under it. It is better presumption even of the *choice* of a nation, far better than any sudden and temporary arrangement by actual election.[2]

Rights are not the expression of some abstract law of reason or nature, but the rules which the experience of many generations has established for the good of all. They are stable because they are encrusted with the sentiments and prejudices which sanctify habit and custom, but their truth cannot be demonstrated like propositions in geometry. Radical theorists propose a system of rights of nature as the only rational and useful system of political principles. But the reason of a handful of theorists, or even of a whole generation of them, is not equal to the task. Their prin-

[1] See for example Richard Price's famous pamphlets, *Observations on the Nature of Civil Liberty*, 1776; *Additional Observations*, 1777; *Discourse on the Love of Our Country*, 1789; and Paine's *Common Sense*, 1776.

[2] *Speech on the Reform of Representation*, 1782, in *Works*, Boston, 1894, Vol. VII, p. 94.

ciples are in fact unreasonable, injurious to the common welfare, and incapable of inspiring that unthinking respect which is the guarantee of stability, the practical advantage of a living constitution over a paper one.

His fanatical hatred and fear of the equalitarianism of the French Revolution led Burke to emphasize the conservative implications of his theory and to defend, perhaps more wholeheartedly than he otherwise would have, all rights of property, however acquired and however abused. 'Equality of mankind' is a 'monstrous fiction'; it makes the poor dissatisfied with that 'real inequality which it can never remove, and which the order of civil life establishes as much for the benefit of those whom it must leave in a humble state, as those whom it is able to exalt to a condition more splendid, but not more happy.'[1] 'The characteristic essence of property, formed out of the combined principles of its acquisition and conservation, is to be *unequal*. The great masses therefore which excite envy, and tempt rapacity, must be put out of the possibility of danger.'[2] Practically, this is accomplished by giving special political privileges to the rich. In England, the House of Lords is the safeguard of great wealth; even in France, the revolutionists saw the wisdom of restricting the suffrage to men of property in direct violation of their supposed principle of natural equality. 'It is easy to perceive . . . how much they were embarrassed by their contradictory ideas of the rights of men and the privileges of riches.'[3] Theoretically, property is secured by prescription. When the mass of men no longer accept that theory, all property is in danger.

With the National Assembly of France, possession is nothing, law and usage are nothing. I see the National Assembly openly reprobate the doctrine of prescription, which, one of the greatest of their own lawyers tells us, with great truth, is a part of the law of nature. . . . If prescription be once shaken, no species of property is secure. . . . I

[1] *Reflections on the Revolution in France*, 1790, Everyman edition, p. 35.

[2] P. 48.

[3] P. 172. Burke adds that the safeguards of property in France were too weak to be effective.

see the confiscators begin with bishops, and chapters, and monasteries; but I do not see them end there. . . . They have at length ventured to subvert all property of all descriptions throughout the extent of a great kingdom. . . . We entertain a high opinion of the legislative authority; but we have never dreamt that parliaments had any right whatever to violate property, to overrule prescription. . . .[1]

If the principle 'that by the laws of nature the occupant and subduer of the soil is the true proprietor, that there is no prescription against nature' is adopted, not only feudal privileges but landlords' rents as well will be destroyed. The foundation of both is the 'old, habitual, unmeaning prepossession in favour' of historical rights.[2] To take away the property of one single individual on the pretext of the public good, particularly, 'to confiscate and extinguish the original gentlemen and landed property of a whole nation, cannot be justified under any form it may assume.'[3] Burke reminded the radically inclined Duke of Bedford that the House of Bedford had been enriched with the spoils of Henry VIII's tyrannical confiscations. But the wealth acquired so unjustly is now legitimate, 'guarded by the sacred rules of prescription. . . . The Duke of Bedford will stand as long as prescriptive law endures—as long as the great stable laws of property, common to us with all civilized nations, are kept in their integrity. . . .'[4] In the end, Burke appealed to the most hackneyed of conservative arguments: unequal possession is a necessary evil in an evil world. Inequality of fortune is inherent in the nature of society; and those who suffer because of it must look for their relief beyond this life.

The body of the people must not find the principles of natural subordination by art rooted out of their minds. They must respect that property of which they cannot partake. They must labour to obtain

[1] Pp. 148–9.
[2] Pp. 219–21.
[3] P. 102; and, in the same volume, *A Letter to a Member of the National Assembly*, 1791, p. 246.
[4] *Letter to a Noble Lord*, *Works*, Boston, 1894, Vol. V, p. 209. A noble class is necessary in a stable society, and the Bedfords serve the purpose better than any new-fangled aristocracy of talent, because 'the *prejudice* of an old nobility is a thing that *cannot* be made.' P. 225.

what by labour can be obtained; and when they find, as they commonly do, the success disproportioned to the endeavour, they must be taught their consolation in the final proportions of eternal justice. Of this consolation, whoever deprives them, deadens their industry, and strikes at the root of all acquisition as of all conservation.[1]

The revolutionary optimism of the English middle class is here abandoned for the pessimism of the typical conservative; the English Revolution may have been 'glorious,' but another revolution can only make a bad matter worse.

The validity of Burke's attack on the natural rights philosophy is obvious to the modern reader. His sense of history, of the fallibility of human reason, of the importance of habit and custom in human life, and his recognition that there is a wide gap between the theories and the accomplishments of revolutionaries, appeal to anyone who is not converted by Tom Paine's zealous faith in the abstract, and never very consistent, dogmas of reason. In the circumstances of the time, Burke was the most vigorous conservative advocate. He pointed out the equalitarian implications of the natural rights theory. These were sufficient to persuade English landlords and business men, who had already won for themselves the privileges which their French counterparts were fighting for, to abandon the theory. In its place Burke substituted an historical theory: the just rights of property are those which have been prescribed and consecrated by history.

By the end of the eighteenth century, English political theorists, radicals apart, had abandoned the theory of natural rights and the theory of property which was a part of it. Even the radical equalitarians began to speak of utility rather than of right. But in one branch of speculation the natural right theory of property reigned supreme at the end of the century. The political economists of the classical school made it, in its technical economic form of the labour theory of value, the hub of their economic theory.

[1] *Reflections*, pp. 240–1. Here religious faith is not an end in itself, but a device for encouraging the industry of the poor and persuading them to respect the wealth of their betters.

'The annual labour of every nation,' according to the opening sentence of the *Wealth of Nations*, 'is the fund which originally supplies it with all the necessaries and conveniences of life which it annually consumes.'[1] Labour, moreover, is the measure of the exchangeable value of all commodities:[2] 'If among a nation of hunters, for example, it usually costs twice the labour to kill a beaver which it does to kill a deer, one beaver should naturally exchange for or be worth two deer. It is natural that what is usually the produce of two days' or two hours' labour, should be worth double of what is usually the produce of one day's or one hour's labour.'[3]

The doctrine that labour is the source of economic goods, and that those goods are valued according to the amount of labour required to produce them, does not tell us who owns those goods. The workman creates exchange value, but some other man may own it, as, for example, when the workman is a slave. In fact, the economists were not ostensibly interested in the property rights of individuals. The science of economics, one of them wrote, is 'an enquiry into the laws which determine the division of the produce of industry amongst the classes who concur in its formation.'[4] How it came to pass that one of these classes had land to rent, a second had capital to invest for profit, and a third had only labour to sell for wages, the economists did not usually inquire. They accepted the economic system which existed and tried to analyse its workings.[5] Their references to the rights of private property were incidental.

Nevertheless, the economists usually took for granted the natural rights doctrine that men were born free, and that each individual was his own master and the owner of the commodities he created by mixing his labour with them. 'The property which every man has in his own labour, as it is the original foundation

[1] Edited by Edwin Cannan, 2nd edition, London, 1920, Vol. I, p. 1.

[2] Pp. 32, 38.

[3] P. 49.

[4] Ricardo, quoted in Eric Roll, *History of Economic Thought*, 2nd edition, N.Y., 1942, p. 186.

[5] See Edwin Cannan, *A History of the Theories of Production and Distribution in English Political Economy from 1776 to 1848*, 2nd edition, London, 1903, p. 370.

of all other property, so it is the most sacred and inviolable,'[1] and 'the produce of labour constitutes the natural recompense or wages of labour.'[2] Twice in the First Book of the *Wealth of Nations* Smith wrote that in the state of nature the labourer owned the whole produce of his labour.[3] 'In the original state of things, which precedes both the appropriation of land and the accumulation of stock, the whole produce of labour belongs to the labourer. He has neither landlord nor master to share with him.' But when the original community of land was replaced by private ownership, and when individuals had accumulated capitals and set others to work, the workman no longer enjoyed the whole product of his industry. Smith did not pause to describe how the economic arrangements of the primitive state had come to an end.[4]

He did, however, hint that the result was exploitation.[5] 'As soon as the land of any country has all become private property, the landlords, like all other men, love to reap where they never sowed, and demand a rent even for its natural produce.' And in capitalist enterprises, 'the value which the workmen add to the materials . . . resolves itself . . . into two parts, of which the one pays their wages, the other the profits of their employer. . . .' How large each part shall be is determined by bargaining; and the employer will, 'upon all ordinary occasions, have the advantage in the dispute. . . .' In highly developed economic societies, 'rent and profit eat up wages, and the two superior orders of people oppress the inferior one.'[6] He sometimes recognized that

[1] Adam Smith, *Wealth of Nations*, Vol. I, p. 123.

[2] P. 66.

[3] Pp. 49–51, and pp. 66–8.

[4] From the notes of his lectures at Glasgow it appears that he thought land had been appropriated by the consent of the original commoners. See *Lectures on Justice, Police, Revenue and Arms*, edited by E. Cannan, Oxford, 1896, pp. 108–9. 'Private property in land never begins till a division be made from common agreement. . . .' Apparently he did not, as had Locke, extend the labour theory to include the acquisition of land. Capital, he assumes, is the savings of the industrious and thrifty; *Wealth of Nations*, I, p. 320.

[5] *Wealth of Nations*, Vol. I, pp. 49–51 and 66–8.

[6] *Wealth of Nations*, Vol. II, p. 67. Smith approved high wages because 'it is but equity' that those who create all the wealth 'should have such a share of the produce of their own labour as to be themselves tolerably well fed, cloathed and lodged.' Vol. I, p. 80.

in this theory of economic development the purpose of government was to protect the owner of capital. 'Till there be property there can be no government, the very end of which is to secure wealth, and to defend the rich from the poor.'[1]

The kernel of the Lockean theory of property, with all its radical and equalitarian implications, was contained in the theory of value which Adam Smith bequeathed to the school of classical economists. But neither Smith nor his successors were radical equalitarians. So far as they had axes to grind they were all supporters of the capitalist system and enemies of the feudal survivals and mercantilist regulations which hampered its free development. Smith used the doctrine that a man's labour belonged to himself, not to prove that he should have the whole product of that labour, but to demonstrate that he ought to be free to sell it to any employer he chose.[2] The economists used the labour theory of value, as Locke had used the related theory of property, to attack the political obstacles in the way of capitalist—they thought of it as 'natural'—economic progress. The labour theory made it appear that the property which they wished to protect was natural, hence just, hence in the common interest—the elements of a first-rate apologetic. They were defending the industrious against the parasites who fattened on political privilege. Their arguments seemed plausible in an age when industrial and commercial property was widespread and did not seem to flow into a few hands so long as government did not interfere with its natural course.

On the other hand, they were hard put to it to explain away the radical conclusions to which that theory led. Adam Smith had sensed what those conclusions were and had avoided them by qualifying the labour theory of value in various confusing and contradictory ways. Malthus, Ricardo, McCulloch, James Mill, and Nassau Senior, all wrestled with the same problem and

[1] *Lectures*, p. 15. A similar statement occurs in the *Wealth of Nations*, Vol. II, p. 207.

[2] He was protesting against the Statute of Apprentices which forbade men to work at, or be employed in, certain trades until they had served a set term as apprentices. *Wealth of Nations*, Vol. I, p. 123.

devised theories of population, of capital as stored-up labour, and of abstinence, to prove that capitalism was consistent with the natural right of property.[1] Their technical variants of the labour theory of value have been described and analysed by historians of economic thought.[2] The latter agree that the classical school, beginning with the assumption that labour was the creator of property, was unable to construct an economic theory which was both consistent and did not lead to the conclusion that the man who profited without working was necessarily robbing the workman. Partly, at least, because they were determined to avoid that conclusion, economists abandoned the labour theory of value. By the middle of the century it had almost disappeared from the best-known treatises and was being replaced by other theories of value. Nassau Senior, who played a part in that transformation, stated the difficulty succinctly: the only way to make the labour theory of value correspond with reality was to abolish those classes who profited without working, and to introduce a barbarous economy in which the rationalizations of the economist would have no function. 'If all the labourers were employed in the production, direct or indirect, of commodities for their own use, the rate of wages would depend solely on the productiveness of labour. But it is obvious that this could never be the case unless the labourers themselves were the owners of all the capital and all the natural agents of the country; a state of existence so utterly barbarous as to be without distinction of ranks or division of labour; a state in which a few scat-

[1] Ricardo's famous theory denied that rent could be justified as a natural reward of labour. Nassau Senior wrote that wages and profits were natural rewards for labour and abstinence, 'but a considerable part of the produce of every country is the recompense of no sacrifice whatever; it is received by those who neither labour nor put by, but merely hold out their hands to accept the offerings of the rest of the community.' *An Outline of the Science of Political Economy* (1836), Library of Economics, London, 1938, p. 89.

[2] C. Gide and C. Rist, *A History of Economic Doctrines*, London, 1927; Eric Roll, *A History of Economic Thought*, N.Y., 1942; E. Cannan, *A History of the Theories of Production and Distribution in English Political Economy*, London, 1903; Eli Ginsberg, *The House of Adam Smith*, N.Y., 1934; M. Bowley, *Nassau Senior and Classical Economics*, London, 1937.

tered savage families have sometimes been found, but which exhibits none of the phenomena which it is the business of Political Economy to trace to their causes.'[1] The socialists took up the labour theory of property and value and agreed with Senior that it resulted logically in the expropriation of landlords and capitalists. They insisted, however, that the new economic system would be less barbarous than the old. Later economists recognized, and sometimes lamented, that socialists, however subversive their conclusions, were loyal adherents of the classical tradition.[2]

The economists had clung to some variant of the natural rights theory of property long after that theory had been abandoned by the political theorists in England. Meanwhile, the Lockean explanation of the origin and rights of property had taken root on the Continent and in America, where it continued to appear both in economic and political literature, sometimes as a radical attack, sometimes as a conservative apology, almost to the present century. Some of the best known Continental writers on jurisprudence, followers of the natural law tradition, accepted Locke's theory of property. In Germany Christian Wolff described the negative community of nature and appropriation by labour.[3] In Switzerland, Emer de Vattel elaborated the same ideas.[4] A younger contemporary of Vattel, Jean Jacques Burlamaqui, explained that 'the property of individuals is prior to the formation of states.'[5] In general Burlamaqui was an adherent of the natural rights school, but his theory is ambiguous. Property, he said, was common in the beginning and could only be appro-

[1] *An Outline of the Science of Political Economy*, p. 180.

[2] E. Cannan, *Theories of Production and Distribution*, p. 393.

[3] *Institutions de la Nature et des Gens*, Leyden, 1772, Bk. I, Pt. II, ch. 1. The Latin edition appeared in 1750. Otto Gierke, *Natural Law and the Theory of Society*, E. Barker, translator, Cambridge, 1934, p. 104, refers to a number of German writers who followed Pufendorf and Grotius in thinking that both property and society were conventional.

[4] *The Law of Nations or the Principles of Natural Law*, French text of 1758 and English translation, Washington, 1916, Bk. I, sections 15, 203, 238, and 251.

[5] *The Principles of Natural and Politic Law*, Cambridge, Mass., 1807, Vol. II, Pt. III, ch. v. A translation of the French edition of 1748.

priated by 'some human act,' but he does not say whether the act was mixing labour with things, or entering into a formal agreement—whether it was natural or conventional.[1] The authors of the French *Encyclopédie*, who quoted Burlamaqui, and Jefferson, who owned and presumably read his book, could interpret him in either sense.[2] But the American and French writers who carried on the revolutionary liberalism abandoned by the established middle class in England, generally spoke of private property as an institution of the law of nature.

b. America

All men are born free and equal, and have certain natural, essential, and unalienable rights; among which may be reckoned the right . . . of acquiring, possessing, and protecting property. . . . Massachusetts Bill of Rights, 1780.

The Puritan founders of New England upheld a religious tradition which had long since discovered that the idea of natural right was a useful weapon against ungodly princes. The revolution which Locke justified was also a revolution in America and Governor Andros was as little loved as King James. Finally, in the eighteenth century, American as well as European gentlemen read Grotius, Pufendorf, Locke, Blackstone, *L'Encyclopédie*, Vattel, Burlamaqui, and many lesser interpreters of the law of nature. When the moment came to reject British authority, it was inevitable that the colonists should appeal to those natural rights which, in the opinion of all decent men, were self-evident. One of the best-known chapters of American history describes how the natural rights philosophy was naturalized in the colonies, adopted as the official theory of the Revolution, and engrossed on the sacred parchments of constitutional law.[3] Mr. Dorfman

[1] Vol. I, Pt. I, ch. iv.

[2] R. F. Harvey, *Jean Jacques Burlamaqui*, Chapel Hill, 1937, argues that the Swiss theorist did not believe that property was a natural right and that Jefferson probably excluded property from the Declaration of Independence as a result of reading his work. The argument is plausible although not conclusive.

Blackstone also quoted Burlamaqui frequently.

[3] Some of the best descriptions are B. F. Wright, *American Interpretations of Natural Law*, Cambridge, Mass., 1931; Carl Becker, *The Declaration of Indepen-*

has recently shown us how the natural right of property was subsequently expounded in the colleges, taught in the academies, preached in the Sunday Schools, and simplified for the benefit of working men, until it became a commonplace of popular American theory.

Behind the slogan, 'no taxation without representation,' stood the Lockean theory of property. Because a man's property, acquired by labour, was his by the law of nature, it could not be taken away unless he or his representatives consented. 'It is an essential, unalterable right in nature, ungrafted into the British Constitution, as a fundamental Law, and ever held sacred and irrevocable by the Subjects within the Realm, that what a man has honestly acquired is absolutely his own, which he may freely give, but cannot be taken from him without his consent.'[1] In 1774 the Continental Congress declared that 'by the immutable laws of nature' the colonists were entitled to the 'rights' of 'life, liberty, and property, and they have never ceded to any sovereign power whatever, a right to dispose of either without their consent.'[2] The drafters of such statements did not need to explain in detail what they meant by the natural right of property: they adopted that idea precisely because it was a part of common knowledge.

After the Declaration of Independence, most of the thirteen states adopted new constitutions, prefaced by Bills of Rights which included the natural right of property. The most famous, the Virginia Bill, declared that 'all men are by nature equally free and independent, and have certain inherent rights, of which, when they enter into a state of society, they cannot by any

dence, N.Y., 1922; C. G. Haines, *The Revival of Natural Law Concepts*, Cambridge, Mass., 1930; E. S. Corwin, 'The "Higher Law" Background of American Constitutional Law,' *Harvard Law Review*, Vol. XLII, 1928–9; Joseph Dorfman, *The Economic Mind in America*, 1606–1865, 2 vols., N.Y., 1946.

[1] *Massachusetts Circular Letter*, 1768, reprinted in *Documents of American History*, H. S. Commager, editor, N.Y., 1938. The author was Samuel Adams. He had used the same words two weeks earlier in the *Letter of the Massachusetts House to Lord Camden*, also reprinted in Commager's *Documents*.

[2] *Declaration and Resolves of the First Continental Congress*, reprinted in Commager, *Documents*.

compact deprive or divest their posterity; namely, the enjoyment of life and liberty, with the means of acquiring and possessing property, and pursuing and obtaining happiness and safety.' Massachusetts followed with the declaration that 'all men are born free and equal and have certain natural, essential, and unalienable rights; among which may be reckoned the right of enjoying and defending their lives and liberties; that of acquiring, possessing, and protecting property; in fine, that of seeking and obtaining their safety and happiness.'[1] From this time on, American states acquired the habit of proclaiming property a right of nature. Even in the twentieth century, when American political theorists had abandoned the theory of natural right, makers of constitutions continued to paraphrase the original Bills of Virginia and Massachusetts.[2] A declaration of the natural right of property became one of the traditional elements in a state constitution.

In 1787 all political leaders, whether Federalist or Anti-Federalist, were supporters of the principles of the Revolution and of the natural rights theory which had justified it. Both groups included men who had been prominent in popularizing that theory in the colonies. But now the practical context, which gives meaning to political ideas, had changed; in the new context the idea of natural property meant, as liberal ideas so often have, one thing to those with property, another to those who had none.[3] The radical democrats who opposed the Constitution held the traditional view that natural right was a defence against tyranny,

[1] In both Bills the definition of the right of property is loose. Presumably the right of 'acquiring' property is aimed at the British laws restricting colonial trade and manufactures and granting monopolies. This follows logically from the Parliamentary protest against monopolies in the reign of James I: 'all free subjects are born inheritable to the free exercise of their industry'; quoted in H. J. Laski, *Rise of European Liberalism*, London, 1936, p. 63.

[2] B. F. Wright, *American Interpretations of Natural Law*, gives a clear summary of the facts. I am much in debt to this book for its interpretation as well as its facts.

[3] H. J. Laski, *Rise of European Liberalism*, p. 15. Professor Laski's essay is crammed with suggestive interpretations of the ideas which I have tried to trace.

against any government, autocratic or oligarchic, which was not popularly controlled. But in those states where popular majorities ruled, adherence to this abstract theory of property was formal: it did not restrain the majority of debtors from legislating into their own pockets the property of their creditors. Democrats paid little heed to the right of property when they controlled the government. 'After a bloody war in defence of property, they forgot that property was sacred,' John Adams wrote.[1]

The men of property who favoured the Constitution agreed with their opponents that the theory of natural rights was a weapon against tyranny: they had justified their revolt against King and Parliament by that theory; the Constitution itself proves they were determined to put every obstacle in the way of would-be dictators. But the Federal Convention had not been called to deal with the dangers of autocracy. What the Founding Fathers had good reason to fear was the unrestrained rule of the majority. It was the radical democrat, in the opinion of the propertied classes, who was the real violator of the right of property. The immediate concern of the Convention was to take from the states the power to redistribute property, and erect a central government which, they confidently hoped, would represent an oligarchy of property-owners. For the Federalists the natural right of property was a weapon against democracy; the Constitution, as Mr. Beard has demonstrated, was the means by which they hoped to make that weapon efficient. For the Anti-Federalists, the natural right of property was a weapon against governments which ignored the popular will. To them the Constitution appeared to offer opportunities for the creation of such a tyranny.

The fact that the Federalists wanted to secure the right of property from democratic violation needs no further documentation. That they thought of that right as a natural right is, perhaps, not so obvious. Their concern, as Roger Sherman said in the Convention, was not to define rights in theory, but to discover 'how they may be most equally and effectually guarded in

[1] *Works*, edited by C. F. Adams, Vol. IX, Boston, 1854, p. 560.

society.'[1] But there is little doubt that if they had been pressed to explain the right of property they would have paraphrased Locke. Madison's reference in the tenth *Federalist* paper to 'the diversity in the faculties of men, from which the rights of property originate,' and to the 'different and unequal faculties of acquiring property' from which 'the possession of different degrees and kinds of property immediately results,' are clearly Lockean.[2] To remember that John Adams was the author of the Massachusetts Bill of Rights is to be convinced that he was using the word 'right' in a Lockean sense when he spoke of property in his *Defence of the Constitutions* (1787–8).

The different connotations which that right had for Federalist and Anti-Federalist is revealed with clarity in the debate over a Federal Bill of Rights. The Convention had dispensed with a Federal Bill of Rights because they saw no need to bid a government of property-owners respect property, the basis, as John Adams thought, of all liberty.[3] A Bill of Rights was a proper, if ineffective, element of constitutions when property did not control the government; where property ruled, the legislators' 'soundness of sense and honesty of heart' were better protections of its rights than 'a Bill of Rights, or any characters drawn upon paper or parchment, those frail remembrances.'[4] Alexander Hamilton put the Federalist case with characteristic vigour:

[1] Quoted by Wright, *American Interpretations of Natural Law*, p. 127. Professor Wright points out that the delegates had little occasion in the Convention to refer to the theory of natural right, although many of them were certainly adherents of that theory.

[2] E. M. Burns, *James Madison*, New Brunswick, N.J., 1938, pp. 15 ff. and 176 ff., demonstrates that Madison accepted the Lockean theory of property as derived from labour. He thought that profits from speculation were illegitimate because they were not earned by work. Interpreted in this way, the Lockean theory could be used to exalt the claims of landowners and deny those of Hamiltonian stock-jobbers.

[3] *Discourses on Davila*, in *Works*, edited by Charles Francis Adams, Vol. VI, Boston, 1851, p. 280. Adams had spoken of property as a natural right as early as 1765, see *Works*, Vol. III, pp. 448 ff.

[4] John Dickinson, *Letters of Fabius*, 1788, reprinted in P. L. Ford, *Pamphlets on the Constitution*, N.Y., 1888, p. 186. The Federalist arguments are described in Wright, *American Interpretations of Natural Law*, pp. 138–46.

It has been several times truly remarked that bills of rights are, in their origin, stipulations between kings and their subjects, abridgements of prerogative in favour of privilege, reservations of right not surrendered to the prince. Such was MAGNA CHARTA obtained by the barons, sword in hand, from King John. Such were the subsequent confirmations of that charter by succeeding princes. Such was the *Petition of Right* assented to by Charles I, in the beginning of his reign. Such, also, was the Declaration of Right presented by the Lords and Commons to the Prince of Orange in 1688, and afterwards thrown into the form of an act of Parliament. It is evident, therefore, that, according to their primitive signification, they have no application to constitutions, professedly founded upon the power of the people, and executed by their immediate representatives and servants.[1]

But everyone knew that when Hamilton wrote 'people' he meant 'men of property.' The Anti-Federalists were not deceived. In their opinion the prerogatives of property were as fit to be abridged as those of princes. Consequently, the more radical opponents of the Constitution argued that it should be rejected altogether, and used the omission of a Bill of Rights to prove that its proponents had sinister designs to overthrow the rights of man. The moderate opponents made the inclusion of a Bill of Rights a condition of their support. In Massachusetts, Elbridge Gerry, who was no friend of excessive democratic and levelling principles, nevertheless thought that the natural rights of life, liberty, and property should be safeguarded by a special Bill in the Constitution. He accused the framers of being 'partisans of arbitrary power' and using 'insidious arts' to lock the strong chains of despotism on a country, which by the most glorious and successful struggles 'is but newly emancipated from the spectre of foreign dominion.'[2] Luther Martin of Maryland reveals most clearly, perhaps, the Anti-Federalist attitude to the right of property. An advocate of paper money, stay laws, and other methods of relieving debtors at the expense of their creditors, all of which violated the natural right of property, he opposed

[1] *Federalist*, No. 84.

[2] Wright, *American Interpretations of Natural Law*, p. 133.

in the Convention those clauses of the Constitution forbidding states to impair contracts and juggle the currency. But in the fight over ratification he led the opposition in Maryland and condemned the Constitution because it did not have a Bill protecting natural rights from the despotic acts of government.[1] Obviously Martin thought of the right of property as a protection against oligarchy, but forgot it altogether when democracy ruled. George Mason, who had drafted the Virginia Bill of Rights, defended the rule as well as the right of property: he had argued in the Convention for property qualifications for Congressmen. But he feared the new government would end in corrupt aristocracy or monarchy and argued that a Bill of Rights was, consequently, essential. On the other hand he opposed the Constitution because it forbade the states to violate the right of property; he himself was the owner of lands which the state of Virginia had confiscated from Lord Fairfax, and he candidly admitted that he feared the new Federal courts might invalidate that confiscation.[2] Here again is demonstrated the fact that the natural right of property is used or abused in accordance with changing political contexts.

Other opponents of the Constitution insisted on having an explicit guarantee of the rights of nature[3] and when Jefferson lent his authority to their complaints, the Federalists agreed to support amendments for that purpose. Such amendments, from the Federalist point of view, might be superfluous or illogical, but they could hardly be harmful. The result was the Fifth Amendment stating that no person should be 'deprived of life, liberty, or property, without due process of law; nor shall private property be taken for public use, without just compensation.' The Fifth Amendment enacted into law the *Civil Government* of Mr. John Locke.

The heirs of the Federalists have reason to be grateful to the Anti-Federalists who forced through that amendment. For in time the democracy captured that very government which the

[1] Wright, pp. 133–5; Charles Beard, *Economic Interpretation of the Constitution*, 1935 edition, pp. 205–6.

[2] Beard, p. 129, pp. 206–7; Wright, pp. 135–6.

[3] Wright, pp. 136–8.

Fathers had sought to reserve to men of property. The Fifth Amendment, supplemented by the Fourteenth, which prohibited state as well as federal government from depriving men of property 'without due process of law,' both interpreted by a Supreme Court with strong views on the rights of property, became the chief legal barrier to popular demands for the limitation of private ownership. In England, where, as Hamilton pointed out, Bills of Right restrain kings, Parliament can legally abolish private property; in America, Congress is prohibited by the Bill of Rights from postponing the foreclosure of farm mortgages in a time of catastrophic depression.[1]

No group in the United States has been more faithful to the philosophy of the Founding Fathers than the interpreters of their handiwork, the constitutional lawyers and the judges. In 1795 Justice Patterson set a precedent for Supreme Court decisions by declaring that 'it is evident that the rights of acquiring and possessing property, and having it protected, is one of the natural, inherent, and inalienable rights of man. . . .'[2] Three of the best-known treatises on American Law, the *Commentaries* of Chancellor Kent (1826–30), those of Justice Story (1833), and T. M. Cooley's *Constitutional Limitations* (1868) all expound the same doctrine. In the Massachusetts Constitutional Convention of 1820–1 the conservatives, wanting to retain a property qualification for the suffrage, argued that property was a natural right and voting was not: hence it was sensible to restrict the suffrage in order to protect property. The same argument was used in the Virginia Convention of 1829–30, but by this time some conservative thinkers had begun to doubt the usefulness of the natural rights philosophy and put their arguments on utilitarian grounds.[3] After the Civil War and the passage of the

[1] Louisville Joint Stock Bank Co. *v.* Radford, May 1935.

[2] Quoted in Wright, *American Interpretations of Natural Law*, p. 293. This book, and the same author's *Growth of American Constitutional Law*, New York, 1942, and C. G. Haines' *Revival of Natural Law Concepts* are useful studies of constitutional interpretation and the law of nature.

[3] The use of the theory of natural rights at these Conventions is described by Wright, *American Interpretations of Natural Law*, ch. vii.

Fourteenth Amendment, Justices of the Supreme Court tended to use the words 'due process of law' in place of the now unfashionable 'natural rights,' but the substance was unchanged.[1] Even so the older form lingered on; in 1891 Justice Brewer told the graduates of the Yale Law School that property was an institution of the law of nature, that it began when Eve appropriated the forbidden fruit, and that the duty of the courts was to protect property from democratic majority, just as they had formerly protected it from autocratic monarchs.[2] Except for a short relapse under Chief Justice Taney, the Supreme Court has been, until our own day, a consistent upholder of the theory that property is a right of nature.

That American constitution-makers and interpreters should affirm their faith in the natural right of property is easily understood. The puzzling question is why Jefferson substituted 'pursuit of happiness' for 'property' in the Declaration of Independence. Historians have debated as to whether Jefferson thought property was one of the rights of nature.[3] His statements on the subject are, in fact, inconsistent; they vary according to their context. When he thought of tyranny, he was prone to speak of the violation of the rights of nature; but when he thought of the policy of a free government, he often spoke of preserving a measure of economic equality by legislative action. Sometimes he appeared to believe, as many liberals did, that if the state did not interfere in the interest of privileged classes, the unfettered operation of natural law would lead to a widespread distribution

[1] In addition to the works cited above, see the brilliant essay by Walton Hamilton, 'The Path of Due Process of Law,' in *The Constitution Reconsidered*, New York, 1938.

[2] D. J. Brewer, *An Address*, New Haven, 1891. For cases involving taxation in which, even in quite recent times, Federal judges referred to the natural right of property, see Sidney Ratner's authoritative work, *American Taxation*, N.Y., 1942.

[3] C. M. Wiltse, *The Jeffersonian Tradition in American Democracy*, Chapel Hill, 1935, pp. 136–9; Gilbert Chinard, *Correspondence of Jefferson and Du Pont de Nemours*, Baltimore, 1931, Introduction, Pt. VI; Adrienne Koch, *The Philosophy of Thomas Jefferson*, N.Y., 1943, p. 175; Dorfman, *Economic Mind in American Civilization*, Vol. I, p. 434.

of property; at other times he seems to have sympathized with the agrarians who, in the interests of equality, wanted to exempt land from the objects to be appropriated by the labour of the individual.

Before he wrote the *Declaration*, Jefferson had more than once referred to 'life and property,' 'liberty and property,' and the right of the individual to appropriate unoccupied land,[1] in such fashion as to leave no doubt that he accepted the theory of Locke, whose 'little book on government,' he wrote, 'is perfect as far as it goes.'[2] But he omitted 'property' in the *Declaration* and, as Mr. Chinard has pointed out, he bracketed the word '*propriété*' in the copy of a Declaration of the Rights of Man drafted by Lafayette. In 1785 he wrote that the unequal distribution of landed property in France was the cause of the wretchedness of the French people, and his comments were agrarian in tone.

I am conscious that an equal division of property is impracticable. But . . . legislators cannot invent too many devices for subdividing property, only taking care to let their subdivisions go hand in hand with the natural affections of the human mind. The descent of property of every kind therefore to all the children, or to all the brothers and sisters, or other relations in equal degree is a politic measure, and a practicable one. Another means of silently lessening the inequality of property is to exempt all from taxation below a certain point, and to tax the higher portions of property in geometrical progression as they rise. Whenever there is in any country uncultivated lands and unemployed poor, it is clear that the laws of property have been so far extended as to violate natural right. The earth is given as a common stock for man to labour and live on. If for the encouragement of industry we allow it to be appropriated, we must take care that other

[1] *A Summary View of the Rights of British America*, 1774; *Address to Governor Dunmore*, 1775; *Draft of a Declaration of the Causes of Taking Up Arms*, 1775. All of these are included in S. K. Padover's volume of selections entitled *The Complete Jefferson*, N.Y., 1943.

[2] Letter to T. M. Randolph, May 30, 1790, *Writings*, memorial edition, Washington, 1903, Vol. VIII, p. 31. Quoted by Wiltse, *Jeffersonian Tradition*, p. 47.

employment be provided to those excluded from the appropriation. If we do not the fundamental right to labour the earth returns to the unemployed. It is too soon yet in our country to say that every man who cannot find employment but who can find uncultivated land shall be at liberty to cultivate it, paying a moderate rent. But it is not too soon to provide by every possible means that as few as possible shall be without a little portion of land.[1]

Here Jefferson assumes that land titles are the creation of positive law and are valid only if they do not violate every man's natural right to have access to the common stock. This is clearly a variant of the agrarian theory of natural right and it justifies the principle of progressive taxation. But the conservative interpreters of natural right usually condemned progressive taxation as an unjust attack on the rich and Jefferson returned to this view in 1816.

To take from one because it is thought that his own industry and that of his fathers had acquired too much, in order to spare others, who, or whose fathers have not exercised equal industry and skill, is to violate arbitrarily the first principle of association 'the *guarantee* to everyone of a free exercise of his industry, and the fruits acquired by it.' If the overgrown wealth of an individual be deemed dangerous to the state, the best corrective is the law of equal inheritance to all in equal degree; and the better, as this enforces a law of nature, while extra-taxation violates it.[2]

Here Jefferson had returned to the usual theory of natural property, and he affirmed his belief in it again the same year in a letter to Du Pont de Nemours. 'I believe with you . . . that a right to property is founded in our natural wants, in the means with which we were endowed to satisfy those wants, and the

[1] Letter to Rev. James Madison, October 28, 1745, *Writings*, Vol. XIX, pp. 17–18. Jefferson owned a pamphlet by the English agrarian, William Ogilvie; see Adrienne Koch, *Philosophy of Thomas Jefferson*, p. 120.

[2] Antoine, Comte Destutt de Tracy, *Treatise on Political Economy*, 1817, 'Prospectus.' This introduction by Jefferson to the work of the French economist praises Tracy's account of the origin of the rights of property; that account, pp. 53 ff., is in fact an elaboration of the Lockean theory. For Jefferson and Destutt de Tracy, see Adrienne Koch, *Philosophy of Thomas Jefferson*, ch. xx. In the memorial edition and in Padover's *Complete Jefferson*, this passage from the 'Prospectus' is garbled.

right to what we acquire by those means without violating the similar rights of other sensible beings.'[1] These are Jefferson's last words on the theory of property. But they do not settle the problem of what Jefferson thought about it.

Only three years before he had written that

> it is a moot question whether the origin of any kind of property is derived from nature at all. . . . It is agreed by those who have seriously considered the subject, that no individual has, of natural right, a separate property in an acre of land, for instance. By an universal law, indeed, whatever, whether fixed or movable, belongs to all men equally and in common, is the property for the moment of him who occupies it; but when he relinquishes the occupation, the property goes with it. Stable ownership is the gift of social law, and is given late in the progress of society.[2]

Concerned for the moment in denying that inventors had any exclusive property in their creations other than that which the state might award them for utilitarian reasons, Jefferson denied the natural right of property. His reasoning here is that of Blackstone and Dugald Stewart.

What can be concluded from these conflicting statements? Only that Jefferson's allegiance to the principle of the natural right of property wavered whenever it led to unpalatable conclusions. As a tool it was useful in undermining tyranny. Reshaped by an agrarian apostle of equality, it could be used to break down concentrations of landed wealth. But it had to be abandoned on occasion, when it impeded the efforts of popular government to effect a proper redistribution of wealth.[3] Clearly Jefferson was

[1] April 24, 1816, printed in Chinard, *Correspondence of Jefferson and Du Pont*. Jefferson was arguing here that the vote should not be restricted to property owners; Du Pont argued in the following letter, also printed in Chinard, that the right of property could not be protected if everyone had a vote.

[2] Letter to Isaac McPherson, in S. K. Padover, *Complete Jefferson*, p. 1015.

[3] A paper by Thomas Paine, discovered among the Jefferson Papers by Gilbert Chinard, suggests that Paine and Jefferson were discussing in 1789 the idea that in contracting to form a state, men give up their natural rights to acquire and possess property. The paper is printed in Foner, *Complete Writings of Thomas Paine*, Vol. II, pp. 1298–9. Such a theory, of course, would give the state full power over the property of its citizens.

one of the foremost exponents of natural right; but he was also an exponent of individual independence and equality, and when these seemed to conflict with the natural right of property, his belief in that right wavered. In the American society of Jefferson's day, where ownership was in fact widespread and where most men could reasonably hope to become proprietors, property did not seem to menace liberty and equality. Jefferson, like many Liberal revolutionists, could conclude that natural property, cleansed of the excrescences of aristocratic privilege, would be the foundation of a free society. Even so, he seemed ready to abandon the theory of natural right whenever in practice it led to contrary conclusions.

Jefferson's political disciple, John Taylor of Caroline, was a more consistent upholder of a theory of natural right of property, but like his master he gave it an equalitarian hue.[1] 'The rights of man,' he wrote, 'include life, liberty, and property. . . . The last right is the chief hinge upon which social happiness depends.'[2] 'Our policy is founded upon the idea, that it is both wise and just, to leave the distribution of property to industry and talents; that what they acquire is all their own, except what they owe to society; that they owe nothing to society except a contribution equivalent to the necessities of Government. . . .'[3] But, Taylor implied, the natural right theory, properly interpreted, leads to an equalitarian social structure. For natural property includes only those things 'which are fairly gained by talents and industry, or are capable of existing without taking property from others by law.'[4] It is 'substantial, real, or honest property, comprising accumulations arising from fair and useful industry and talents.'[5] It does not include any 'artificial establishment, which subsists

[1] For Taylor see Benjamin F. Wright, 'The Philosopher of Jeffersonian Democracy,' *American Political Science Review*, Vol. XXII, 1928; Charles Beard, *Economic Origins of Jeffersonian Democracy*, ch. xii, N.Y., 1915; E. T. Mudge, *The Social Philosophy of John Taylor of Caroline*, N.Y., 1939.

[2] *Construction Construed, and Constitutions Vindicated*, Richmond, 1820, p. 78.

[3] *An Inquiry into the Principles and Policy of the Government of the United States*, Fredericksburg, 1814, p. 282.

[4] P. 113.

[5] P. 564

by taking away property: such as hierarchical, kingly, noble, official and corporate possessions, incomes, and privileges. . . .'[1] It is contrasted with 'legal, factitious or fraudulent property, comprising every species resulting from direct and indirect modes of accumulation by law, at the expense of others. . . .'[2] His distinctions between 'natural' and 'artificial' property are not always clear, but in general Taylor opposed national banks, tariffs, and Hamiltonian funding and credit operations, and shared the suspicion of finance and big business which was typical of agrarian radicalism. Capitalism, he thought, has its legal privileges as well as feudalism; both are a violation of natural rights of property and create such great and unjust inequalities of wealth that they lead desperate men to propose violent measures such as the equalization of property by law or the total abolition of private ownership.[3]

In spite of his inconsistencies—he included slaves, for example, under 'natural' property—the tendency of Taylor's thought is apparent. He was using the theory which had been developed to combat feudal privilege, for the purpose of attacking the newer privileges of large-scale capitalist enterprise. He wanted to establish equality of opportunity by withdrawing the protection of government from those forms of enterprise which made it possible for a few to get rich quick. His work is a clear illustration of how the natural rights theory could be given a strong equalitarian bent if the definition of 'natural' was properly restricted. Jefferson had not developed a theory which would limit the government from interfering with that property which he prized, and yet permit it to destroy that which he thought was oppressive. Taylor tried, not without some success, to supply that theory. Clearly, Taylor shared the views of those generous liberals who thought that the abolition of legal privilege would be enough to insure the triumph of equal opportunity.

As Jeffersonian Republicanism declined, the philosophy of the rights of nature became less fashionable with political theorists and yielded to the more popular, and apparently less

[1] P. 113. [2] P. 564. [3] Pp. 562–4.

radical, doctrines of Jeremy Bentham. The changing temper is illustrated in the works of two writers, Judge Nathaniel Chipman of Vermont and President Thomas Cooper of South Carolina College. Before 1800 both had defended the natural right of property, although they were, respectively, supporters of Hamilton and Jefferson. But thirty years later, both adopted the utilitarian argument, and Cooper denounced the philosophy which his friend Thomas Jefferson had embedded in the Declaration of Independence.[1] Another attempt to supplant the Lockean theory was made by a German refugee, Francis Lieber. Using the terminology of natural right, he poured out a confused variant of Hegel and Kant and a transcendental theory of property, designed to cut the ground from under any proposal to limit in any way the privileges of owners. His influence was short-lived and he can best be remembered as the author of the most shameless defence of the abuses of property.[2]

But if the natural right of property was no longer expounded by professional theorists, it was still deeply embedded in popular thinking. In the *American Democrat* (1838), James Fenimore Cooper spoke of property as 'the base of all civilization,' and of the rights of ownership as created by labour, human or animal: 'the food obtained by his toil, cannot be taken from the mouth of man, or beast, without doing violence to one of the first of our natural rights.' There is an echo of the theory of natural right in Thoreau's anarchism: the state, he wrote in *Civil Disobedience* (1849), 'can have no pure right over my person and property but what I concede to it.' In his essay on *Politics* Emerson suggested that property derived from work had

[1] Chipman, *Sketches of the Principles of Government*, 1793, pp. 175 ff.; *Principles of Government*, 1833, pp. 67–74. Cooper, *Propositions Respecting the Foundations of Civil Government*, London, 1787; *Lectures on the Principles of Political Economy*, Columbia, S.C., 1826. For Cooper, see Dorfman, *Economic Mind*, Vol. II, and the references cited there.

[2] Lieber's principal work, *Political Ethics*, was published at Philadelphia in 1838–9. His popular work, designed for the benefit of the poor, is *Essays on Property and Labour*, N.Y., 1841. Dorfman, *Economic Mind*, Vol. II, gives a comprehensive account of Lieber's career, but does not mention his obvious connection with the German Idealist school.

stronger claims than that which was inherited. Daniel Webster occasionally referred in passing to property as a right of nature.[1] Finally, in the great debate over slavery, the natural right theory of property had a temporary revival and, in a perverted interpretation, served the apologists of slavery as well as the abolitionists.

The men who invented arguments justifying slavery could hardly make use of the philosophy of natural rights in so far as that emphasized liberty and equality. But they were able to use at least the terminology of the natural right theory of property. The most effective Southern argument was that interference with slavery was interference with property; it convinced many a Northerner that the Abolitionists were dangerous opponents of the established order, Northern as well as Southern. The Lecompton (slavery) Constitution of Kansas in 1857 declared that 'the right of property is before and higher than any constitutional sanction.' When the Abolitionists replied that this was not true of slave property they were accused of being socialists. 'European Socialists,' Senator Jefferson Davis told the Senate in 1860, 'who in wild radicalism (including the assassination doctrine) are the correspondents of the American Abolitionists, maintain the same doctrine as to all property, that the Abolitionists do as to slave property. The famous theory of the Socialist Proudhon is that property is theft.'[2] Several of the authors of the famous *Pro-Slavery Argument* of 1852 tried to show that slavery was not incompatible with the natural law which gives to each the fruit of his labours. While these men proved that slave property was protected by the law of nature, George Fitzhugh, perhaps the most famous defender of the slavocracy, proved that the property of Northern capitalists was a violation of natural right. Taking a leaf from the socialists' text, he argued that rent, interest, and profit, are stolen from the

[1] See Wright, *American Interpretations of Natural Law*, p. 175.

[2] Quoted in Dorfman, *Economic Mind*, Vol. II, p. 633. Davis was quoting from a letter of Caleb Cushing. Other Southern writers who referred to property, including slaves, as natural are mentioned by Dorfman, Vol. I, p. 402, and Vol. II, p. 891.

workman whose labour has created them. 'I never read Proudhon. If this is what he means when he exclaims, "Property is a Thief!" he is right.'[1] He did not, of course, advocate the abolition of exploitation, but maintained that slavery was a more beneficent and stable method of exploiting, in which each received according to his needs.

The Abolitionist reply to these arguments made full use of the argument from nature. Men are born free and equal; men cannot be made property; slavery is unnatural because, for one thing, it deprives the slave of the fruits of his work. 'Every man,' declared the Anti-Slavery Convention of 1833, 'has a right to his own body' and 'to the products of his own labour.'[2] 'Justice,' said William Ellery Channing, 'is a greater good than property'; but he did not admit that the abolition of slavery would in fact be a violation of property. Property is protected by the natural law, but by that very law men themselves can never be property.[3]

Abraham Lincoln once spoke of the Republicans as following Jefferson in their 'superior devotion to the personal rights of men, holding the rights of property to be secondary only and greatly inferior.'[4] But he usually denied that slaves were rightful property. Slavery is based upon the principle of 'you toil and work and earn bread, and I'll eat it.' The Negro may not be our equal in all respects, but according to the principles of the Declaration of Independence, 'in the right to put into his mouth the bread that his own hands have earned, he is the equal of every other man, white or black.'[5]

In answer to the charge that capitalism as well as slavery violated the right of property by depriving the workman of his

[1] Quoted by Harvey Wish, *George Fitzhugh*, Baton Rouge, La., 1943, p. 176. Fitzhugh's most famous works are *Sociology for the South*, 1854, and *Cannibals All; or Slaves Without Masters*, 1857.

[2] Wright, *American Interpretations of Natural Law*, p. 212.

[3] *Essay on Slavery*, Boston, 1835. Relevant passages are quoted by Wright, *American Interpretations of Natural Law*, pp. 225 ff.

[4] Letter to H. L. Pierce, April 6, 1859.

[5] Speech at Springfield, Ill., July 17, 1858. Similar sentiments are to be found in the speech at Galesbury, Ill., October 7, 1858; speech at Chicago, July 10, 1858; speech at Alton, Ill., October 15, 1858.

just reward, Lincoln replied in effect that capitalism was not widespread in the United States. In the free states every man has a chance of rising above the status of a hired labourer: so many in fact do so that 'their case is almost, if not quite, the general rule.' The majority of Americans, even including the citizens of the South, 'neither work for others nor have others working for them. . . . [They] work for themselves, on their farms, in their houses, and in their shops, taking the whole product to themselves, and asking no favours of capital on the one hand, or of hirelings or slaves on the other.'[1] Slavery apart, the economic system of the United States, Lincoln believed, secures to most men the full value of their industry: in its most radical and equalitarian form, the natural rights theory of property squares well with the facts of ownership in America.

Lincoln's observation about the nature of American economic society was, perhaps, not far wide of the mark in 1859, but it could hardly serve as a justification of those concentrations of wealth which already existed. It said in effect that great wealth was tolerable because not typical. The economists, meanwhile, had done service by elaborating a safer theory of the rights of the rich owner. All the important American writers took over from the classical English and French economists the labour theory of value and the related idea that property belonged to him who had created it by his industry. They accepted the principles laid down by the Reverend Joseph Haven of Amherst, subsequently of the Chicago Theological Seminary: 'Man has not only the right to life and liberty, but also to property, or the possession and enjoyment of whatever he may, by his own industry or good fortune, or the gift of others, have honestly acquired.' If anyone objects that 'we possess many things which we call property, on which we have not bestowed labour—many values which we have not ourselves created, as for example,

[1] Speech at Milwaukee, Wis., September 30, 1859. In some notes, written on December 1, 1847, he had said: 'To secure to each labourer the whole product of his labour, or as nearly as possible, is a worthy object of any good government.' A speech in New York, March 21, 1864, stated that 'property is the fruit of labour.'

property inherited or bequeathed, I reply, these values were originally created by labour; they became the property of the original owner in that way, and the right of possession has been conferred by him on the present possessor.'[1] Theories which describe property as a conventional rather than a natural institution, wrote one economist, are more dangerous than the doctrine of atheism.[2]

Faced with the problem of justifying profits and rent as the reward of labour, the economists resorted to those solutions common to the classical school. Eventually, because those solutions, as socialist critics quickly pointed out, were unsatisfactory, economists abandoned the whole theory of labour as the source of value and the source of property rights. In the first volume of *Capital*, Karl Marx quoted the works of the three most prominent American economists, Reverend Samuel Newman, Reverend Francis Wayland, and Henry Carey, as examples of the confusion which accompanies any attempt to hold to a labour theory of value and yet avoid the conclusion that the labourer is exploited. Meanwhile, however, the economists prior to the Civil War had kept alive the tradition that property was a natural right.

c. France

The aim of every political association is the preservation of the natural and imprescriptible rights of man. These rights are liberty, property, security, and resistance to oppression. *Declaration of the Rights of Man and Citizen*, 1789.

The liberalism which, in the seventeenth century, made England the nurse and teeming womb of regicides and revolutionists, crossed the narrow seas in the eighteenth century and settled in the Kingdom of France. In the course of time the philosophy of natural rights came to be thought of as a French theory, and the natural right of property was adopted as an

[1] Quoted from Haven's *Moral Philosophy* in Dorfman, *Economic Mind* , Vol. II, p. 704.

[2] R. H. Garnett, quoted in Dorfman, Vol. II, p. 892.

axiom of French political thought. But in the beginning natural rights and liberalism were not necessarily connected in the French mind. More than one notable French liberal put his hopes in enlightened despotism and looked forward to reforming France and the world, not by attributing rights to the *canaille*, but by catching the ear of an absolute monarch. When the clergy protested against an unprecedented tax of Louis XV, enlightened anti-clericalists joined the royal lawyers in asserting that all property was held at the king's pleasure.[1] Radical equalitarians, before they realized that the natural right theory could be turned to their purposes, clung to the idea that property was a creature of convention. Montesquieu, whose historical and genetic approach to politics was in direct opposition to the logical abstractions of the natural right school, wrote that property had been created by the state and that its distribution ought to be regulated by the state at all times. He agreed that in the state of nature men had been equal and property common; but he argued that men had assigned to the state the power of distributing property and granting legal and political privileges. Modern states, he insisted, ought to pursue a liberal policy in respecting the property of the individual, not because such a policy safeguards natural rights, but because it promotes prosperity and happiness.[2] Thus conservatives, liberals, and radicals, however they differed as to ends, often agreed that the institution of private ownership was the conventional creation of human law. They might support Bourbons, enlightened despots, or imaginary philosopher-kings, but in any case they adopted the property theory of absolutism.

But if the natural right theory of property was not popular with French thinkers in the first half of the eighteenth century it was, nevertheless, not unknown to them. Grotius and Pufendorf were standard authorities and the most popular translations of their writings were equipped with notes explaining the

[1] André Lichtenberger, *Le Socialisme au XVIIIe Siècle*, Paris, 1895, pp. 383 ff.

[2] *Spirit of the Laws* (1748). The relevant passages are Bk. V, 3, 4, 5, 15; Bk. VIII, 4; Bk. XVII, 5; and Bk. XXVI, 15.

superiority of the Lockean labour theory of property.[1] Locke himself was well known and Burlamaqui and Vattel were popular authorities.[2] As the century wore on the terminology of natural rights was increasingly adopted by French thinkers. By the second half of the century, that terminology had become so common that Rousseau adopted it, and quoted the 'wise Locke,' in those works which were in fact direct and influential attacks upon the whole system of natural rights, including that of property.

Rousseau's remarks on property exhibit the changes of mood and the apparent contradictions which are characteristic of his political theory. In 1755 he said:

> The first man who, having enclosed a piece of ground, bethought himself of saying, *This is mine*, and found people simple enough to believe him, was the real founder of civil society. From how many crimes, wars and murders, from how many horrors and misfortunes might anyone have saved mankind, by pulling up the stakes, or filling up the ditch, and crying to his fellows, 'Beware of listening to this imposter; you are undone if you once forget that the fruits of the earth belong to us all, and the earth itself to nobody.'[3]

Three years later he said, 'It is certain that the right of property is the most sacred of all the rights of citizenship, and even more important in some respects than liberty itself. . . .'[4] Finally, in 1762 he wrote that 'the state, in relation to its members, is master of all their goods by the social contract, which, within the state, is the basis of all rights. . . .'[5] These passages register the shift from individualism to popular sovereignty, from anarchism to the organic state.

The *Discourse on the Origin of Inequality* sets before the reader a vision of the golden age when men were equal and had no

[1] Jean Barbeyrac's (1674–1744) annotated French translations went through several editions, and were translated into English before 1740.

[2] Daniel Mornet, *Les Origines Intellectuelles de Révolution Française*, Paris, 1933, and Kingsley Martin, *French Liberal Thought in the Eighteenth Century*, Boston, 1929, describe the growth of the natural rights philosophy in France.

[3] *A Discourse on the Origin of Inequality* (1755), Everyman's Library, p. 207.

[4] *A Discourse on Political Economy* (1758), Everyman's Library, p. 271.

[5] *The Social Contract* (1762), Everyman's Library, p. 19.

property, each being content with the spontaneous gifts of nature. This primitive state of nature is in every way the opposite of the state of society where man is civilized, corrupted, and enslaved. Private property, Rousseau wrote, is the fundamental institution of the social state and he sketched the origin of this institution whose introduction destroyed the golden age. The development of family life and permanent habitations, the invention of weapons for hunting and fishing, and the gradual expansion of men's desires, all contributed to the birth of the idea of private ownership. But the primitive state was not essentially altered until men began to co-operate in agricultural and manufacturing enterprises. 'It was iron and corn which first civilized men, and ruined humanity.' 'From the moment one man began to stand in need of the help of another; from the moment it appeared advantageous to any one man to have enough provisions for two, equality disappeared, property was introduced, work became indispensable and . . . slavery and misery were soon seen to germinate and grow up with the crops.'[1]

In one passage Rousseau seems to accept the theory that property derived from labour is natural, 'It is impossible to conceive how property can come from anything but manual labour: for what else can a man add to things which he does not originally create, so as to make them his own property? It is the husbandman's labour alone that, giving him a title to the produce of the ground he has tilled, gives him a claim also to the land itself, at least till harvest; and so, from year to year, a constant possession which is easily transformed into property.'[2] This suggests the familiar distinction of the agrarians who accepted the labour theory of property but excluded land from the list of objects which could be appropriated. In fact, Rousseau makes clear that the right of property in land is a creation of positive law and is 'different from the right deducible from the law of nature.'[3] Moreover, the right established by labour is further limited by the rule that men can appropriate only the bare necessities of life. 'Even those who had been enriched by their

[1] Pp. 214–15. [2] Pp. 216–17. [3] P. 217.

own industry, could hardly base their proprietorship on better claims.' The poor could say to them, 'You ought to have had the express and universal consent of mankind, before appropriating more of the common subsistence than you needed for your own maintenance.'[1] In effect, then, except for a few articles of consumption which a man appropriates for his own use and by his own labour, property is not natural. It is 'only a convention of human institution.'[2]

To justify their usurpations, the rich 'conceived at length the profoundest plan that ever entered the mind of man': they persuaded the poor to exchange real equality for equality of right, and to consent to the establishment of property and government. Thus anarchy gave way to the state, 'which irretrievably destroyed natural liberty, eternally fixed the law of property and inequality, converted clever usurpation into unalterable right, and, for the advantage of a few ambitious individuals, subjected all mankind to perpetual labour, slavery and wretchedness.'[3] Nevertheless, Rousseau concludes, the system of property and government is now legitimate since men have in fact consented to it. They cannot go back to the state of nature and their only hope is that wise princes will mitigate the evils of inequality.

But in spite of this disclaimer, *The Discourse on the Origin of Inequality* was a source of inspiration to many socialist dreamers. It contributed much to the formulation of that Utopian tradition, especially prominent in France, which rejected theories about the natural right of property, denied that any system of private ownership whatsoever could be anything but artificial and bad, and insisted that communism was the only natural and good system. Rousseau himself continued to preach that property was conventional rather than natural. But he finally abandoned the opinion that the ways of nature were altogether preferable to the ways of man.

In the article on political economy, written for the *Encyclopédie* in 1758, the change is already apparent. The advantages of the social state are no longer questioned: the problem now is to

[1] P. 220. [2] P. 227. [3] Pp. 220–1.

determine the principles which should guide the state in regulating those economic questions which are its proper concern. Having assumed the propriety of political organization, Rousseau goes on to say that the right of property is sacred, 'because property is the true foundation of civil society.'[1] This is the usual modern argument: the state cannot in reason attack the institution which it has been created to protect. Taxes can be levied only with the consent of the citizens.[2]

But if the state ought to respect the rights of property it ought also to prevent that extreme inequality of fortune which makes any impartial administration of justice impossible. Moreover, it is an essential duty of government to provide for the subsistence of its citizens, by creating sufficient opportunities for gainful employment. These duties of the state, Rousseau admits, may conflict with its obligation to protect the property of the individual. But it is generally impossible to protect property without making regulations about contracts and wills and the like, regulations which do in fact restrict the right of property. Moreover, there are two obviously legitimate methods of regulating the distribution of property. When a man dies his right to his property ends and the state may prescribe the rules of inheritance. Secondly, since all the advantages of society are monopolized by the rich, it is only just that taxation should be progressive.[3]

In the essay on political economy Rousseau maintains his thesis that property is conventional. But he now accepts the institution without hesitation and adopts an attitude acceptable to the middle class: property should be sacred, taxation should rest on consent, and extremes of wealth should be discouraged in the interests of equality of opportunity. In the circumstances of the time, of course, extreme wealth could only mean the estates of the privileged aristocracy.

Finally, in the *Social Contract*, Rousseau stated his theory of property in its most developed form. Here the social state, with

[1] *Discourse on Political Economy*, Everyman's Library, p. 271.

[2] P. 278.

[3] Pp. 267, 271–2, 279–82.

its institutions of property, is described as more desirable than the state of nature. Now the freedom of the savage is licence and only the citizen enjoys that true liberty which consists in obedience to laws of his own choosing. In describing the transition from savagery to civilization, Rousseau repeats many of his earlier ideas about property. In the state of nature land may be appropriated, provided that it is still unoccupied, that the appropriator occupies only what he needs for his subsistence, and that he establishes his claim by labour and cultivation. All other possession is usurpation.[1] Here Rousseau has included land as one of the legitimate objects of natural property, but otherwise the theory is the same as in the earlier writings.

Modern property rights cannot, according to this view, be rights of nature. They are, Rousseau continues, conventional rights created by the social contract. When men contract with one another to form a state they give up all their property and possessions to the sovereign power. Henceforth, the only legitimate rights of property are those which the law creates and protects. But, Rousseau adds, 'the peculiar fact about this alienation is that, in taking over the goods of individuals, the community, so far from despoiling them, only assures them legitimate possession, and changes usurpation into a true right and enjoyment into proprietorship.'[2]

Here Rousseau's theory bears obvious similarities to that of Hobbes. Property is a human convention with no basis in natural law. Only by creating an absolute sovereign power, which will enact laws of property, can men secure legitimate and guaranteed titles of ownership. Like Hobbes, Rousseau assures men of property that the sovereign power will not in practice assert its claims and confiscate their possessions. And like Hobbes again, his assurances are not persuasive. He asserts that every act of the general will or sovereign must be general in its application; the sovereign does not and cannot enact laws which apply only to particular individuals; the supreme legislator will never single out individuals and take from them the rights of property which it has conferred

[1] Everyman edition, pp. 19–20.

[2] P. 21.

upon the general body of citizens.[1] But political theorists have constantly remarked that Rousseau does not demonstrate how it happens that the sovereign never exceeds the limits of its power. Moreover, even if the sovereign confines itself to general conventions, the rich are not secure. Solon introduced a general law abolishing all debts: the law was legitimate by Rousseau's criterion since it applied equally to all citizens, but in fact it benefited the poor at the expense of the rich.[2]

From the various statements of Rousseau, different groups chose those which suited their own views. German nationalists developed the concept of the sovereign state which admitted no limitations of its powers, which claimed to be the source of all rights and benefits, but which in fact would secure and enlarge the property of its citizens. The radical equalitarian and communist groups developed those passages which asserted that all private ownership was a violation of right in the state of nature, and which gave the sovereign the title to all property in the social state. French socialists of the eighteenth century, whether Utopian moralists such as Mably, or spokesmen of the Fourth Estate such as Babeuf, adopted Rousseau's theory that property was a conventional, and bad, institution. They did not attempt to base their proposals on a radical interpretation of the natural right theory of property.[3]

On the other hand, French liberals could find ammunition in Rousseau. They could point out that many of his statements were not unlike those of Montesquieu, whom he often quoted with approbation. Both men asserted that property is a conventional institution founded on the will of the sovereign; but both

[1] Bk. II, ch. iv.

[2] In his proposals for a Corsican constitution (1764) Rousseau stated that government ownership of all land would be best, but that in any case the state should retain the right of confiscating private estates. C. E. Vaughan, *Political Writings of Jean Jacques Rousseau*, Cambridge, 1915, Vol. II, pp. 151–2.

[3] The theories of the socialists are fully described in the two classic studies of André Lichtenberger, *Le Socialisme au XVIIIe Siècle*, Paris, 1895, and *Le Socialisme et La Révolution Française*, Paris, 1899. Some new material is included in Kingsley Martin, *French Liberal Thought*, ch. ix.

assumed that the sovereign will not change its will suddenly or for light reasons. In the *Social Contract*, Rousseau still exhibits a partiality for equality, but it is now hardly more than that traditional maxim of policy which Bacon, Montesquieu, and a host of earlier writers had commended. He refers the reader to the *Spirit of the Laws* for examples of how the legislator may discourage the extremes of wealth and poverty.[1] Moreover, his references to common liberal assumptions—that in society equality of right and opportunity replace the actual equality of the state of nature, that inequalities of wealth ought to originate in the natural inequalities of men's talents and not flow from grants of special privilege, and that the middle classes are the worthiest elements in the community[2]—made Rousseau acceptable to the liberal political thinkers.

In any case, French liberals were not yet committed to the philosophy of natural rights and, in the circumstances of the time, saw many advantages in the theory that property was conventional. Those men who wanted an enlightened monarch to redistribute the property of France, and those revolutionary legislators who actually carried out such a distribution, found it convenient to think that property was a creature of that sovereign general will of which they were the representatives. A middle class fearful of the confiscations of autocrats and democrats turns readily to the idea of the natural right of property. But a middle class which hopes to lay hands on the state power and confiscate feudal property turns as readily to a convention theory of the rights of ownership. Thus it was that the theory of property as an artificial creation of man, the theory adopted by Rousseau, continued to flourish in eighteenth-century France. The men of the Revolution proclaimed in the Declaration of the Rights of Man that property was natural; but they confiscated the property of the Church and the aristocracy on the theory that property was subject to the sovereign will of the people. Not until Ther-

[1] *Social Contract*, pp. 46–7.

[2] *Discourse on Inequality*, pp. 217, 238; *Discourse on Political Economy*, pp. 266–7; *Social Contract*, p. 21–2.

midor, when the revolutionary confiscations had been completed and ominous rumblings were heard from the Left, did French property-owners give whole-hearted allegiance to the natural rights theory of property. Meanwhile the convention theory had been perpetuated and its revival in the nineteenth century, a revival in which the writings of Rousseau figured prominently, was one of the causes of the decline of the natural rights philosophy.

Voltaire illustrates most dramatically the fact that the *philosophes* found it inconvenient to commit themselves irrevocably to any one theory of property. A great admirer of the Lockean tradition, he paraphrased many of the natural rights doctrines: men are born equal, the law ought to recognize their equality of right, feudal privileges are unjust, and a sound agricultural system is one in which the peasants own the land.[1] It is not surprising that he also adopted, on occasion, the theory that property is a natural right. ' "Liberty and Property" is the great national cry of the English. It is certainly better than "St. George and my right," or "St. Denis and Montjoie"; it is the cry of nature.' The English did well, he remarks, in confiscating Church lands and preventing priests from fattening on the fruits of other men's labour.[2] Other passages in the *Philosophical Dictionary* assert that property is a natural right[3] and, in the articles on 'Natural Law' and 'Man,' Voltaire attacks Rousseau for denying that property is an institution of the law of nature. That law grants to every man the sole dominion of the products of his industry. Voltaire was apparently a partisan of the Lockean theory, at least in the *Philosophical Dictionary*.

But in the same book he wrote, 'In society we hold not any good, or any possession, as a simple natural right, since we give up our natural right and submit it to the order of civil society, in return for security and protection. It is, therefore, by the law that

[1] *Philosophical Dictionary* (1764), articles on 'Equality,' 'Government,' 'Impost,' 'Natural Law,' and 'Property.'

[2] Article on 'Property,' in the *Philosophical Dictionary*.

[3] Article on 'Government.'

we hold our possessions.' The switch in theory is explained by the fact that this quotation comes from the article on 'Canon Law' where Voltaire tried to prove that the Church has no title to its property other than the permission of the law. The implication was that the King of France, or any enlightened despot, might confiscate the wealth of the Church at any time.

Other *philosophes* wavered in the manner of Voltaire. Diderot insisted that governments should not interfere with the rights of property; but he also hoped that benevolent autocrats would redistribute property by imperial ukase.[1] The article '*Propriété*' in the *Encyclopédie* deliberately avoids the question whether property is a natural or a political right; wise government, the author asserts, will secure to its citizens the wealth their labour has amassed, but he does not tell us whether the wise state acts on grounds of utility, or in obedience to the law of nature. Similarly, the article '*Droit Naturel*' does not distinguish the early theorists of natural law, who taught that property was founded on human agreements, from the disciples of Locke, who sought to prove that it was founded in the law of nature. Helvetius spoke of the right of property as sacred, but he argued that rights were based on utility rather than any supposed law of nature, and he urged the state to cut off the extremes of wealth and poverty.[2] Of all the *philosophes* Holbach was the one who held most firmly to the Lockean theory. 'The laws of nature,' he wrote, 'give to each man a right which is called *property*, and which is nothing else than the power of exclusive enjoyment of those things which his talent, labour, and industry have procured.' Property is based on the necessary connection which is established between a man and the fruit of his labour: a field, for example, 'becomes in some fashion a part of the person who cultivates it. . . .' Watered with his sweat, it is in some sense identified with him. Holbach points out that from this theory it follows that property should be

[1] Laski, *Rise of European Liberalism*, p. 217.

[2] *De L'Homme*, Section VII, in *Oeuvres*, Vol. IV, Paris, 1795. See also Kingsley Martin, *French Liberal Thought*, p. 186, and Harold Laski, *Rise of European Liberalism*, pp. 218–19.

unequally divided because men's talents are naturally unequal, and that the state cannot deprive a man of that which is his by right of nature. In fact the state was created to guarantee the right of property.[1] Thus Holbach was an adherent of the Lockean theory. He also, on occasion, spoke of property rights as having no other basis than utility, and urged the state to see that property was well distributed; but since he assumed that, in the absence of artificial restraints and privileges, property would distribute itself naturally in such a way as to promote the general welfare, he did not involve himself in serious contradiction.[2] Another *philosophe*, Condorcet, made the same assumption, and it was an axiom for the physiocratic economists, who were the most important French exponents of the natural right of property.[3]

The economists also preferred enlightened despotism to constitutional regimes: 'in France,' one of them explained, 'reforms changing the whole face of the country can be accomplished in the twinkling of an eye, while in England the very slightest reform can be frustrated by the hostility of parties.'[4] Nevertheless, they were all professors of the Lockean theory of property. Quesnay was of the opinion that the land itself could not be appropriated by labour—at some period the ground must have been parcelled out in equal lots to all the citizens—but labour was a sufficient title to all other goods.[5] But both Dupont de Nemours and Nicolas Baudeau included land among those objects

[1] Holbach's theory is fully stated in *La Politique Naturelle*, London, 1773, Pt. I, sections xxv–xxvii. His views are summarized in W. H. Wickwar, *Baron d'Holbach*, London, 1935.

[2] *Politique Naturelle*, IV, xxvii; *La Morale Universelle* (1776), Pt. IV, section ix; *Système de la Nature* (1770), Pt. I, section ix.

[3] For Condorcet's views on property, see his *Esquisse d'un Tableau Historique des Progrès de l'Esprit Humain*, Paris, 1795, p. 246; Kingsley Martin, *French Liberal Thought*, pp. 293–4; and J. S. Schapiro, *Condorcet*, N.Y., 1934, ch. viii.

[4] Le Trosne, quoted by Professor Salvemini, 'Concepts of Democracy and Liberty in the Eighteenth Century,' in *The Constitution Reconsidered*, Conyers Read editor, New York, 1938.

[5] *Oeuvres*, Auguste Oncken editor, Paris, 1888, pp. 331, 366–7, 647–9, 694. Quesnay's convention, which awarded each man an equal share of land, was less awkward than those of Grotius and Pufendorf which asserted that men had agreed to an unequal division.

to which man could gain a 'natural title' by work. It is a common error, wrote Baudeau, to attribute property to the civil law. Before societies and laws existed, wrote Dupont, men had rights, including that of property in things acquired by the labour of their bodies.[1] Mercier de la Rivière repeated the same ideas and added that property was the foundation of the whole social order. 'It is from the right of property, maintained in all its natural and primitive fullness, that all the institutions which make up the essential form of society *necessarily* flow: you can think of the right of property as a tree, and all the institutions of society are the branches which it shoots forth, which it nourishes, and which perish when they are detached from it.'[2] Finally, Turgot agreed with the other economists that labour gave a natural title to property. But he added, as other theorists had done before, that in the state of nature property in land lasted only so long as the appropriator continued to occupy and cultivate: permanent property in land was a creation of the civil law. These civil extensions of the right of property were justified by their general utility, but they should be revised whenever they conflict with the original right of nature. Thus the privileges of the aristocracy, he advised the king, are civil rights which deprive others of their natural right to enjoy the produce of their own industry: these privileges ought, consequently, to be suppressed.[3]

The French physiocrats found it as difficult as did the English economists to hold fast to the Lockean theory that property is derived from labour, and yet avoid the conclusion that rent, interest, and profits are the fruits of exploitation. Their solutions to that problem, according to the historians of economic thought, were no more successful than those of their English successors. But in both countries it was the liberal economists who clung

[1] Dupont, in *Collection des Économistes*, Vol. I, Paris, 1910, pp. 11–15, 33; Baudeau in the same, Vol. II, pp. 21, 23, 107–9.

[2] *L'Ordre Naturel et Essentiel des Sociétés Politiques* (1776), in *Collection des Économistes*, Vol. III, pp. 337, 8–14, 21.

[3] *Oeuvres*, Gustav Schelle editor, 5 vols., Paris, 1913, Vol. I, pp. 380–1, 439; Vol. II, pp. 539–40, 596–7; see also Kingsley Martin, *French Liberal Thought*, pp. 223–4.

most faithfully to the Lockean theory, and who were largely responsible for its adoption as the official theory of the middle class.

When the Estates met at Versailles in the spring of 1789, no one theory of property could be called official. The feeling of the deputies was generally in favour of abolishing, with compensation, feudal rights, and establishing the reign of absolute property everywhere. Everything, and particularly the land, was to be given a sole owner whose rights should be as extensive as those which the bourgeois owners of *la propriété mobilière* had long enjoyed. Such a reformation was practically desirable. But in accordance with what theory of ownership it should be carried out, the deputies had not decided. Some were Rousseauists, believing that all rights were definable by the sovereign power; some were Lockeans who wished to distinguish between natural and artificial property; others were attracted by the theory of prescription and were ready to oppose any great and sudden subversion of existing rights. Probably the majority had no decided opinions on matters of theory.

If the deputies dipped into the flood of pamphlets which appeared in the course of the summer, they would have found that many of them spoke of property as a convention which needed overhauling if it was to promote the general welfare. But the authors agreed that once the proper rights had been instituted they should be declared inviolate.[1] The lists of grievances which poured in from the whole of France also demanded a reformation of property rights; they sometimes spoke as if feudal privileges were violations of natural property.[2] They agreed that the true rights of property should be fully protected by law: according to the summary prepared for the National Assembly, all the *Cahiers* asked that 'property will be sacred.'[3]

Those deputies who had no set opinions on the theory of

[1] Lichtenberger, *Le Socialisme et La Révolution*, ch. ii.

[2] Pp. 23–4.

[3] Reported on July 27, 1789. Printed in L. G. Wickham Legg, *Select Documents of the French Revolution*, Oxford, 1905, Vol. I, p. 103.

property were forced by circumstances to make a decision in the course of the summer of '89. The National Assembly had frequently been urged to issue a declaration of rights. In August the proposal was put to debate and the members found themselves involved in a long discussion of the philosophical theory of property.[1] From the start a number of deputies were opposed to issuing any declaration at all, on the grounds that such a document would be dangerous. In America, where property, unburdened either with arbitrary taxes or feudal incidents, is equally divided, the various declarations merely confirm existing rights. But to declare that all Frenchmen are equal and enjoy the same rights, when in fact the inequalities of the feudal regime still exist, is to invite rebellion. Using the time-honoured conservative argument that all metaphysical discussions of fundamental justice are potentially dangerous, these deputies voted against the proposal to issue a declaration of rights.[2] But the opponents and defenders of the proposal were not always in disagreement as to the nature of the right of property.

One opponent argued that men had no rights in a state of nature: all rights are social. He was answered by a member who agreed that rights were civil: the immortal Rousseau had settled that. But, he argued, a declaration is necessary to teach men that the rights of property, which obligated no one in the state of nature, are now inviolable. A declaration of rights will not be dangerous: it will impress upon men a respect for property, and it will protect them from the dangers of despotism.[3] A third speaker pointed out that a declaration of the right of property would be a useful weapon against anyone who argued for an

[1] Wilhelm Rees, *Die Erklärung der Menschen-und-Bürgerrechte von 1789*, Leipzig, 1912, discusses in detail the controversial question of the origin of the Declaration of 1789; B. Schickhardt, *Die Erklärung der Menschen-und-Bürgerrechte*, Berlin, 1931, is a study of the work of the National Assembly in formulating the Declaration.

[2] See the debates of August 1, 1789, printed in the *Réimpression de L'Ancien Moniteur*, Vol. I, Paris, 1858, pp. 257 ff., particularly the speeches of Malouet and the Bishop of Auxerre.

[3] Count d'Antraigues, in a reply to Biauzat, August 3rd, both reported in *Réimpression de L'Ancien Moniteur*, Vol. I, pp. 268–9.

equal division of the land.[1] The lines of theoretical disagreement were still further blurred by a speaker who professed to believe in the principles of natural right, including the right of property, as they had been defined by Locke, Hume, and Rousseau.[2] Many of the members, in fact, apparently made no distinction between Locke and Rousseau: both were regarded as defenders of property and natural right.[3]

In the end, the proposal to issue a declaration was adopted and on August 17th Mirabeau read the draft which had been prepared by a committee of five members. This document adopted without qualification the principles of the *Social Contract*. The general will is sovereign, and since its aim is the welfare of all, property will be secure.[4] Article XVII emphatically distinguished civil equality, which the law must always recognize, from equality of property. But nowhere are property rights described as natural, existing before the social contract, or superior to the rights of the sovereign.[5] Had the National Assembly accepted this draft, the natural right of property would not have become the official theory of the French nation. But the work of Mirabeau's committee was rejected.

On August 19th, the National Assembly voted to accept as a basis for discussion a draft declaration which, in contrast to that of Mirabeau's committee, was wholly Lockean in its assumptions.[6]

[1] Barnave, quoted in Rees, *Die Erklärung*, p. 117.

[2] Landine on August 1st, *Réimpression de L'Ancien Moniteur*, Vol. I, p. 264.

[3] This fact was ignored by Georg Jellinek, *Declaration of the Rights of Man and of Citizens*, translated by Max Farrand, N.Y., 1901. His argument, that Rousseau's writings could not have inspired the Declaration because Rousseau did not believe in natural rights, is unconvincing. The members of the National Assembly may have interpreted Rousseau wrongly, but some of them did regard him as a believer in natural rights.

[4] Articles V, XI, XII, and XVII concern property. The document is printed on *Réimpression de L'Ancien Moniteur*, Vol. I, pp. 339–40.

[5] Presumably Mirabeau would not have objected to calling individual rights 'natural.' In defending the work of his committee he twice referred to 'natural rights.' Speeches on August 18th, *Réimpression de L'Ancien Moniteur*, Vol. I, pp. 350–1. Apparently he did not distinguish the theory of Rousseau from that of the natural rights school.

[6] Printed in *Réimpression de L'Ancien Moniteur*, Vol. I, pp. 362–3.

The preamble states that men possess rights before they enter societies. Articles II, III, and IV proclaim that every man is naturally free to make use of his natural endowments and that he has a right to the property which he acquires in the exercise of that freedom. But, as articles V and VI explain, nature has not endowed all men alike, hence inequality arises; society has been instituted to maintain equality of rights in the midst of the natural inequality of endowments. Finally, Article XXII states that every man has the right to consent to taxation since the public revenue is 'a sum deducted from the property of each citizen.'

None of these articles defining the right of property was adopted without change in the final Declaration of the Rights of Man and of Citizen which was adopted on August 26, 1789. In the discussions of the various articles the question of whether rights are natural or civil continued to be debated. But the concept that property was a right of nature was finally adopted, and thereby became the official theory of the French nation. The new preamble declared the intention of the Assembly to define the 'natural, inalienable, and sacred rights of man.' Article II summed up the Lockean concepts: 'The aim of every political association is the preservation of the natural and imprescriptible rights of man. These rights are liberty, property, security, and resistance to oppression.' Robespierre objected to saying that taxes were deductions from each citizen's property: that implied that the citizens lost control of the money they paid over to the government. In fact, the taxpayer merely deposits his property with a public administrator who is to use it as the body of taxpayers directs.[1] Robespierre's objection emphasized the individual's right at the expense of the right of the state. The Assembly agreed with his argument and omitted the offending clause from the Article (XIV) on taxation. Finally, on the last day of the discussion, several members suggested a final article, devoted particularly to the protection of property. Article XVII declared that "property being a sacred and inviolable right, no one can be deprived of it unless a legally established public necessity evidently

[1] Speech on August 26th, in *Réimpression de L'Ancien Moniteur*, Vol. I, p. 383.

demands it, under the condition of a just and prior indemnity.' On August 26, 1789, the natural right theory of property became part of the fundamental law of France.

The adoption of the natural rights theory was a victory for the radical liberals. These men were not consecrating feudal dues when they declared that property rights were natural and inviolable. They had voted, in the dramatic night of August 4, 1789, to abolish the feudal system for the very reason that it was in conflict with the system of natural property: 'in a free state,' it was said, 'properties ought to be as free as persons.'[1] They thought of the natural right of property as a weapon which would destroy feudal property and absolutism with one blow. The moderates who opposed issuing a declaration understood this well. They feared that a declaration would encourage a too rapid course of reform and lead to the sudden destruction of those old rights which they also wished to extinguish, but gradually, and with compensation. Everyone saw that natural right was the enemy of prescriptive right, and that the victory of the former was a victory for the radicals.

Nevertheless natural right was a double-edged sword. Two months after the famous Declaration had been adopted, defenders of the old order were appealing to the natural right of property, and radical reformers were denying it. The occasion was the famous proposal to solve financial problems by taking over the property of the Church.[2] Defending the property of the Church,

[1] From the draft of the resolution abolishing feudalism, presented to the National Assembly on August 6th; *Réimpression de L'Ancien Moniteur*, Vol. I, p. 293. This sentence was omitted from the final resolution passed on August 11th.

The declaration of grievances of one of the Paris electoral districts had stated that property should be inviolate, but that those privileges which violated natural right were not rightfully property. The text is printed in Jean Jaurès, *Histoire Socialiste*, Vol. I, Paris, n.d., p. 166.

[2] The debate, which lasted from October 10 to November 2, 1789, can be followed in *Archives Parlementaires*, Première Série, Tome IX, Paris, 1877. The best account of the debate is in Ph. Sagnac, *La Législation Civile de la Révolution Francaise*, Paris, 1898. See also Sagnac, 'La Révolution et sa Conception de la Propriété,' in *Cahiers d'Histoire de la Révolution Française*, 1947, No. 1, N.Y., 1946.

Abbé d'Eymar reviewed the whole theory of natural right and insisted that the property system 'is founded on the principles of natural right, anterior and superior to the conventions of the social pact' and is not to be abrogated by those conventions.[1] Defending the right of the state, Mirabeau declared that all property is 'a benefit (*bien*) acquired by virtue of the laws': the state can deprive individuals and corporate bodies of their goods, without paying them compensation.[2] Theories of property were obviously weapons which men picked up and discarded as the needs of battle dictated.

Other speakers chose other weapons. A number of anti-clerical members followed M. Thouret in distinguishing, as radical liberals have often done, between individual and corporate property. Individuals, he said, existed prior to society, and they have rights which were not created, but are merely recognized and protected by the law. Such rights, including that of property, can no more be destroyed by the law than the individuals themselves. Corporations, on the other hand, have been created by the law, and can be destroyed by it. For the same reason that the suppression of a corporation is not a homicide, the revocation of its property rights is not a spoliation. Practically, he added, the proposal is advantageous since it will increase the number of landowners: propertyless men are a danger in every state, and men who own their own land are the most industrious farmers.[3] Another group, composed partly of radical priests, argued that the clergy were not the owners of Church property, but the administrators of it; the government could, as French kings had done in the past, take over the administration of this national

[1] *Archives Parlementaires*, IX, p. 420. Similar views were expressed by Abbé Maury, pp. 424–31, and the Bishop of Clermont, p. 484.

[2] P. 607. A translation of this speech of October 30, 1789, and of a second which was written out, but not delivered, was published in London, 1792—*Speeches of M. de Mirabeau*, by James White, Esq. A few years earlier in England, Bishop Butler adopted the same theory in defending the right of the lay holder of what had once been Church property; *Property, Its Duties and Rights*, N.Y., 1922, p. xx.

[3] *Archives Parlementaires*, p. 485. M. Treilhard, pp. 490–2, and M. Durand de Maillane, pp. 499–500, repeated the substance of this argument.

endowment on condition that it provide for the expenses of religion and the relief of the poor.[1] This argument, as well as that which insisted that the clergy ought to follow apostolic example and own no property,[2] avoided the difficult problem of defining the right of property: whatever that right was, the Church did not enjoy it.[3]

The defenders of the clergy answered with various arguments, most of which were summed up in an able speech by M. Camus. To the argument that clerical property was a national endowment, he replied that the donors had given the property for the support of individual clergymen and churches, and for specific purposes. To those who tried to distinguish between corporate and individual property, he replied that all property was civil. All property, corporate and individual, is created by the law, and the state has as much right to confiscate one as the other. In fact, he added, neither corporations nor individuals ought to be deprived of their rights except for a just cause. Finally, to the argument that it would be useful to multiply the number of landowners, he replied that the large landowner was useful too because he supplied capital to his tenants and smaller neighbours.[4]

Camus's argument implied that it was dangerous to begin a policy of confiscation. The state had the legal power to deprive individuals as well as corporations of their property: it might begin with the Church and end with rich individuals. The Bishop of Uzés made that argument explicit. The spoliation of the Church will, he warned, be merely the prelude to a general attack on property.[5] Sir Thomas More had sounded the same warning one hundred and fifty years earlier. Indeed, many of the speeches of 1789 were reminiscent of the arguments which had preceded Henry VIII's confiscations. The problem was the same

[1] Talleyrand was one of the leading supporters of this theory, which could be squared with the canon law; see Sagnac, *La Législation Civile*, pp. 162–3. Other speakers who supported it are reported in *Archives Parlementaires*, IX, pp. 423–4, 484–5, 492, and 496.

[2] *Archives Parlementaires*, IX, p. 511.

[3] The Comte de Clermont-Tonnerre was convinced that owners have a natural right to their property, but, he added, the clergy are not the owners of Church property. *Archives Parlementaires*, IX, pp. 496 ff.

[4] Pp. 416–18.

[5] Pp. 487 ff.

in both cases: how can the Church be despoiled without weakening the indivdual right of property? Tudor theorists tried to solve the problem by pretending that the clergy had voluntarily surrendered their property, and that the Crown would use it for the welfare of religion and the poor. On September 24, 1789, Dupont de Nemours, who had the liveliest respect for the natural right of property and at the same time wished to nationalize Church property, asserted that the clergy had in fact given up all their property on the memorable night of August 4th.[1] But the clergy demurred. Consequently, the National Assembly adopted the other argument: the state would take over the administration of the Church estates—who owned them was left undecided—and use them for religious purposes. The decree adopted on November 2, 1789, read: 'All the ecclesiastical estates are at the disposal of the nation, on condition of providing in a suitable manner for the expenses of worship, the maintenance of its ministers, and the relief of the poor. . . .' Many members who voted for this decree would have rejected it had they known that within five years the clergy would receive no income from their former property, Notre Dame would become a Temple of Reason, and the Cathedral of Metz would be put up for rent. Whatever the theory, the fact was that the ancient domains of the Church became the property of peasants and speculators.

On two other occasions the National Assembly debated at length the theory of property. In 1791 a resolution was offered declaring that the mines of France were the property of the nation; landowners could claim only the surface of the earth. Dupont de Nemours opposed the resolution and asserted that landowners had a natural right to the mineral resources lying under their properties: the state had no power to touch these resources. Mirabeau, however, asserted again that property rights were civil: whoever had been the owners of the mines, the state could take them over if it chose.[2]

[1] P. 509.

[2] The debate is reported in *Archives Parlèmentaires*, Tome XXIV, and is summarized in Henri Hayem, *Essai sur Le Droit de Propriété*, Paris, 1910, pp. 198–9.

A more famous debate, begun in April 1791, argued the question of the right of testators.[1] The radicals generally wanted to regulate inheritance and limit the right of testators in order to divide wealth more equally. Robespierre demanded from the first that inheritance be regulated on the principle that a 'too great inequality of fortunes is the source of political inequality, of the destruction of liberty. According to this principle, the laws ought always to tend to diminish this inequality.'[2] As the Revolution progressed, inheritance was ever more stringently regulated. In 1791 Dupont de Nemours supported the proposed regulations and pointed out that they did not violate natural right, for right dies with the individual. 'What property can a man have who is no more?'[3] Cazalès and others who opposed limiting the right of testators, asserted that it was a logical part of the natural right of property.[4] But Mirabeau again argued that the legislators could do as they wished since all rights of property were civil,[5] and M. Tronchet agreed: social conventions and laws, he said, 'are the true source of the right of property.'[6]

Thus in spite of the famous Declaration men still did not agree on the theory of property. Nevertheless, the natural right theory was enshrined in the Constitution of 1791 as well as in the Declaration, which served as a preamble. Title I of the Constitution guaranteed 'the inviolability of property, or a just and prior indemnity for that of which a legally established public necessity may demand the sacrifice.' But the next clause announced that the property of the Church had been confiscated without indemnity. 'Property intended for the expenses of worship and for all services of public utility belongs to the nation and is at all times at its disposal.' The compromise of 1789 which had avoided the question of who owned the property of the Church was now

[1] Reported in *Archives Parlementaires*, XXIV, and in P.-J.-B. Buchez and P.-C. Roux, *Histoire Parlementaire de la Révolution Française*, Vol. IX, Paris, 1834. The history of regulation of inheritance during the Revolution is described by Sagnac, *La Législation Civile*, I, iv.

[2] Buchez and Roux, IX, p. 299. [3] *Archives Parlementaires*, XXIV, p. 555.

[4] Buchez and Roux, IX, p. 313. [5] P. 287. [6] Pp. 302–3.

abandoned: the property was not merely 'at the disposal' of the nation, it 'belonged' to the nation.

Thus the very document which proclaimed that property was a natural right also proclaimed the power of the French nation to treat property as if it were a creation of the state. After 1791, the rulers of France paid less and less attention to the principle of natural property. The income from the Church lands was devoted entirely to secular purposes; the privileged classes were deprived of their rights without compensation; the estates of emigrés were confiscated; rigid rules were established regulating gifts and testaments, and in 1794, these rules were made retroactive to 1789 so that men who had once been legal heirs were deprived of their property by *ex post facto* legislation. Meanwhile, radical pamphleteers were demanding agrarian laws whose aim was the complete elimination of unequal landed property.

The radical leaders were enamoured with equality, but the proposals of the agrarians were dangerous politics. The peasants who had gained their land were not averse to soaking the rich, but they would not support a general redivision of landed property. Consequently, the radical leaders were quick to dissociate themselves from the agrarians, quick to reaffirm the right of property, at the very time that they were ignoring it most. On the day that monarchy was abolished, Danton proposed that the Convention allay the suspicions of those excellent citizens who were afraid the friends of liberty 'might destroy the social order by exaggerating their principles.' 'Let us declare,' he said, 'that all property, landed, personal, and industrial, will be maintained for ever.'[1] In March 1793, the Convention voted the death penalty for anyone proposing an agrarian law. In June, the Jacobins, at the very moment they were arresting the more moderate Girondins, affirmed their faith in the right of property and claimed that they were ready to die in its defence.[2] On

[1] Speech of September 21, 1792, printed in *Orators of the French Revolution*, edited by H. M. Stephens, Vol. II, pp. 171–2, Oxford, 1892. Again on April 27, 1793, Danton, proposing a heavy tax on the rich, denounced agrarian laws; *Orators*, Vol. II, pp. 240–1.

[2] J. M. Thompson, *The French Revolution*, N.Y., 1945, pp. 388–90.

June 3rd, Marat dissociated himself from the agrarians and said, 'we do not wish to violate property.' But he added that the bread of the poor was the most sacred property and that the rich would be driven from France, and their property distributed to the needy, if they did not support the revolution.[1]

Thus it is not surprising that the Jacobin Constitution, adopted on June 24, 1793, reaffirmed the natural right of property. The new Declaration of Rights listed property among the natural and imprescriptible rights of man, and declared it inviolable, using almost the words of the Declaration of 1789. But a new definition of property was added: 'the right of property is that which belongs to every citizen; to enjoy, and to dispose at his pleasure of his goods, income, and the fruits of his labour and his skill.' Moreover, the Jacobins added that everyone had a right to the property necessary to live: 'Public relief is a sacred debt. Society owes maintenance to unfortunate citizens, either in procuring work for them or in providing the means of existence for those who are unable to labour.'

These clauses in the new Declaration of 1793 are an indication of the Jacobins' theory of property. They accepted the natural rights theory, partly because it was expedient to reassure peasants and shopkeepers that their rights were safe, but mostly because they believed in a regime of private property and individual rights, in opposition to the agrarian and communist radicals. They whole-heartedly favoured that property which a man's labour and skill had acquired for him. But the Jacobins were also equalitarians. They distrusted the rich and had little respect for their property rights; they wanted to make sure that everyone had an equal opportunity to acquire property. Among the last acts of the Jacobin rulers were the famous Laws of Ventôse which appear to have been the prelude to a general policy of levelling economic inequalities.[2]

[1] F. A. Aulard, *La Société des Jacobins*, Vol. V, Paris, 1895, p. 227.

[2] E. N. Curtis, *Saint-Just*, N.Y., 1935, ch. xx; R. R. Palmer, *Twelve Who Ruled*, Princeton, 1941, pp. 284–5, 312–15. General accounts of the Jacobin attitude toward property can be found in Lichtenberger, *Le Socialisme et La Révolution*, ch. iv, and Crane Brinton, *The Jacobins*, N.Y., 1930, ch. v.

In the circumstances of the time the Jacobins chose to support their programme by the theory of natural right. By insisting that natural property was that which a man gained by his own labour, and that everyone should have the chance to labour, the Jacobins were choosing the radical possibilities latent in the doctrine of natural rights. They could both affirm the right of property and confiscate the fortunes of the rich. But as it turned out they did not succeed in convincing the small owner that his property was sacred while that of the rich was not. Peasants and shopkeepers joined with men of wealth to guillotine the Jacobins and put all estates, large and small, under the protection of the law of nature.

It was this difficulty of squaring a policy of redistribution with the theory of the natural right of property which had led Robespierre to follow the tradition of Rousseau and deny that property rights were natural. His most famous statement was made during the debates on the Constitution of 1793. Proposing to speak on the theory of property, he assured those sordid souls who valued only riches that he did not intend to touch their treasures, however impure their source. 'You must know that this agrarian law, of which you have talked so much, is only a phantom created by rascals to terrify fools.' Extreme inequality of fortune is certainly the cause of many evils, but 'equality of goods is a chimera.' What is the right of property? You have said that liberty, the most sacred of the rights of nature, has as its limits the rights of others.

Why have you not applied this same principle to property, which is a social institution, as if the eternal laws of nature were less inviolable than the conventions of men? You have multiplied articles to guarantee the greatest freedom for the exercise of the right of property, and you have not said a single word to determine its nature and legitimacy, so that your declaration seems made not for men, but for the rich, for monopolists, for speculators, and for tyrants. I ask you to correct these vices by consecrating the following truths:

I. Property is the right which each citizen has, to enjoy and dispose of the portion of goods which the law guarantees him.

II. The right of property is restricted, as are all the others, by the obligation to respect the possessions of others.

III. It cannot prejudice the security, nor the liberty, nor the existence, nor the property of our fellow-creatures.

IV. All possession, all traffic which violates this principle is essentially illicit and immoral.[1]

At the end of this speech, Robespierre presented the draft of a new Declaration of Rights which included the four articles quoted, a fifth which made it the duty of the state to provide either work or a dole for everyone, and a sixth which stated that 'the relief of poverty is a debt owed by the rich to the poor; it belongs to the law to determine the manner in which this debt must be discharged.'[2] This draft spoke of natural rights, but it made clear that property was not one of them. Only the fifth of these articles was included in the Declaration of Rights adopted in 1793; the Convention preferred to uphold the theory that property was a natural right. Robespierre's theory that property was a civil right was perhaps better suited to Jacobin practice; but it was less palatable to the proprietors.[3]

With the reaction of Thermidor the natural right theory of property, interpreted conservatively to cover all existing properties, was once more reaffirmed. The Convention, after sending the Robespierrists to the guillotine in July, proclaimed in October 1794 its regard for the rights of owners. The Constitution of the Year III (adopted August 22, 1795) was prefaced with a new Declaration of Rights which included property, but omitted all mention of the state's duty to provide work and subsistence for its citizens. The Constitution itself impressed citizens with the

[1] Speech of April 24, 1793, printed in Stephens, *Orators of the French Revolution*, Vol. II, pp. 367–74.

[2] P. 371. Other statements of Robespierre asserting that property is a social institution can be found in his *Oeuvres*, Paris, 1840, Vol. III, pp. 34 ff.—where he says that property necessary for the subsistence of the citizens belongs to the community, and the excess belongs to individuals—and in Lichtenberger, *Le Socialisme et La Révolution*, ch. iv.

[3] The communist Babeuf preferred Robespierre's draft to the official one: Albert Mathiez, *The Fall of Robespierre and Other Essays*, London, 1927, ch. xii.

duty of recognizing that 'it is upon the maintenance of property that the cultivation of the land, all the production, all means of labour, and the whole social order rest' (Art. 8). It again guaranteed that individual owners would be indemnified when public necessity led the state to take their property (Art. 358). Finally, it restricted the electorate to property owners. As one of its authors said, 'a country governed by property-owners is a true civil society; one where men without property govern is in a state of nature.'[1]

But the men of Thermidor, anxious as they were to prevent future confiscations, could not help approving those of the past upon which their power was built. Like the Englishmen of 1660, they were determined to call a halt to revolution; but they had no intention of restoring the *ancien régime*. Consequently, Articles 373 and 374 assured the holders of property which had once belonged to the Church, to the *emigrés*, and to other enemies of the Revolution, that their titles would never be challenged. But to make sure that the era of confiscation was ended, the Directory decreed, on April 16, 1796, that any one proposing 'the pillage or partition of individual properties, under the name of an agrarian law, or in any other manner,' shall suffer death or deportation.

The final result of the Revolution, which had abolished feudal property and transferred a large measure of the wealth of France from one set of owners to another, was to consecrate the Lockean theory of the natural rights of property. The new peasant proprietors, the buyers of national lands, and all those who had profited by the destruction of the old order, became ardent defenders of the rights of ownership. For these men, the Lockean theory expressed the real meaning of the Revolution. It was, accordingly, written into the Civil Code and remained for a hundred years the official theory of the French nation.

The authors of the Code which Napoleon issued in 1804 thought of themselves as the codifiers of the revolutionary tradition. They viewed their work as the final victory against feudalism

[1] Laski, *Rise of European Liberalism*, p. 230.

and the old regime,[1] the victory of peasant proprietor and business-man. Their work was summed up in the substitution of modern absolute property rights for the chaotic bundles of rights which were characteristic of feudal ownership. 'Its grand and principal object,' wrote one of the authors of the Code, 'is to regulate the principles and the rights of property.' 'Its most precious maxim,' said another, 'is that which consecrates the right of property; everything else is but the logical consequence of this fact.'[2]

The Code itself avoided any entangling references to the theory of property. It confined itself to defining property as 'the right of enjoying and disposing of things in the most absolute manner' (Art. 544), to guaranteeing that individuals should enjoy that right, subject to the necessary limitations established by law (Art. 537), and to enacting that no property should be taken by the state, except for public necessities, and with indemnification (Art. 545).[3] But the remarks and speeches of the lawyers who drafted the Code make clear that they were supporters of the theory of natural right. The Code guarantees property, Treilhard said, because 'property is the foundation, and one the most powerful springs, of society.' Society was made to secure property and we must all be protected in the enjoyment of the 'fruit of our labour and of our industry.'[4] That property is a natural right, said Grenier, is a 'dogma which men, whatever their condition, cannot fail to recognize when they use their reason,'[5] 'Property is the base of all legislation, the

[1] Hayem, Henri, *Essai sur Le Droit de Propriété et ses Limites*, Paris, 1910, pp. 256 ff.

[2] Quoted by Laski, *Rise of European Liberalism*, p. 228, from J. G. Locré, *La Législation Civile de La France*, Paris, 1827, Vol. XXXI, p. 169, and Vol. XVI, p. 499.

[3] Some of the Councillors of State were not happy about the limitations on ownership contained in the last two clauses, but in the end they agreed that there was no practical way to free the owner from all control by the state power; P. A. Fenet, *Recueil Complet des Travaux Préparatoires du Code Civil*, Paris, 1827, Vol. XI, pp. 83–4.

[4] J. G. Locré, *Procés-Verbaux du Conseil D'État*, Paris, 1803, Vol. IV, pp. 49–50.

[5] Fenet, *Recueil Complet*, Vol. XI, pp. 154–5.

source of all the moral affections, and of all the happiness to which man may aspire.'[1]

The most extensive remarks on the theory of property were made by Portalis, one of the ablest and most renowned architects of the Code.[2] Property, he began, is a right of nature and is acquired by labour; the remainder of his speech was an exposition of the pure Lockean doctrine. Some writers, he said, have held that the land was once common, but this is true only in the negative sense that it belonged to no one and was open for anyone to occupy. It was of this negative community that Cicero spoke when he said that the world was originally like a theatre in which seats became the property of those who first occupied them. The theory that the land once belonged to all men, in the sense of a positive community of ownership, is false and is used primarily as an excuse for depriving individuals of their rights. Historically, all societies have recognized the natural right of property, although experience and reason have taught men how to make the exercise of that right more effective. 'But the principle of the right is in us; it is not the result of a human convention or a positive law; it is in the very constitution of our being. . . .' Some philosophers have been puzzled by the problem of how labour can give a title to land, which it cannot create. The answer is that labour is the principal source of value: land to which labour is not applied is practically worthless. Other philosophers have regretted the loss of equality and innocence which they imagine existed in the state of nature before the land was appropriated. But inequality is rooted in nature, since men's capacities differ; and the innocence of the noble savage is a myth: he is in fact lazy, ignorant, and quarrelsome. 'What would become of agriculture and the arts without landed property, which is merely the right to possess with continuity that portion of the earth to which we have applied our painful industry and our just hopes?' 'It is property which has created human society.' The state, of

[1] P. 158.

[2] Portalis's speech is reprinted in Fenet, Vol. XI, pp. 112 ff., and in Locré, *Procés-Verbaux*, Vol. IV, pp. 57 ff.

course, must in certain cases regulate the right of property in the general interest. But the state is in no sense the owner of the property of the citizen; as Seneca said, 'property belongs to the citizen, empire to the sovereign.' The feudal regime confused the two, but we have re-established the true relation once more, and laid the basis for the good society. Portalis concluded with a flowing peroration:

'A man cannot cherish his property without cherishing the laws which protect it. In consecrating maxims favourable to property, you will have inspired the love of the laws; you will have not worked solely for the happiness of individuals or of particular families; you will have opened the true fountains of general prosperity, you will have prepared the happiness of all.'[1]

To Portalis and his fellow jurists, who stood at the beginning rather than the end of the liberal tradition, who saw around them a nation of small peasant proprietors, the guarantee of the right of property seemed to be the fulfilment of individual liberty. They continued to think of that right as a revolutionary weapon directed against feudalism and privilege. They did not foresee that the right which they had proclaimed could come to be the negation of liberty.[2]

From France the liberal theory of property as a right of man spread all over the world and was incorporated in constitutional charters wherever liberalism was successful. In France itself, the theory of property enshrined in the Declaration was repeated in the Constitutions of 1814, 1830, and 1848. In the course of the nineteenth century, from Norway to Portugal, and from Japan to Chile, instruments of government proclaimed the inviola-

[1] In discussing the regulation of inheritance, Portalis remarked that natural right ceased with the death of the individual; see Hayem, *Droit de Propriété*, p. 297. One or two other speakers said the state could regulate inheritance since all property was in fact civil, but they were in a minority; see Sagnac, *La Législation Civile*, p. 351.

[2] F. Dugast, *La Propriété Devant Le Droit Naturel*, Paris, 1904, attacks the Code for protecting property rights which defraud the workman of the product of his labour.

bility of the right of property, often in the very words of the great Declaration.[1]

In France, as in America, the theory of natural property grew from a young and radical doctrine into an old and conservative one. When, in the course of the nineteenth century, French liberalism had achieved that freedom for property which the middle classes demanded, and which the natural right theory of property was intended to justify, liberalism became a defence of the existing system. The task of adapting a theory of property, designed for a society of peasant-owners, artisans, and small shopkeepers, to a society of big-scale capitalist enterprises, was not easy. One solution was to assume, baldly and without argument, that all existing property rights were natural. One of the first works using this solution was written by the famous statesman, Adolphe Thiers. Thiers' little book on property was meant to be an answer to socialist critics of the property system.[2] The first chapters explain in simple terms the Lockean concept of appropriation by labour as a law of nature, and demonstrate that inequality of talents leads inevitably to inequality of fortunes. 'Property is unequal because this man, with these talents, remains poor all his life, that man, with these talents, becomes rich and powerful. This is the real reason one has little, another much.'[3] Thiers avoids any real discussion of rent and profits as violations of natural property, and leaves the reader with the distinct impression that all forms of capitalist property are included under the Lockean formula. In one short passage he does twist Cicero's famous analogy into a justification of landed property. Cicero had said the state of nature was like a theatre which belongs to all the people, but in which each seat becomes the temporary property of the first occupant. The seats, Thiers concedes to the

[1] Examples can be found in W. F. Dodd, *Modern Constitutions*, 2 vols., Chicago and London, 1909. A short discussion of the influence of the Declaration in Germany is to be found in Georg Jellinek, *Declaration of the Rights of Man and of Citizens*, English translation, N.Y., 1901.

[2] *De La Propriété*, Paris, 1848. Immediately after the February revolution, it was republished in a one-franc edition by the contemporary French version of the National Association of Manufacturers.

[3] Bk. I, ch. iv.

critics, are now all permanently occupied. But, he adds, the occupants built the theatre and late-comers have no right to be seated: these should be grateful if some of the occupants are willing to rent their seats.[1]

Thiers' argument that inheritance is not a violation of natural property is no less perverse. The son who lives idly on the fortune left him by his father does not injure society or deprive other men of the fruits of their labour: he merely lives on the labour of his father instead of on his own.[2] Capital, in short, is nothing more than the stored-up labour of the capitalist. Consequently, a primary concern of socialist government will be to prevent men from saving and automatically becoming capitalists: every citizen will have to submit to examinations as intimate as those given to workers in the Mexican diamond mines.[3] To these shallow arguments which amount to no more than an assertion that all existing property is natural in the Lockean sense, Thiers adds all the usual arguments, most of them as old as Aristotle, based on utility and 'human nature.' Without doubt his work is a caricature of serious thought. But as the work of a former Prime Minister and a future President of France, it demonstrates precisely the corruption to which the liberal tradition was liable whenever it abandoned its original emphasis upon equality.

Other French statesmen who claimed to be the heirs of the liberal tradition followed the general argument of Thiers: they exalted the natural right of property, assumed that the rights of existing owners were all natural, and cast off the ideal of equality.[4] Another Prime Minister, Guizot, emphasized that private property was an institution of the law of nature. Equality,[5] he asserted, means equality before the law, and not economic or political equality. He opposed democracy because it was no respecter of property. Alexis de Tocqueville was sympathetic to democracy, but he too was concerned with protecting property from demo-

[1] Bk. I, ch. xiv. [2] Bk. I, ch. x. [3] Bk. II, ch. ii.

[4] Among early liberals, the theory that property was a convention to be regulated by society was still popular. See the account of Benjamin Constant (1767–1830) in Roger Soltau, *French Political Thought in the Nineteenth Century*, Yale, 1931, pp. 40 ff.

[5] *De La Démocratie en France*, Paris, 1849.

cratic majorities. Recognizing that the French Revolution had consecrated property as a natural right, he feared lest democracy destroy that right in the name of equality.[1] Two other liberal democrats, the poet, historian, and statesman Lamartine, and the popular historian Jules Michelet, were adherents of the natural right theory.[2] But except for the fact that Michelet recognized in general that industrialism threatened equality, neither offered a consistent theory of property which would combine the concepts of natural right and equality. In the latter part of the century, Hippolyte Taine again stressed the conservative implications of the right of property. His famous *History* condemned the Revolution: 'Whatever the great names, Liberty, Equality, Fraternity, with which the Revolution decks itself out, it is, in essence, a *transfer of property*.'[3] His respect for property led Taine, as well as other conservative liberals, to condemn democracy and equality.[4]

These random examples illustrate how 'agrarian categories of property and contract passed into an industrial age, whose need was not so much a statement of individual rights as a conception of purpose and social organization.'[5] The difficulties of the liberal position are demonstrated in a work by one of the leading French liberals of the early twentieth century. Paul Leroy-Beaulieu was a consistent upholder of the rights of property, but he found it necessary to publish a bulky refutation of socialist writers who had appropriated the theory of natural right and used it to condemn capitalism for depriving the wage-earner of the

[1] De Tocqueville's views are to be found in his history, *L'Ancien Régime et la Révolution Française*, Paris, 1853, and his *Democracy in America* (1835–40), revised English translation, N.Y., 1945. His political philosophy is summarized by Soltau, *French Political Thought*, pp. 50 ff.

[2] Lamartine's political theory is described by Soltau, *French Political Thought*, pp. 104 ff.; Michelet's ideas are to be found in his popular book *Le Peuple*, Paris, 1846.

[3] Quoted from *Les Origines de la France Contemporaine: La Révolution* (1878–84) by Paul Farmer, *France Reviews Her Revolutionary Origins*, N.Y., 1944, p. 32.

[4] See Soltau, *French Political Thought*, pp. 240 ff.

[5] Kingsley Martin, *French Liberal Thought*, p. 304.

fruits of his industry.[1] He made some attempt to demonstrate that the wage-earner is justly rewarded and that capital is natural property.[2] But his chief argument was utilitarian: capitalism has produced wealth for all, socialism would result in 'the material impoverishment and moral weakening of humanity . . . owing to the want of personal interest.'[3] The socialist adoption of the theory of natural right, and the obvious discrepancies between the fact of property and its theory, were forcing conservative liberals to abandon the venerable liberal doctrine.

[1] *Collectivism*, translated by Sir Arthur Clay, N.Y., 1908.

[2] See the argument on p. 17 that 'great trusts are one of the most characteristic and in some ways the most triumphant forms of individualism.'

[3] P. 329.

CHAPTER NINE

The Nineteenth Century

Property and law are born together and must die together. Before the laws there was no property: take away the laws, all property ceases.

. . . . .

Secure to the cultivator the fruits of his labour, and you most probably have done enough.

Jeremy Bentham, *Principles of the Civil Code.*

In political economy there is a current confusion between two very different kinds of private property, one of which is based upon the producer's own labour, whilst the other is based upon the exploitation of the labour of others.

Karl Marx, *Capital.*

Eighteenth-century liberalism adopted as its official doctrine the natural rights theory of property. In the nineteenth century, liberals were as likely to quote the utilitarian formula which had been popularized by Jeremy Bentham, but which had been stated by David Hume as early as 1739.[1]

Against all theories of formal right Hume urged the principle of utility—the rules of justice are conventions which experience has shown to be useful for the promotion of happiness. We obey them, not because we are obligated, but because our self-interest leads us to promote our own happiness in promoting that of the public. Applying this general principle to property, Hume argued that private ownership and its laws had no other origin or justification than utility. If we suppose a society in which nature granted an unlimited supply of goods, we can see that there no laws of property would arise. 'For what purpose make a partition of goods, when every one has already more than enough? . . .

[1] The origins of the Benthamite philosophy are discussed in the two principal authorities, Sir Leslie Stephen, *The English Utilitarians*, 2 vols., London, 1900, and E. Halévy, *The Growth of Philosophical Radicalism*, English translation, N.Y., 1928.

Why call this object *mine*, when, upon the seizing of it by another, I need but stretch out my hand to possess myself of what is equally valuable? Justice, in that case, being totally USELESS, would be an idle ceremonial.'[1] Also, if everyone felt the same interest for others as for himself, laws of property would be useless; and in times of famine and war, the laws of property are in fact suspended because they are no longer useful: 'can we imagine that men will see any means of preservation before them, and lose their lives, from a scrupulous regard to what, in other situations, would be the rules of equity and justice?'[2] But in fact men are not commonly found in these extreme situations. They are by nature selfish, but capable of perceiving the advantages of respecting the interests of others: nature is not liberal, but by labour men can produce an abundance. 'Hence the ideas of property become necessary in civil society: Hence justice derives its usefulness to the public: And hence alone arises its merit and moral obligation.'[3]

Against the Lockean theory Hume protested that labour cannot be joined to an object except in a figurative sense: labour merely alters the original object.[4] Moreover, the connection between the labourer and the object of his labour imposes no obligation on other men to regard that object as his property: at most it leads to an association of ideas out of which the concept of property is born.[5] With the theory of Grotius, that property is a convention, Hume indicates his agreement, provided that convention is properly defined, not as a promise—for what obliges us to keep promises?—but as a sense of common interest which leads each man, 'in concurrence with others, into a general plan or system of actions, which tends to public utility. . . .'[6]

The laws of property, then, are conventions which men obey because it is to their common interest to do so. But what parti-

[1] *Essays, Moral, Political, and Literary*, edited by T. H. Green and T. H. Grose, 2 vols., London, 1875, p. 180. Hume's most important statements about property are found in this essay, 'Of Justice.'

[2] Pp. 180–3.

[3] P. 183.

[4] *Treatise of Human Nature* (1739–40), Everyman edition, Vol. II, p. 209, n. 1.

[5] Pp. 206–16. *Essays*, Vol. II, p. 277, n. 1.

[6] *Essays*, Vol. II, pp. 274–5.

cular pattern of ownership is most useful? Some men, Hume recalled, have preached that a man's property ought to be proportionate to his virtue.

But were mankind to execute such a law; so great is the uncertainty of merit, both from its natural obscurity, and from the self-conceit of each individual, that no determinate rule of conduct would ever result from it; and the total dissolution of society must be the immediate consequence. Fanatics may suppose, *that dominion is founded on grace*, and *that saints alone inherit the earth*; but the civil magistrate very justly puts these sublime theorists on the same footing with common robbers. . . .[1]

Other theorists have argued, Hume continues, that an absolutely equal division of property would produce the greatest happiness.

It must, indeed, be confessed, that nature is so liberal to mankind, that, were all her presents equally divided among the species, and improved by art and industry, every individual would enjoy all the necessaries, and even most of the comforts of life; nor would ever be liable to any ills, but such as might accidentally arise from the sickly frame and constitution of his body. It must also be confessed, that, wherever we depart from this equality, we rob the poor of more satisfaction than we add to the rich, and that the slight gratification of a frivolous vanity, in one individual, frequently costs more than bread to many families, and even provinces. It may appear withal, that the rule of equality, as it would be highly *useful*, is not altogether *impracticable*; but has taken place, at least in an imperfect degree, in some republics; particularly that of SPARTA; where it was attended, it is said, with the most beneficial consequences. . . . But historians, and even common sense, may inform us, that, however specious these ideas of *perfect* equality may seem, they are really, at bottom, *impracticable*; and were they not so, would be extremely *pernicious* to human society.[2]

Assuming that this equalitarian scheme would be introduced into a society where property was privately owned—Hume never considers seriously communistic theories—he finds several major

[1] P. 187.

[2] P. 188.

difficulties. Either the equality would be destroyed by men's varying exercise of thrift and industry, or the suppression of these virtues would result in universal misery; and the government would be either a tyranny, inquiring into every man's wealth and punishing those who have a penny too much, or anarchy, for levelling property would also level power.[1]

In the end, Hume adopted the conclusions of those philosophers whose arguments he had demolished. The true system of property, he concluded, is that which the theorists of natural right have defended, for the wrong reasons.

> Who sees not . . . that whatever is produced or improved by a man's art or industry ought, for ever, to be secured to him, in order to give encouragement to such *useful* habits and accomplishments? That the property ought also to descend to children and relations, for the same *useful* purpose? That it may be alienated by consent, in order to beget that commerce and intercourse which is so *beneficial* to human society? And that all contracts and promises ought carefully to be fulfilled, in order to secure mutual trust and confidence, by which the general *interest* of mankind is so much promoted?
>
> Examine the writers on the laws of nature; and you will always find, that, whatever principles they set out with, they are sure to terminate here at last, and to assign, as the ultimate reason for every rule which they establish, the convenience and necessities of mankind. . . . What other reason, indeed, could writers ever give, why this must be *mine* and that *yours*; since uninstructed nature, surely, never made any such distinction?[2]

That Hume should come, by a different path, to the same end as John Locke is not surprising: they were both defending the same social system, they were both admirers of that economic society which Adam Smith was to describe so persuasively, they agreed that the protection of free, individual property was the chief end of the state.[3] The Utilitarians from the beginning had no quarrel with the aims of the natural rights theorists.

But their new arguments led in some cases to slightly different

[1] Pp. 188–9.

[2] P. 189.

[3] *Treatise of Human Nature*, Vol. II, pp. 196–7.

conclusions. For one thing, Hume's theory put more power into the hands of the state, which is the guardian of the general welfare. 'All questions of property,' he wrote, 'are subordinate to authority of civil laws. . . .'[1] Such a theory accorded well with political fact in eighteenth-century England where no constitution or Bill of Rights protected the property-owner from an omnipotent Parliament; but it might serve as an attack on property if that Parliament should become the instrument of propertyless men. Secondly, Hume's theory presented a new argument for equality: equality, he admitted, would bring the greatest happiness if the problems of incentive and political organization did not oppose practical difficulties. Later theorists could claim that those problems could be solved and demand economic equality on Hume's principle. Hume himself shared the liberal belief that a large measure of equality was desirable and that it would in fact result from the operation of laws which secured to each man the fruits of his industry.[2] Finally, Hume's theory could also serve as a defence of inequality: against the radical interpreters of natural right who wished to abolish the kinds of property which deprived men of the fruits of their labour, the utilitarian could argue that these forms of property promoted the general welfare and were more useful in the particular circumstances than the principle of awarding property to the workman who made it. The utilitarian theory was eventually used in all these ways, but for the moment Hume had supplied a new argument for the protection of the property system of his day. Locke and his followers were always convinced that natural right harmonized with utility; Hume added that utility alone justified the laws which the insufficient theory of natural right had tried to sustain.

But as early as 1768 the radical implications of the utilitarian theory were becoming apparent. Joseph Priestley's *Essay on the First Principles of Government* adopted Hume's argument that 'nothing is properly *a man's own*, but what general rules, which

[1] *Essays*, Vol. II, p. 190, and p. 191, n. 2.
[2] *Essays*, Vol. I, 'Of Commerce.'

have for their object the good of the whole, give to him.'[1] Priestley agreed that utility prescribed securing to each the reward of his industry.[2] But he also emphasized that it was the duty of the state to revoke those rights of property which did not contribute to the general welfare.[3] The implications of that emphasis, especially when coming from a Priestley, were radical.

A few years later, a whole-heartedly conservative interpretation of the utilitarian theory was published by the famous divine, William Paley. Paley began with a striking paragraph outlining the apparent absurdities of the system of unequal private ownership.

If you should see a flock of pigeons in a field of corn; and if (instead of each picking where and what it liked, taking just as much as it wanted, and no more) you should see ninety-nine of them gathering all they got into a heap; reserving nothing for themselves but the chaff and the refuse; keeping this heap for one, and that the weakest perhaps, and worst pigeon of the flock; sitting round and looking on all the winter, whilst this one was devouring, throwing about, and wasting it; and if a pigeon, more hardy or hungry than the rest, touched a grain of the hoard, all the others instantly flying upon it, and tearing it to pieces: if you should see this, you would see nothing more than what is every day practised and established among men. Among men, you see the ninety and nine toiling and scraping together a heap of superfluities for one, getting nothing for themselves all the while, but a little of the coarsest of the provision which their own labour produces (and this one, too, oftentimes the feeblest and worst of the whole set—a child, a woman, a madman, or a fool); looking quietly on, while they see the fruits of their labour spent or spoiled; and if one of them take or touch a particle of it, the others join against him, and hang him for the theft.[4]

The paradoxical truth, Paley concluded, is that such a state of affairs is advantageous for everyone, because it supplies the necessary incentive to make men produce. Even the poorest 'in

[1] Second edition, London, 1771, p. 41.

[2] P. 69.

[3] P. 41.

[4] *The Principles of Moral and Political Philosophy* (1785), London, 1817, pp. 68–9.

countries where property and the consequences of property prevail' are better off than any inhabitants of lands where most property is common.[1]

Paley's argument was striking, but it contained a logical flaw. He supported the principle that men should enjoy the fruits of their own labour because it incited them to industry; he agreed that inequality was an evil, on utilitarian grounds, but that the inequality inherent in rewarding men according to their different talents was necessary; he agreed, finally, that inequalities which do not arise from differences of labour ought to be abolished.[2] But the figure of the remarkable society of pigeons expressly stated that the workmen did not enjoy the fruits of their labour in modern society. The conclusion appears inescapable: eighteenth-century society violates both the principles of utility and those of natural right, and, since it is the business of the state to establish useful rules relating to property,[3] property ought to be redistributed by law. Paley, of course, drew no such conclusion and persistently ignored the flaw in his own theory.[4]

Jeremy Bentham and his disciples added little to the theory of property propounded by Hume and Paley. But it was their writings which made it popular. Englishmen wanted a theory which would sustain liberal reforms but ward off revolution. The natural rights theory, connected in men's minds with the Revolution in France, was not respectable; the Benthamites publicized the utilitarian theory and it served the purpose.

Bentham himself pointed out the inadequacies and dangers of the natural rights theory. Analysing the Declaration of Rights, he argued that the famous 'right of property' implies that everyone ought to have some property—a radical conclusion; that all property is sacred—even that which conflicts with the general welfare; and that it puts an end to many activities of government, for it asserts that property shall only be taken for 'public necessities,' but many of the actions of government are merely

[1] P. 71. [2] Pp. 56, 71. [3] P. 76.

[4] The chapters on rent, profits, and wages do not raise the question of how these are related to labour.

convenient.[1] The entire concept of natural right, he concluded, is a logical muddle which leads to hopeless tangles in practice. There is no natural property.[2] Rights are no more than rules of utility defined by law. 'Rights are . . . the fruits of law, and of the law alone. There are no rights without law—no rights contrary to law—no rights anterior to the law.'[3] 'Property and law are born and must die together.'[4]

Bentham accepted the conclusion of the earlier utilitarians that an equal distribution of wealth, other considerations aside, would provide the greatest happiness. Assuming that men were equally susceptible of pleasure and pain—a necessary assumption if the utilitarian calculus was not to be hopelessly complex—he worked out the principles of marginal utility and proved that a particle of wealth would always give most pleasure to the man who had least. It followed that in distributing wealth the legislator ought to strive for equality.[5]

But, Bentham added at once, there always are other considerations, and equality is only one of the aims of the utilitarian legislator. Equality of wealth, for instance, will not produce happiness if there is no wealth to equalize. The legislator must first make sure that men will work and produce. Once again Bentham followed the example of Hume and Paley and asserted that in order to incite men to work the law ought to secure to each man the results of his industry. Locke had argued that this was a principle of natural right; Bentham and his predecessors accepted it as a counsel of utility.

In legislation, the most important object is security. If no direct laws are made respecting subsistence, this object will be neglected by no one. But if there are no laws respecting security, it will be useless to have made laws respecting subsistence: command production—

[1] *Anarchical Fallacies*, especially pp. 503, 521, 532, in *Works*, edited by John Bowring, Vol. II, Edinburgh, 1843.

[2] *Principles of the Civil Code*, *Works*, Vol. I, p. 308.

[3] *Pannomial Fragments*, *Works*, Vol. III, p. 221.

[4] *Principles of the Civil Code*, *Works*, Vol. I, p. 309.

[5] *Principles of the Civil Code*, *Works*, Vol. I, pp. 305–6; *Pannomial Fragments*, *Works*, Vol. III, pp. 228–30.

command cultivation, you will have done nothing: but secure to the cultivator the fruits of his labour, and you most probably have done enough.[1]

Over and over again the *Principles of the Civil Code* insisted that the security of the workman, the guarantee that he will enjoy the rewards of his work, is a more important end of the law than equality. Following Hume, Bentham assumed that the equalitarians wished to divide all wealth equally within the framework of a system of private ownership. He repeated all of Hume's remarks on the absurdities and iniquities of such a scheme and added a few of his own: all large libraries, museum collections, laboratories, as well as all concentrations of capital needed to carry on large enterprises, would have to be dispersed.[2]

Sometimes, in his eagerness to avoid revolutionary conclusions, Bentham concluded that any system of secure ownership, even one which did not award things to their creators, was inviolate. Any system is better than the anarchy which will follow from its sudden subversion.[3]

In consulting the grand principle of security, what ought the legislator to direct with regard to the mass of property which exists? He ought to maintain the distribution which is actually established. . . . There is nothing more diversified than the condition of property in America, England, Hungary, Russia: in the first country the cultivator is proprietor; in the second he is a farmer; in the third he is attached to the soil; in the fourth he is a slave. Still the supreme principle of security directs the preservation of all these distributions, how different soever their natures, and though they do not produce the same amount of happiness. . . . When security and equality are in opposition, there should be no hesitation: equality should give way. . . . The establishment of equality is a chimera: the only thing which can be done is to diminish inequality.[4]

[1] *Principles of the Civil Code*, *Works*, Vol. I, p. 303.

[2] *Principles of the Civil Code*, *Works*, Vol. I, pp. 311–12, and appendix 'On the Levelling System,' pp. 358 ff. Bentham put all these arguments against levelling into a manuscript entitled *Radicalism Not Dangerous* which is now printed in the *Works*, Vol. III.

[3] *Principles of the Civil Code*, *Works*, Vol. I, p. 309.

[4] P. 311.

These words, however, do not mean that Bentham had abandoned his belief in the utility of equality or in the wisdom of protecting the labourer in the enjoyment of his produce. They merely emphasize his belief that progress should follow the path of gradual reform rather than violent revolution. He had a number of schemes for abolishing useless rights and injurious concentrations of wealth which would not violate the principle of security. By a judicious regulation of inheritance, he wrote, large fortunes may be dispersed without depriving present proprietors or seriously violating the expectations of heirs.[1] Confiscation is always an unwise policy, but the same ends may be accomplished in other and more gradual ways. Henry VIII was right in thinking the monasteries ought to be dissolved, but instead of confiscating the property at one swoop, he should have taken the slower method of forbidding the various houses to accept new members: in the end the property would have fallen to the crown and no one would have been alarmed or injured. Annuities and pensions can always be used to cushion the shock which accompanies the abolition of old rights.[2]

But more important than these politic devices, Bentham thought, were the economic doctrines of Adam Smith and the classical school. A large measure of equality, and the proper distribution of goods in accordance with industry, will automatically result from the spontaneous action of economic law if the absurd hangovers of feudalism and mercantilist policy are abandoned.

> If the laws do not oppose it—if they do not maintain monopolies—if they do not restrain trade and its exchanges—if they do not permit entails—large properties will be seen, without effort, without revolutions, without shock, to subdivide themselves by little and little, and a much greater number of individuals will participate in the advantage of moderate fortunes.[3]

[1] P. 312. Bentham's complicated schemes for regulating inheritance are found on pp. 334 ff.

[2] P. 320. Bentham likewise condemned the French, not for confiscating the property of the Church, but for doing it without regard to the principle of security; Halévy, *Growth of Philosophical Radicalism*, p. 172.

[3] *Principles of the Civil Code*, *Works*, Vol. I, p. 312.

A moderate inequality, coupled with a large number of middle-sized fortunes will be the ideal result of this policy.[1] Utilitarianism rejected the metaphysical arguments of the natural rights school; but it accepted the practical doctrines which the natural rights theory of property sustained. Whatever their differences, utilitarians and natural right theorists were all advocates of middle-class liberalism. They could agree that 'the greatest possible happiness of society is attained by insuring to every man the greatest possible quantity of the produce of his labour.'[2]

Thus it was not strange that the classical economists of the early nineteenth century were both utilitarians, and exponents of the rights of property as those were defined in the Lockean tradition. The idea that each man ought to own what his industry created was, according to one's philosophical preferences, either a rule of natural justice or a correct counsel of expediency. Ricardo and his interpreters could defend private ownership on either ground. Their only problem was to demonstrate that a liberal economic society did in fact distribute property on this principle.

The coalescence of the conclusions of natural right and utility in classical economic thought is clearly demonstrated in one of the last important texts of that school. John Stuart Mill's *Principles of Political Economy* stated:

> The institution of property, when limited to its essential elements consists in the recognition, in each person, of a right to the exclusive disposal of what he or she have produced by their own exertions, or received either by gift or fair agreement, without force or fraud, from those who produced it. The foundation of the whole is the right of producers to what they themselves have produced.[3]

Mill's work is also a good example of the difficulties which

[1] *Pannomial Fragments*, *Works*, Vol. III, p. 230.

[2] James Mill, article on 'Government' in the supplement to the fifth edition of the *Encyclopaedia Britannica* (1816–32), reprinted in E. A. Burtt, *English Philosophers from Bacon to Mill*, Modern Library, N.Y., 1939, p. 859.

[3] *Principles of Political Economy*, edited by W. J. Ashley, London, 1909, p. 218. This text includes all of Mill's revisions through the last edition in 1871.

beset the attempt to justify existing institutions of property by this combination of natural right and utilitarian theory. He himself accepted the logical conclusion that landed property could not be justified by this theory, unless the proprietor were also the cultivator.[1] He recognized that large transfers of property by inheritance might result in divorcing ownership from labour.[2] He still clung to the Ricardian tradition which attempted to define capital in such a way that profits would be justified as payments for labour expended, although in one case he spoke of profits as 'tribute' paid by workmen 'out of the produce of their industry.'[3] Nevertheless, the organization of the working classes of Europe and the development of socialist theory had proceeded so far by Mill's time that he was attracted by the possibility of securing to each the fruits of his labour by abolishing private ownership in the means of production.[4] He saw no insuperable difficulties in a socialist reconstruction of society and suggested

> that if the institution of private property necessarily carried with it as a consequence, that the produce of labour should be apportioned as we now see it, almost in an inverse ratio to the labour. . . , if this or communism were the alternative, all the difficulties, great or small, of communism would be but as dust in the balance.[5]

But Mill was convinced that the system of private property, properly reformed, might still be made to work for the general welfare, although he prophesied that at some time in the future capital would be collectively owned.[6] Consistently a friend of reform and an enemy of revolution, Mill might properly be called one of the first Fabian socialists.

After Mill many economists, unwilling either to accept the reforms which he regarded as necessary if property was to be justified on the usual utilitarian grounds, or to recognize the possible advantages of a socialist reconstruction, abandoned the

[1] Pp. 230–1. [2] Pp. 221–9. [3] Pp. 773–4.

[4] The story of Mill's growing interest in socialist theory is recorded in his *Autobiography* (1873), World's Classics, and in the additions which he made to the discussion of socialism in the later editions of the *Principles*.

[5] *Principles*, p. 208. [6] P. 773.

theory that property ought to be the property of the producer. Recognizing that modern economic systems do not distribute property in accordance with that theory, they argued that the present system was still justified on the grounds of utility since it provided for the maximum of production. By substituting 'production' for 'happiness' they were able to maintain the general arguments based on utility and yet discard the natural right concept of the proper relation between work and ownership. The history of this development, and particularly the story of how the classical labour theory of value was replaced by the theory of marginal utility, has been described by the historians of economic thought. But a few quotations from some of the better-known texts of modern economic theory will suffice here to indicate how the old natural rights theory of property came to be abandoned by modern utilitarians.

In his *Principles of Economics*, Alfred Marshall noted that

> the tendency of careful economic study is to base the rights of property, not on any abstract principles, but on the observation that in the past they have been inseparable from solid progress; and therefore it is the part of responsible men to proceed cautiously and tentatively in abrogating or modifying even such rights as may seem to be inappropriate to the ideal conditions of social life.[1]

The same idea was expressed more vigorously by F. W. Taussig in his *Principles of Economics*—for many years the standard textbook in American colleges.

> The theory that property rests on labour, and therefore on what is conceived to be the 'natural' right of each man to that which he has produced, has gone into the lumber room of discarded theories. It was elaborated by Locke, accepted more or less through the eighteenth century, and used freely by the English economists of the first half of the nineteenth century. But it plays little part in modern discussion. 'Natural' rights have quite gone out of fashion. Where there is a highly complex division of labour, such as characterizes existing society, it is impossible to distinguish how much any one individual has contributed to the whole output—to say, this is his specific output,

[1] Eighth edition, London, 1938, p. 48

therefore rightly his property. Even if it were possible so to distinguish, no natural or inherent right would thereby be established. Least of all is it possible on such reasoning to justify inheritance. As the institution of inheritance can be sustained only on a basis of utilitarianism, so can that of property in general.[1]

Modern economists, Taussig concludes, have demonstrated that men ought to be paid, as on the whole they are, 'according to what they contribute to society; or, to be accurate, according to the marginal contribution of their sort of labour.'[2]

These statements indicate that the utilitarian theory of property was redefined in such a way as to leave out the natural right thesis, which the early classical economists had accepted, that property should belong to the producer. They also indicate that the redefinition was made necessary, in part, by the difficulty of applying the natural right theory to modern society without concluding that much modern property was unjustified. The fact that influential socialist thinkers had adopted the natural rights theory and used it as an argument for socialism helps to explain why the defenders of capitalism abandoned that theory.

The works of Herbert Spencer, one of the most popular nineteenth-century exponents of *laissez-faire*, illustrate the difficulties which beset the conservative exponents of natural right. Spencer began as a defender of the natural right of property; he ended as an advocate of the principle of utility, flavoured with a dash of Darwinianism which robbed it of all equalitarian tendencies. His first important work, *Social Statics* (1850), accepted the Lockean theory of property as that had been developed by the agrarian radicals: labour establishes a natural claim to property, but not to land because land is not created by labour and its appropriation leads to a monopoly which destroys equality of right.[3] Spencer concluded that the only just policy was for the state to resume ownership of the land and rent it to individuals. He apparently thought all other property in the England of 1850

[1] Third edition, Vol. I, N.Y., 1921, p. 273.

[2] P. 477.

[3] *Social Statics*, N.Y., 1880, pp. 131–54. Pp. 111–12 ridicule the Benthamites for their rejection of natural right.

conformed to the principles of natural right and had nothing to say about it except that its owners ought to have complete freedom to use it as they chose: he was already the champion of the most ruthless policies of *laissez-faire*.

But by the 1880's Spencer had virtually abandoned his earlier theory of property. In *Man versus the State* (1884) he identified natural law with the biological concepts of struggle for existence and survival of the fittest, denounced all forms of state interference with private property as violations of this new natural law, and castigated Henry George, whose theory of social ownership of the land he had once defended.[1] Finally, in *Justice* (1891) he once more observed that, by the dictum of the absolutist ethics of natural right, land ought to be owned by society. But he now gave a number of remarkable arguments to prove that the landowners had in fact paid for their exclusive right so that no real violation of the theoretical rights of property had taken place.[2] Finally, he resorted to the argument of utility in its Darwinian dress. The present system suffices to maintain that 'natural discipline by which every kind of creature is kept fit for the activities demanded by the conditions of life,'[3] and any radical change in the property system, however 'equitable in the abstract,' would result in a state of things 'less desirable' than the present one.[4]

Spencer's ultimate conclusion was that the system of *laissez-faire* is the most useful because it gives free play to the natural principle of the survival of the fittest: all state interference with the economic system upsets this principle. Nevertheless he was never able to free himself entirely from the old concept that the most useful system of property was the same as the natural right

[1] *Man versus the State* was reprinted in N.Y. in 1892 with an abridged edition of *Social Statics* which omitted all the original passages about the natural right of property.

[2] American edition, N.Y., 1891, chs. xi and xii, and Appendix B. Here he confesses that he 'overlooked' these arguments in 1850. In 1892 he printed the arguments from *Social Statics* and his answers to them, from *Justice*, in parallel columns in a volume called *Mr. Herbert Spencer on the Land Question*.

[3] P. 101.

[4] P. 270

system which guaranteed to each the produce of his labour. In economic terms, natural selection means either that the best man wins in a race in which the rules are the same for all, or that the strong make the rules for their own benefit and take whatever they want. Spencer apparently chose the first alternative and always asserted that natural justice consists in guaranteeing to each man the benefits which his effort has created.[1] He attacked socialists and liberal reformers alike for denying 'that each man should receive benefits proportionate to his efforts.'[2] But his consistent refusal to consider whether the economic system of England in the eighteen-eighties did observe this rule of justice, his apparent ignorance of those socialist writers who denied that capitalism was consistent with the liberal theory of property, make it obvious that he actually chose the second alternative and praised *laissez-faire* as a system of natural warfare in which the strong devoured the weak. It is this conflict in his own thinking which accounts for the rapid decline of his popularity. Once widely heralded as the prophet of *laissez-faire*, his admirers quickly discovered that his acceptance of the natural right theory of property could be turned against the very institutions which he had so strenuously defended.[3]

The principal non-socialist writers, except for the Spencerians, rejected the natural right theory of property and thereby closed a chapter in the history of that theory. But the new utilitarian theory could also be used as the basis of a socialist argument and it was quickly adapted to that purpose. As early as 1793 William Godwin had emphasized the radical equalitarian implications of the greatest happiness principle. Rejecting the theory that every man has an exclusive right to the property he creates, Godwin wrote that 'every man has a right to that, the exclusive possession

[1] For example, in *Justice*, pp. 98, 100. [2] P. 100.

[3] William Graham Sumner and Thomas Nixon Carver elaborated versions of the Spencerian theory and became entangled in the same difficulty: they rejected natural right for utility, yet defended capitalism because it insured 'that each shall enjoy the fruit of his labour.' For Sumner, see especially 'The Challenge of Facts,' in *Essays*, edited by A. G. Keller and M. R. Davie, Yale, 1934, Vol. II; for Carver, see especially *Essays in Social Justice*, Cambridge, Mass., 1915, ch. v.

of which being awarded to him, a greater sum of benefit or pleasure will result, than could have arisen from its being otherwise appropriated.'[1] Since men are equal in their wants, it follows that an equal distribution would be the most beneficial. Godwin was firmly convinced that men could be educated to operate an equalitarian, communistic organization of economic society. Many English socialists in the nineteenth century began as disciples of Bentham. In modern times the Fabians, who substituted marginal utility for the classical labour theory of value and argued that a socialist redistribution of wealth was desirable, not primarily because it would secure to each man the fruit of his industry, but because it would produce a maximum of happiness, were following the pathway of English and Utilitarian radicalism.[2]

Interpreted conservatively or radically, the utilitarian theory of property became a serious rival of the natural right theory, not only in England, but in other parts of the world as well.[3] Meanwhile, another attack on the philosophy of individual rights, including the natural right of property, was gaining a wide audience. The theory of the organic state, revived by Rousseau and developed by Hegel and the German Idealists, popularized once again the old theory that property is a creation of the state.

The outlines of this Idealist version of the old theory were indicated in the political writings of Kant. In the *Principles of*

[1] *Political Justice* (1793), Philadelphia, 1796, Bk. VIII, "Of Property."

[2] The best general accounts of the Fabians are Edward Pease, *History of the Fabian Society*, N.Y., 1928; M. Beer, *History of British Socialism*, 2 vols., new edition, London, 1929. Their economic theory was set down in *Fabian Essays*, by Shaw, Webb and others, London, 1889. One of the clearest statements of the utilitarian, as opposed to the natural right, arguments for socialist redistribution is to be found in an early work by the recent Labour Chancellor of the Exchequer: Hugh Dalton, *Some Aspects of the Inequality of Incomes in Modern Communities*, London, 1920. R. H. Tawney, *Equality*, 3rd edition, London, 1938, is one of the most persuasive defences of a large measure of equality as a rule justified by the general welfare.

[3] Examples are given in B. F. Wright, *American Interpretations of Natural Law*, Cambridge, Mass., 1931, chs. viii and x, and with particular reference to the theory of property in Richard Ely, *Property and Contract*, N.Y., 1914. Ely adopted the utilitarian theory of property and rejected the natural right theory: see Vol. I, pp. 543–5.

Political Right (1793), he adopted some of the major premises of liberal thought: justice requires that men enjoy equality of right; equality of right entails inequality of possessions since these ought to be the rewards of talent.[1] Three years later, in the *Philosophy of Law*, Kant outlined in more detail his theory of property. A man, he wrote, acquires property not by the mechanical operation of mixing his labour with external things, but by the transcendental operation of directing his will upon a given object.[2] But because no man is obliged to respect my will unless I respect his, there must be a union of wills—the recognition of a general will, Rousseau had said—which can convert the individual's possession into right. 'In a word, the mode in which anything external may be held as one's own in the *state of nature*, is just *physical* possession with a presumption of right thus far in its favour, that by union of the Wills of all in a public Legislature, it will be made juridical. . . .'[3] Kant assumed, as Rousseau had done and the later Idealists did, that the general will would in all normal circumstances substantiate the claims of the individual owner; but it was inherent in the theory that property was a social creation and subject to social control.

The ideas which Rousseau had revived and Kant had touched upon were developed by Hegel and became the standard Idealist theory of property. 'A person,' Hegel wrote, 'has the right to direct his will upon any object as his real and positive end. The object thus becomes his. As it has no end in itself, it receives its meaning and soul from his will.'[4] The appropriation of things as private property is one of the important ways in which the individual will objectifies itself and realizes external freedom; hence private property is an institution essential for the realization of liberty. If two or more individuals own things in common, freedom is limited since no one of them can direct those things

[1] English translation by W. Hastie, Edinburgh, 1891, especially pp. 38, 41, and 44.

[2] English translation by W. Hastie, Edinburgh, 1887, p. 92.

[3] P. 79.

[4] *Philosophy of Right* (1821), translation by S. W. Dyde, London, 1896, p. 51.

entirely according to his will and ends. Plato was wrong in supposing that the ideal man owned nothing, because ownership is included in the idea of spiritual freedom. Modern states did wisely in destroying monasticism: by assigning monastic property to individual owners they extended liberty.[1] For the same reason feudal property was inferior to modern property: it belonged to more than one person and entailed a confusion and limitation of wills, a confusion and limitation of freedom. The abolition of feudal property was as great a triumph of freedom as the abolition of slavery.[2] Like Kant, Hegel rejected the Lockean theory of labour and insisted that the act of willing was sufficient to establish title; and he remarked that the labour theory could not justify the appropriation of land, since this was not created by labour, but that appropriation by an act of the will could be applied to the earth as well as to other things.[3]

Unlike Kant, Hegel did not insist that men must have the consent of others before appropriating the common property. But he arrived at the same conclusions about the power of the state by a slightly different route. In the political philosophy of the Idealists the individual was not the only embodiment of spirit. The family, corporate bodies of various kinds, and the national state itself are the embodiments of corporate spirits or general wills whose claims are superior to those of the individual, for it is only as a member of society, and particularly as a citizen of a national state, that the individual can enjoy freedom. By this reasoning Hegel was able to state, as Rousseau had done before, that individual rights of property do not hold good against the commands of the state, of the general will. The rights of owners are always subject to the 'higher spheres of right, to a corporate body, e.g., or to the state.'[4] In fact, once political society has been established, the law alone determines ownership.[5]

But if in the end Hegel concluded that the rights of property are defined by the state, he did not mean that the state might define those rights arbitrarily. The rule that the individual enjoys

[1] Pp. 48–9, 52–3.

[2] Pp. 65–8.

[3] Pp. 58 and 61.

[4] P. 53.

[5] P. 214.

perfect freedom only when he has absolute control over a portion of the external world still holds good; the state consequently must favour private rather than communal ownership. To this Hegel added that justice requires an unequal division since human personalities are unequal and need unequal amounts of things to realize their fullest development.[1] In practice, then, the state confines itself to establishing modern absolute property in order to ensure the greatest possible amount of freedom, and interferes with established rights only when these have ceased to fulfil their proper function. The state, for example, could extinguish the rights of monastic houses because during the Reformation 'the spirit of confession and therefore of these buildings had fled'[2] and the legal right no longer expressed an actual realization of will.

Hegel's political thinking was part of a general reaction against the philosophy of natural right and the ideas of the era of middle-class revolution, and his theory of property became one of the principal rivals of the classical liberal theory of Locke. It was a revival in part of the traditional theory of convention. But it could be used to justify any number of different systems of property. In the first part of the nineteenth century the German economists who preached a doctrine of mystical nationalism agreed with Hegel that property should be divided unequally among individuals, but that private rights are always subordinate to the demands of the totalitarian state.[3] In the course of time the Hegelian concept of property was adopted by the apologists for Prussian autocracy, Italian Fascism, and National Socialism.[4] In these cases it served as a defence of private ownership, a justification of state regulation for the purpose of developing military power, and particularly as an answer to the critics of *laissez-faire* liberalism who pointed out that the freedom granted to property-owners injured other men. The Hegelians agreed that private

1 Pp. 55–6.

2 Pp. 69–70.

3 Eric Roll, *History of Economic Thought*, 2nd edition, N.Y., 1942, ch. vi, is a good survey of the doctrines of the German romantic economists.

4 The development of Hegelian thought is outlined in G. H. Sabine, *History of Political Thought*, N.Y., 1937.

rights should be subject to social control; the Nazis adopted the principle in their propaganda and used it to bolster their pretence that they were socialists whose purpose was to rescue the working man from the tyranny of capitalist property.[1]

Another interpretation of Hegel's theory of property was expounded by his English admirers in the latter part of the nineteenth century. The school of Oxford Idealists, led by Thomas Hill Green, were heirs of the middle-class liberal tradition. But they were aware that the evils of industrial capitalism, which had already made government regulation a practical political necessity, also necessitated a revision of the old liberal doctrine that all property rights are sacred. The theory of Hegel was admirably suited to their purpose. By balancing the idea of property as a necessary expression of personality, against the idea of the state as the instrument of the general will and the guardian of the general welfare, the neo-Hegelians produced a justification of capitalism and state regulation admirably adapted to the middle-class temper of the eighties and nineties. Green himself held the balance between freedom for property and state regulation fairly evenly.[2] Other followers of Hegel tended to weight one or the other. David Ritchie stressed the idea of the general will and reached conclusions similar to those of the Fabian socialists.[3] Bernard Bosanquet emphasized the idea that property is a necessary instrument of personal development and supported a programme of Tory philanthropy.[4]

But whichever aspect of Hegel's theory of property his English disciples preferred to stress, the idea that ownership is essential for individual liberty always prevented them from adopting a full

[1] The whole theory is stated by Dr. Heinrich Brunner in *Die Wirtschaftsphilosophie Fichtes*, Nürnberg, 1935, as well as in the better known treatises of Nazi economists.

[2] His views are expressed in his *Principles of Political Obligation*, in *Works*, Vol. II, 2nd edition, London, 1889.

[3] His general theory is expounded in *Principles of State Interference*, London, 1891, and *Natural Rights*, London, 1895.

[4] *Aspects of the Social Problem*, 'The Principle of Private Property,' London, 1895, and *The Philosophical Theory of the State*, London, 1899, 3rd edition, 1920.

socialist theory. They made use of Hegel's conclusion that all men should have property since each has a personality to express,[1] to urge state regulation and social legislation. The authors, most of whom accepted the philosophical tenets of Idealism, of *Property, Its Duties and Rights*,[2] were severely critical of unregulated capitalism, and criticized Hegel for his failure to probe the problem of how conflicts between persons who had a reasonable claim to the same thing should be settled.[3] They recognized that modern socialist theory does not demand the abolition of private property. 'Professor Bosanquet and many other philosophical critics of Socialism seem to forget that Socialism does not aim at the extinction of private property but only at that of private capital. Under any scheme which is socialistic without being communistic, private property might very well exist in the only sense in which the vast majority of . . . employees now own property.'[4] But in the end most of these writers concluded that private ownership, however regulated, of all kinds of property, including capital, is necessary if people, or at least some people, are to enjoy full liberty. 'It may be of extreme importance that *some* should enjoy liberty—that it should be possible for some few men to be able to dispose of their time in their own way—although such liberty may be neither possible nor desirable for the great majority.'[5]

The Hegelian theory, then, like the Lockean identifies property with liberty. It supports, as the pure Lockean doctrine does not, a large amount of state regulation. But it is likely to balk at the complete elimination of private capital and to maintain that a regulated capitalism, while providing the same security for the mass of people as socialism, will in addition preserve that freedom

1 *Philosophy of Right*, p. 56.

2 Second edition, with an Introduction by Charles Gore, Bishop of Oxford, N.Y., 1922.

3 'The Philosophical Theory of Property,' by Hastings Rashdall, p. 56.

4 The same, p. 66.

5 The same, p. 65. The essays by L. T. Hobhouse, A. D. Lindsay (now Lord Lindsay), and Henry Scott Holland, express the same general attitude toward property and personality.

for the few which the private ownership of capital now confers. In the twentieth century this version of the Hegelian theory has largely replaced the classical Lockean theory as a weapon against socialism: to-day we hear less frequently the argument that 'free enterprise' is the system of nature, and more often that it is the bulwark of liberty, while socialism is not often spoken of as a violation of natural right, but is frequently attacked as a return to serfdom.

Yet another attack on the natural rights theory of property grew out of the belief, which grew increasingly strong in the nineteenth century, that the historical method and the study of history are the only roads to an understanding of man and society. One of the characteristics of *Historismus* was its substitution of the doctrine of historical rights for the old theory of natural rights. In reaction against the philosophy of the revolutionary era, the historians, particularly in Germany where the new science of history enjoyed its greatest vogue, insisted that rights are no more than the persistent custom of a nation. Claims of right are not to be judged by comparing them with some criterion of universal and ideal justice, but by ascertaining whether or not they are an organic part of the traditional, national custom. The effect of the theory of historic rights was anti-revolutionary.

> Admitting that rights were founded in nature, it identified nature with history, and affirmed that the institutions of any nation were properly but an expression of the life of the people, no more than the crystallization of its tradition, the cumulative deposit of its experience, the résumé of its history. It implied that every people has, therefore, at any given time, the social order which nature has given it, the order which is on the whole best suited to its peculiar genius and circumstance, the order which is accordingly the embodiment of that freedom which it has achieved and the starting point for such further freedom as it may hope to attain. Welcomed because it opened the door to progress in terms of nationality while refusing admission to revolutionary methods, the new doctrine . . . became the accepted creed of all those who wished to be classed neither with the reactionaries nor with the revolutionists, those liberal-conservatives and

conservative-liberals who realized that they lived in a changing world but ardently prayed that it might not change too rapidly.[1]

The theory of property which grew from this historical philosophy was not unlike those of Burke and Hegel, and was in large part a conscious derivation from them. It denied that there was any one just right of property, any one system of property valid at all times and in all places, or any *a priori* method of determining what rights should be recognized here and now. For all this it substituted the idea that the best laws of property were those which protected the traditional and prescriptive rights which had evolved within the framework of each national culture. No doubt these rights would vary from age to age and from nation to nation; no doubt they would continue to change; but the change would be evolutionary, not revolutionary. The outlines of the new theory were set down by the distinguished legal authority, Friedrich Karl von Savigny, one of the creators and notable practitioners of the historical rights school, in a number of articles and historical works which were widely influential.[2] Adopted by historians and students of jurisprudence in country after country, the historical rights theory was one more attack on the theory of natural rights, one more rejection of that classical theory which had justified a middle-class revolution and was, now that revolutions were out of fashion, being discarded.

But like all the rivals of the theory of natural right, the new theory could also be turned to revolutionary ends and the opponents of the existing rights of property were not slow to seize the opportunity. The result was a furious debate, half historical and half political, which has not yet entirely subsided. All over Europe historians, mindful that they ought to investigate the origins of national institutions in order to understand and appraise them, industriously assembled and criticized the

[1] Carl Becker, *The Declaration of Independence*, N.Y., 1933, pp. 265–6.

[2] The article 'Savigny' by Hermann Kantorowicz in *The Encyclopedia of the Social Sciences* gives a concise account of the ideas of historic right. J. W. Thompson, *A History of Historical Writing*, Vol. II, New York, 1942, traces the development of the new historical concepts.

records of the early history of their nation. Particularly in Germany, the home of the new philosophy, historians were bent on defining the German national spirit as that which had been manifest in the forests of northern Europe before the culture of the south had influenced or corrupted it. One of their discoveries was the *Mark*, the free village community whose lands were jointly owned by all the freemen. Stimulated by the example of the Germans, investigators began to discover traces of primitive communal ownership everywhere, in England, Java, India, Russia, prehistoric Greece and Rome, and in Gaul.[1] Somewhat later the anthropologists joined in with evidence that communal ownership was typical of primitive societies.[2] Some of these investigations were works of sound scholarship whose conclusions, although much revised, are still acceptable. But their popularity rested on the fact that they reinforced ideas which men had previously adopted. Romantic disciples of Rousseau were delighted to find that the ideal state of nature had been an historical fact; German nationalists could prove that the Teutonic concept of property was different from the Roman Law idea of absolute ownership, or the French and English ideas of natural right and utility; Englishmen were less interested in the idea of common property, but English liberals were happy in the knowledge that the original Anglo-Saxon conquerors had been free men—serfdom and feudal privilege were not native creations but French importations. Everyone found something in the discovery of primitive communism which he could turn to his purpose. It was inevitable that socialists would seize the opportunity, particularly since the myth of the state of nature, which now seemed

[1] The literature is enormous. Some of the most noteworthy works are listed in Thompson, *History of Historical Writing*, Vol. II, in the Introduction and Bibliography to W. J. Ashley's edition of Fustel de Coulanges, *The Origin of Property in Land*, London, 1892, and scattered through the text of Sir Henry Maine's *Village Communities*, 7th edition, London, 1913. The first important German work on the *Mark* was G. L. von Maurer, *Geschichte der Markverfassung*, Erlangen, 1856.

[2] The most famous work was Lewis Morgan's *Ancient Society*, N.Y., 1877.

to be endowed with historical truth, had always been a fruitful source of communistic speculation.

In the seventies and eighties a number of socialist writers repeated and added to the evidence in favour of primitive communism and stated or implied that common ownership was in some sense the natural system of property, a system which had been destroyed by force and fraud.[1] In America, Henry George was quoting the historians to prove that 'historically, as ethically, private property in land is robbery'[2] and to demand a return to the primitive and natural system of common ownership. Marx had referred to the fact of primitive communism,[3] and in 1877 Engels had adopted it to illustrate the 'negation of the negation'—one of the mystic formulas of the dialectic, inherited from Hegel. Common ownership was the primitive form, he argued, and this was 'negated' into private property; the inevitable 'negation of the negation' will be common ownership, or socialism, sometime in the future.[4] But with the publication of Lewis Morgan's *Ancient Society* in 1877, Engles found a more fruitful method of using the evidence in favour of primitive communism. Morgan's work was, although the author had probably never heard of Marx, an almost perfect example of the Marxian historical method, and Engels at once wrote his *Origin of the Family, Private Property, and the State*,[5] based primarily on Morgan's research. Morgan himself had suggested the possibility of establishing a new system of property which would recapture some of the

[1] For example, Charles Letourneau, *L'Evolution de la Propriété*, Paris, 1889; E. de Laveleye, *On Property and Its Primitive Forms* (1874), English translation, London, 1878—perhaps the best-known of these works. Jan St. Lewinski, *The Origin of Property*, London, 1913, is a late volume belonging to the same tradition.

[2] *Progress and Poverty* (1879), Modern Library edition, p. 370. George quoted Laveleye, Maine, and the German scholar, E. Nasse.

[3] *A Contribution to the Critique of Political Economy* (1859), English translation, Chicago, 1904, p. 29.

[4] *Herr Eugen Dühring's Revolution in Science*, English translation, London, 1935, 'Dialectics, Negation of the Negation.'

[5] English translation, Chicago, 1902. For Morgan, and Engels' opinion of his work, see Ralph Gabriel, *The Course of American Democratic Thought*, N.Y., 1940, pp. 163–8.

values of the original system of common ownership, and Engels was able to follow those suggestions without getting entangled in the toils of the Hegelian trilogy of thesis, antithesis, and synthesis.[1]

The most popular argument against these socialist manipulations of the theory of primitive communism was formulated by Sir Henry Maine, himself one of the foremost exponents of the theory. His most famous work, *Ancient Law* (1873), began with an attack on *a priori* theorizing about the nature of rights and demanded the use of the 'Historical Method.' Dismissing all theories based on the concept of natural law and natural rights, he examined the evidence for primitive common ownership in India and elsewhere and concluded that 'private property, in the shape in which we know it, was chiefly formed by the gradual disentanglement of the separate rights of individuals from the blended rights of the community.'[2] Underlying his description of the historical development of rights was the assumption of the historical school that this development was progressive and good so long as it was an organic and evolutionary growth. Maine himself expressed the fundamental idea by his celebrated formula of the progress from status to contract, a progress in which individual freedom gained, since relations between men came more and more to rest on choice rather than on unalterable custom. In a later book he used these arguments to refute socialist contentions.

There are a few perhaps who may conceive a suspicion that, if property as we now understand it, that is, several property, be shown to be more modern not only than the human race . . . but than ownership in common . . . some advantage may be gained by those assailants of the institution itself whose doctrines from time to time cause a panic in modern Continental society. I do not myself think so. . . . Nobody is at liberty to attack several property and to say at the same time that he values civilization. The history of the two cannot be disentangled. Civilization is nothing more than the old order of the Aryan world, dissolved but perpetually reconstituting itself under a

[1] Marx's son-in-law, Paul Lafargue, developed many of the same arguments in *The Evolution of Property from Savagery to Civilization*, Chicago, 1910.

[2] Fifth edition, N.Y., 1875, p. 261.

vast variety of solvent influences, of which infinitely the most powerfu have been those which have, slowly, and in some parts of the world much less perfectly than others, substituted several property for collective ownership.[1]

The argument that private property is synonymous with civilization became a commonplace of conservative thought,[2] and Maine himself used it to combat democracy, whose most dangerous characteristic, he wrote, is its tendency to destroy the rights of property.[3]

A final chapter in the history of the theory of primitive communism—an attempt to deny the theory of the German *Mark*, to deny that the German invaders of England and France had been freemen whose communal system of holding land had been incorporated in the manorial system and was an essential part of feudalism—created a great stir in historical circles. Frederic Seebohm's *English Village Community* (1883), and numerous works of the French historian, Fustel de Coulanges (1830–1889), were not contributions to the debate between conservatives and radicals.[4] But the English historian W. J. Ashley noted that their work was nevertheless related to that debate: 'The history of the mark has served Mr. George as a basis for the contention that the common ownership of land is the only natural condition of things; to Sir Henry Maine it has suggested the precisely opposite conclusion that the whole movement of civilization has been from common ownership to private. Such arguments are alike worthless, if the mark never existed.'[5]

[1] *Village Communities* (1871), 3rd edition, London, 1913, pp. 229–30.

[2] Ludwig Felix, *Entwicklungsgeschichte des Eigenthums*, 4 vols., Leipzig, 1883–1903, is a ponderous documentation of Maine's thesis.

[3] Maine's political views are admirably expounded in B. E. Lippincott, *Victorian Critics of Democracy*, University of Minnesota, 1938.

[4] Fustel de Coulanges was more probably motivated by anti-German sentiments which led him to deny that the Germanic invaders had contributed anything to the development of institutions in France. He did, however, note that the theory of the *Mark* was cherished by men who admired the equalitarian political philosophy of Rousseau; *The Origin of Private Property in Land*, Ashley translation, London, 1892, pp. 150–3.

[5] Introduction to Fustel de Coulanges, *Origin of Property in Land*, p. xliv.

Modern historians have revived a modified theory of the *Mark*,[1] and modern anthropologists have found conclusive evidence that much primitive property was communal.[2] But the bewildering variety of ancient and primitive custom has convinced modern students of the impossibility of establishing a general pattern of development. No universal law of progress, apparently, forces human societies to adopt the same institutions of property at parallel stages of their history. Consequently, both the arguments of Sir Henry Maine and of his socialist opponents have been undermined, to the benefit of both political theory and the study of the past. For the question of what system of ownership will best serve the modern industrial world cannot be answered by a study of origins, by a reference to the practice of ancient Germans or modern Hottentots, and the student who sets out with that question in mind will certainly end as a corrupter of history and science.

But on another level the habit of thinking historically, and the realization of the importance of genetic investigation, from which the theories of historical right and primitive communism grew, has had a lasting effect on the theory of property. If modern anthropologists have found no one system of property among primitive peoples, they have found a bewildering variety of perfectly workable systems, some predominantly communal, some predominately individual. The result has been to undermine all those arguments in favour of any one pattern of ownership as being the only one consistent with 'human nature,' and hence necessary for social order and individual satisfaction. To the defenders of the private ownership of capital who repeat these arguments—most of them as old as Aristotle—the anthropologist points to societies where communal ownership and equality were

[1] But see the latest attack on that theory, with a short sketch of its origin and development, by Professor Carl Stephenson, 'The Problem of the Common Man in Europe,' *American Historical Review*, April 1946, and also Alfons Dopsch, *The Economic and Social Foundation of European Civilization*, translated by M. G. Beard and N. Marshall, London, 1937.

[2] L. T. Hobhouse, G. C. Wheeler, and M. Ginsburg, *The Material Culture and Social Institutions of the Simpler Peoples*, London, 1930.

the rule and observes that 'human nature did not rebel.'[1] A well-known modern authority has noted that the conclusions of anthropological study call

> for a recasting of many of our current arguments upholding our traditional institutions. These arguments are usually based on the impossibility of man's functioning without these particular traditional forms. Even very special traits come in for this kind of validation, such as the particular form of economic drive that arises under our particular system of property ownership. This is a remarkably special motivation and there are evidences that even in our generation it is being strongly modified. At any rate, we do not have to confuse the issue by discussing it as if it were a matter of biological survival values. Self-support is a motive our civilization has capitalized. If our economic structure changes so that this motive is no longer so potent a drive as it was in the era of the great frontier and expanding industrialism, there are many other motives that would be appropriate to a changed economic organization. Changes may be very disquieting, and involve great losses, but this is due to the difficulty of change itself, not to the fact that our age and country has hit upon the one possible motivation under which human life can be conducted. Change, we must remember, with all its difficulties, is inescapable.[2]

In the end, the study of primitive property patterns has redounded to the advantage of the critics of modern property rights. Socialists can no longer argue that common ownership is 'natural,' but they can show that it is feasible; the defenders of private ownership, on the other hand, have lost their once-powerful argument that individual property is 'natural,' but have gained no new argument to compensate for their loss.

Eventually, too, the theory of historical right turned out to be a better radical than conservative weapon. Wrought to combat the subversive implications of the theory of natural right, the theory that property rights are historical growths was conservative only so long as history grew slowly. Sir Henry Maine

[1] Ernest Beaglehole, *Property—A Study in Social Psychology*, London, 1931, p. 237. This study combats the theory that men are born with an 'acquisitive instinct.'

[2] Ruth Benedict, *Patterns of Culture*, Penguin edition, N.Y., 1946, pp. 32–3.

noted that Continentals were thrown into panic by socialist criticism, but he was impressed with the fact that traces of primitive forms of ownership persisted in England even in the nineteenth century, and he remarked that the rights of private property in land had as yet achieved their full development only in America.[1] To the proponents of historic right it seemed likely that private ownership, unless it was destroyed by revolutionaries who did not understand historic right, would be safe for some hundreds of years to come. But even before Maine wrote, the socialists had seized upon the idea that change is inevitable, that rights or customs cannot endure forever, and prophesied that major developments were just around the corner. In 1848 the *Communist Manifesto* noted that 'all property relations in the past have continually been subject to historical change' and proclaimed that the time was ripe for the transformation of private capital into common property.[2] In 1867 appeared the first volume of *Capital*, a work which made full use of the theory that capitalism and the property rights which go with it are ephemeral historical phenomena. In fact it might be argued that the distinctive characteristic of Marx's economic thought and socialist theory is that they are historically-minded; *Capital* is a work of history as well as a treatise on economics, and Marx was, along with Ranke and Sir Henry Maine, a devotee of the 'Historical Method.'

In the end the attempt to find a suitable substitute for the potentially subversive theory of property as a right of nature failed. Utility, convention, and historical right were all adopted by the critics of the existing order and used to undermine it. But the natural rights theory itself was almost submerged in the process. Only one substantial group remained faithful to the old liberal doctrine of property: the various socialist groups all used the principle that property belongs to the man that makes it. Their argument from that premise—that profits and rent are

[1] *Village Communities*, p. 228.

[2] In the English edition of 1888 Engels added a reference to the theory that primitive property had been common.

unjust deductions from the earnings of workmen—explains in part why the theory had been abandoned by conservative thinkers.[1]

English socialists were following in the footsteps of the radical agrarians of the late eighteenth century when they attacked private property in land as a violation of natural right. In the circumstances of the new age they broadened the attack to include the private ownership of capital, but the theory of right remained unchanged. Robert Owen and his followers, particularly John Gray and John Bray and William Thompson, were all defenders of the doctrine that labour is the only title to property.[2] Later generations of British socialists, including those of our own day, usually rejected the technical theory of exchange value which the classical economists had formulated and which Marx fashioned into a club to belabour capitalism; but they did not depart from the more general doctrine that property not acquired by labour is unjust.[3]

French socialists were also attracted to the theory of natural right, although their use of it was sometimes more critical than that of the early English radicals. The disciples of Saint-Simon were aware that 'property' was an ambiguous word which had been used to denote a multitude of human relationships not included in the Lockean theory. They criticized the proponents of

[1] As early as 1853, Richard Hildreth had pointed out that the Lockean theory, as interpreted by Adam Smith, was the original error from which socialism was derived. See Joseph Dorfman, *The Economic Mind in America*, Vol. II, N.Y., 1946, p. 710.

[2] Owen, *Report to the County of Lanark* (1821), in *A New View of Society and Other Writings*, Everyman edition; Gray, *A Lecture on Human Happiness* (1825) and *The Social System* (1831), and Bray, *Labour's Wrongs and Labour's Remedy* (1839), all reprinted by the London School of Economics, 1931; Thompson, *Labour Rewarded*, London, 1827; Max Beer, *A History of British Socialism*, Vol. I, London, 1929, pp. 188 ff., review the influence of the classical Lockean theory on British socialist thought. The Introduction and Bibliography by H. S. Foxwell for Anton Menger's *Right to the Whole Produce of Labour*, translated by M. E. Tanner, London, 1899, are valuable for the study of early English socialism.

[3] An explicit statement of this position is to be found in G. D. H. Cole's Introduction to the Everyman edition of Marx's *Capital*.

natural right as well as those of utility for not analysing in detail the forms of property characteristic of capitalism, and noted that the supposed conflict between utility and right was frequently used to prevent a reformation of property rights: rights which are admittedly unjust are defended as useful, and vice versa.[1] But the Saint-Simonian proposals, as they were elaborated by the followers of the master, followed in the natural rights tradition and were intended to reward men according to the value of the labour they performed, and prevent 'the riches created by labour' from being 'distributed according to birth and consumed for the most part by idleness.'[2]

Professor Dorfman has described in detail how the American followers of these early French and English radicals adopted the labour theory of property, as had their masters before them, and used it to attack large concentrations of landed and capitalist property.[3] Whatever their particular plans for Utopia might be, and whether they were Owenites, like W. Maclure, or Saint-Simonians, like Orestes Brownson, they all held that the product of labour belongs to the labourer. Likewise, the most famous of all native American radicalisms, Henry George's single tax scheme, rested squarely on the 'natural law' that 'as a man belongs to himself, so his labour when put in concrete form belongs to him.'[4] Because land was not created by labour it ought not to be owned individually: 'to affirm that a man can rightfully claim exclusive ownership in his own labour when embodied in material things, is to deny that any one can rightfully claim exclusive ownership in land.'[5] The Lockean theory was as firmly a part of American, as it was of English and French, radical tradition.

The fantastic Utopia designed by Charles Fourier, another French radical who was popular in America—Brook Farm, the

[1] *Doctrine de Saint-Simon* (1829), edited by C. Bouglé and Elie Halévy, Paris, 1924, 'Septième Séance' and 'Huitième Séance.' This is the official text of the Saint-Simonians.

[2] The same.

[3] Joseph Dorfman, *The Economic Mind in America*, Vol. II, especially pp. 638 ff.

[4] *Progress and Poverty*, Modern Library edition, p. 334.

[5] Pp. 336–7.

most famous of American community experiments, was in its last phase managed by disciples of Fourier—did not adhere to the Lockean formula. Talent and capital as well as labour were to receive their appropriate rewards.[1]

But the schemes of Fourier's younger contemporary, Pierre-Joseph Proudhon, were all firmly tied to the labour theory of right. He stated the theory at length in his most famous work, *Qu'est-ce que la Propriété* (1840),[2] and again in the posthumous *Théorie de la Propriété*.[3] He followed in the radical tradition by insisting that land, because it is not created by labour, ought to remain common property, and that capital, because it is created by labour, ought to belong to the labourers.[4] But Proudhon adhered to that tradition of radicalism of which the French Utopian socialists of the eighteenth century, the revolutionary conspirator, Babeuf, the American reformer, Edward Bellamy, and in our own day, George Bernard Shaw, are the most noted representatives, which insists upon absolute economic equality. Consequently he tried to prove that the labour theory of property, as well as all other theories, are in fact based upon the premise of equality: *Qu'est-ce que la Propriété* is still the most persuasive and fullest exposition of all the formal arguments in favour of an equal division of wealth. More important, however, than his various arguments for equality is his application of the labour theory to the system of modern production. That theory, he argued, leads to the conclusion that the total product of industry belongs to the producers. But in a system of social production, he added, no one man can say that he has produced a given thing: things are produced in common and belong to the whole body of labourers in common. For the concept of individual appropriation by the labour of each, modern society must substitute the concept

[1] See the article on Fourier (1772–1837) by E. S. Mason in *The Encyclopedia of the Social Sciences*. Fourier's American followers are described in the second volume of Dorfman, *The Economic Mind in America*.

[2] Vol. V of *Oeuvres Complètes*, edited by C. Bouglé and H. Moysset, Paris, 1926, pp. 192, 210, 212–18.

[3] Paris, 1866, pp. 95 ff.

[4] *Qu'est-ce que la Propriété*, pp. 192, 212, 215, 218.

of social appropriation by the labour of all.[1] Proudhon himself went on to argue that individuals ought to share equally in the social product; the later Marxian socialists adopted the principle of 'to each according to his needs' which was more or less equalitarian, according to the interpretation of the word 'needs.' But whatever principle of distribution the radical interpreters of natural right have chosen, they have all been aware, since the days of Proudhon, that the old individualistic interpretation of the Lockean theory cannot be applied to a modern system of industrial production. Property rights can no longer be defined as a relation between the individual and the material objects which he has created; they must be defined as social rights which determine the relations of the various groups of owners and non-owners to the system of production, and prescribe what each group's share of the social product shall be. The labour theory can still be used to assert that the people who do the work ought, as a class, to own what their labour creates; it no longer suffices to determine how the products of industry should be divided among individuals.

The Marxians followed in the footsteps of the early socialists in making full use of the labour theory of property; and like Proudhon, they thought of labour as the co-operative effort of a class rather than as the isolated effort of the individual. Marx himself used the labour theory in two different ways and for two different purposes. As the labour theory of value it was a technical economic doctrine designed to explain the mechanism of exchange: the exchange-value of an object is determined by the amount of 'socially necessary labour' required to produce it. This theory, which was an adaptation of the classical economists'

[1] Proudhon was not the first to see the difficulty of applying the labour theory in a system of social production. The English radical, Thomas Hodgskin, had wrestled with the difficulty in his pamphlet, *Labour Defended Against Capital*, London, 1825. It was inescapable whenever the radical interpretation of the Lockean theory was applied to an industrial society. Proudhon's practical proposals for reforming society varied: he was at different stages an anarchist opposed to all private ownership, a co-operator, and a proponent of a system of small proprietors.

theory of exchange-value, might be regarded simply as a scientific explanation of what happened in the market-place, quite apart from any considerations of what ought to happen or what was just. But Marx, of course, was aware that the theory had possible ethical connotations. He knew that the older socialist writers had combined the natural right theory of ownership with the economists' theory of value and argued that if labour alone created value, then labourers ought to be the sole owners of these values.[1] Marx's main argument was that capitalism would inevitably collapse for economic reasons; but in order to hasten that collapse he also used the argument that capitalism was an unjust system because it deprived men of the property which their labour created. In adopting this moral argument, Marx was following directly in the tradition of the radical interpreters of natural right.

Engels, who was suspicious of appeals to moral principle, explained that Marx did not base his communist conclusions upon this 'moral sentiment,' and that the labour theory itself was merely a product of an economic situation: 'if the moral sentiment of the mass regards an economic fact . . . as unjust, that proves that this fact itself is a survival; that other economic facts are established thanks to which the first has become insupportable, intolerable.'[2] But those passages in *Capital* which denounce capitalism for depriving workmen of the fruits of their labours demonstrate that Marx was not afraid of mixing morals and science. He quoted Luther's fiery denunciation of usury;[3] he spoke of capitalists as imposing 'tribute' upon the working class just as 'conquerors' 'robbed' the vanquished;[4] he ridiculed the contention that capitalism rewards men according to their work in an ironical paragraph which ended by comparing the workman to 'a man who is bringing his own skin to market, and has nothing to expect but a tanning';[5] and he made a satirical com-

[1] *The Poverty of Philosophy* (1847), translated by H. Quelch, Chicago, n.d., pp. 74 ff.; *The Critique of Political Economy* (1859), translated by N. I. Stone, Chicago, 1904, p. 71, n. 1.

[2] Preface to Marx's *Poverty of Philosophy*, pp. 14–15.

[3] Everyman edition, p. 186, n. 1.

[4] Pp. 639–40.

[5] Pp. 164–5.

parison between the theological legend of the Fall of Man—which explains why man must eat his bread in the sweat of his face—and the economic theory that capitalist profits are the reward of labour—which explains why some men need do nothing of the kind.[1]

In all these examples the fundamental assumption is that just ownership is derived from labour, and that capitalism violates this principle. Marx made the point directly in another passage describing how the 'law of private property' is transformed under capitalism into its direct opposite: 'At the outset, the right of ownership seemed to be based upon the owner's personal labour. . . . Nowadays, however, property appears to mean, as far as the capitalist is concerned, the right to appropriate others' unpaid labour, or the product thereof; and, as far as the worker is concerned, the impossibility of appropriating the product of his own labour.'[2] However much Engels might minimize its importance, the theory that property rights should be based on labour was fundamental in Marx's work.

But Marx was aware of the social nature of modern production and the relation of that fact to the labour theory of property. The expropriation of capital, according to the communist proposal, would transfer property from the capitalist class to the workmen whose labour had created it; but the new owners would hold their property in common, not as individuals. The problem of how the social product should be divided among individuals remained to be solved. Neither Marx nor his more practical followers were very much interested in solving hypothetical problems of this type and were critical of the Utopian prophets who blue-printed in detail the society of the future. But in the *Critique of the Gotha Programme* (1875), Marx laid down the bare formulas which he thought would be applied in the immediate and the distant futures, respectively. Rejecting equality

[1] P. 790.

[2] P. 641 and again on p. 848. The idea that the natural right theory of property applies to societies of 'small industry and petty trade,' but not to advanced industrial societies was elaborated by Thorstein Veblen, *The Theory of Business Enterprise*, N.Y., 1904, ch. viii.

as either an immediately attainable, or ultimately desirable, ideal, he proposed that in the first stage of socialist society, when rent, interest, and profit had been abolished as forms of private property, individuals should be rewarded according to the different value of their work, measured according to its duration and intensity, or quantity and quality; ultimately, he suggested, the principle of 'from each according to his ability, to each according to his needs' would regulate work and distribution.[1] Substantially these same formulas were repeated by Lenin and Stalin and were adopted in the programme of the Communist International in 1928; and in the Soviet Union, apparently, an attempt was made to set wages on the basis of the value of the labour performed.[2]

The Marxian theorists, then, have used the labour theory of ownership to condemn capitalism, to demand that capitalist property be owned in common by those whose co-operative labour produces it, and as a rule to regulate distribution in the initial stages of socialist organization. But they have also held to the view, expressed by Engels, that the natural right theory is not a principle of absolute justice, but an historical formulation of economic demands growing out of particular economic institutions. With the passing of those institutions, they predict, the famous principle of 'securing to each the fruits of his labour' will be replaced by the more generous rule of 'to each according to his needs.' Despite some isolated variations, such as Shaw's insistence, in *The Intelligent Woman's Guide to Socialism and Capitalism*, that a true socialist society would enforce absolute equality of income, most modern socialists have followed the

[1] *Critique of the Gotha Programme*, N.Y., 1938, pp. 8–10.

[2] Lenin's remarks are in his *State and Revolution* (1917); they are reprinted in the edition of the *Critique of the Gotha Programme* quoted above. For Stalin, see Report to the Seventeenth Congress of the Communist Party, *Stalin Reports on the Soviet Union*, London, 1934. A translation of the *Programme of the Communist International* was issued in London in 1929. For the wage system ot the Soviet Union see A. Bergson, *The Structure of Soviet Wages*, Cambridge, Mass., 1944. An illuminating short discussion of the Marxist theory of distribution is to be found in John Strachey's *Theory and Practice of Socialism*, London, 1936.

Marxian doctrine that personal property ought to be based on labour in the immediate future, and on need in the ideal society of the more distant future.[1] Modern socialists are at once the foremost exponents of the natural right theory, as an argument which meets the defenders of capitalism on their own grounds, and the foremost exponents of a theory of distribution based on need, which dispenses with the idea of natural right.

[1] H. N. Brailsford's *Socialism for Today*, London, 1925, which is more typical of English socialist thought than Shaw's book, adopts the Marxian position. The definitions of 'need,' however, vary widely and can be debated at length by those who wish to solve all the problems of the future in advance. Compare the discussion of 'need' in H. J. Laski, *Grammar of Politics*, New Haven, 1925, ch. 5.

CHAPTER TEN

☆

Conclusion

The theory of the natural right of property achieved its classical statement as a defence of the early capitalist societies of the seventeenth, eighteenth, and nineteenth centuries. But even then, as Locke saw, it was in fact subversive of the legal rights of landlords and other important groups of owners, and in the modern capitalist world none of the important forms of property can be linked to the natural right theory. Analyses of the dominant form of property in the United States, the giant corporation in which labour, ownership, and management have been divorced from one another so that the basic concept of 'private property' no longer applies, have made it impossible to defend modern property rights in the traditional Lockean terms.[1] The socialist critics of capitalism, who were once attacked with the natural right theory, have made that theory their own.

Here and there attempts are still made to defend the rights of modern owners by repeating the labour theory. One of the last upholders of the conservative interpretation of the natural right of property was the Church of Rome. That the Church should accept a doctrine born of the Enlightenment and promulgated by the French Revolution is surprising. But apparently it was the fear of socialism which led Leo XIII to state in the famous Encyclical *Rerum Novarum* (1891) that each man 'makes his own that portion of nature's field which he cultivates—that portion on which he leaves, as it were, the impress of his individuality; and it cannot but be just that he should possess that portion as his very own, and have a right to hold it without any one being justified in violating that right. . . . Hence it is clear that the

[1] The classic analysis is *The Modern Corporation and Private Property*, by A. A. Berle, Jr., and G. G. Means, N.Y., 1932. A recent study is David Lynch, *The Concentration of Economic Power*, N.Y., 1946.

main tenet of Socialism, community of goods, must be utterly rejected, since it . . . is directly contrary to the natural rights of mankind.' The Lockean doctrine in this, its simplest form, had little relation to the facts of economic life in 1891, but it nevertheless stood as the official doctrine of the Church until 1931. In that year Pius XI's Encyclical *Quadragesimo Anno* recognized that corporate property and monopoly had replaced the regime of free competition to which the earlier Encyclical had applied. Pius XI did not accuse the socialists of wishing to violate the natural right of property: he omitted any reference to the argument from natural right. In its place he put the popular modern argument that socialism is a threat to liberty: 'Society . . . as socialism conceives it, is impossible and unthinkable without the use of obviously excessive compulsion.'

From time to time the writers of Constitutions repeat the traditional phrases; the New Jersey Constitution of 1947 includes property among the natural rights listed in its first article. But the New Jersey Solons were behind the times. The most famous constitutional document made after the First World War, the Weimar Constitution of the German Republic, made no reference to the natural right of property and gave the state full power to confiscate property without compensation. The 1946 Constitution of the French Republic, although its Preamble 'reaffirms . . . the Declaration of Rights of 1789,' makes no mention of compensation in asserting that 'all property and all enterprises that now have, or subsequently shall have, the character of a national public service or a monopoly in fact, must become the property of the community.'[1] The only important modern constitution which defines at length the right of property is the Soviet Constitution of 1936 which sets forth the socialist interpretation of the classical theory—the net product of labour shall belong, collectively, to those who labour; individuals

[1] The proposed constitution rejected on May 5, 1946, was even more explicit in rejecting the natural right theory: it copied, almost in his words, the social theory of property proposed by Robespierre; above, p. 229. The text was printed in the *New York Times*, April 23, 1946.

shall be rewarded according to the quantity and quality of their work; and the holding of personal property acquired by labour is a right guaranteed by law.[1]

The liberal critics of capitalism, men who are historically the direct heirs of the natural rights tradition, have also abandoned the classical theory of property and have adopted the utilitarian arguments for a more equal distribution of wealth. Their aim is freedom from want, a distribution which will increase the general welfare rather than reward each man fairly according to some abstract and complex rule of natural justice. Or, if they speak of right, they are likely to mean the right of subsistence, the right to a decent standard of living.[2] Occasionally, however, non-socialist critics do use the natural right theory to attack modern capitalism, to demonstrate that it has departed from its own standard of right, even though they do not follow the socialists in adopting that standard as their own.[3]

Finally, in America, the classical theory of natural right is so deeply embedded in popular thought that the spokesmen of big business sometimes repeat the familiar phrases, although their manner of doing so often betrays that they are not unaware of the contradictions between the classical doctrine and the institutions which they uphold. The theorists employed by the National Association of Manufacturers to write *The American Individual Enterprise System* assert again and again that each man has a right to that which his own labour creates. But each time they qualify the classical theory: each man owns by right what he

[1] Chapters i and x, and the Summary by Beatrice and Sidney Webb, in the Appendix to Vol. I of *Soviet Communism*, 2nd edition, London, 1937.

[2] The right of subsistence as a liberal substitute for the labour theory was proclaimed by Anton Menger, *The Right to the Whole Produce of Labour*, translated by M. E. Tanner, Introduction by H. S. Foxwell, London, 1899. The German edition appeared in 1886. Menger wanted to discard the labour theory because (1) it is socialist and revolutionary, and (2) it is difficult to apply in practice in a system of social production.

[3] For example, in *Christianity and Property*, edited by Joseph Fletcher, Philadelphia, 1947, pp. 196–8. This volume is a more recent and more forceful statement of the Anglican view of economic justice previously developed in *Property, Its Duties and Rights*, discussed above, p. 260.

'creates or *acquires*,' 'by his labour' or by his '*efforts*' and '*activities*,' 'either alone or *in co-operation with others*.'[1] The qualifications are doubtless intended to adapt the theory in the light of modern facts. But they destroy whatever logical rigour the theory has and prove its uselessness as a defence of the modern capitalist system. In the end, the spokesmen for the National Association of Manufacturers do not emphasize the argument from natural right, but turn to the most popular of all modern arguments against socialism, the argument used by Pius XI in the Encyclical of 1931, the argument which appears in every contemporary American magazine and newspaper, the argument from liberty. Today we hear a great deal about the suppression of civil liberty in socialist countries, but nothing about their violation of the natural rights of property. Modern property, the conservative agrees, cannot be justified by the outmoded theory of natural right; but private ownership, he adds, is necessary for liberty, and free men should prefer that liberty to the security which socialism offers.[2]

Today the natural right theory of property, restated to fit a complex system of co-operative production, is the officially-recognized rule for the distribution of wealth in those parts of the world where socialism has prevailed. In other lands, where that theory was originally developed, and where capitalist economic institutions predominate, the natural right theory lingers on as a popular tradition, but has been rejected by the more thoughtful defenders of the existing system. In general, theories of formal right, especially if they profess to be based on the immutable laws of nature, are not likely to be popular in this historically-minded age. Nevertheless, men are still fascinated by the theory that just ownership is based on labour. The natural right of property is not yet a dead idea, and its future is clearly linked with the outcome of that struggle between rival social systems which dominates the thinking and acting of our age.

[1] *The American Individual Enterprise System*, by the Economic Principles Commission of the National Association of Manufacturers, 2 vols., N.Y. and London, 1946, Vol. I, pp. 5, 7, and 25, and Vol. II, p. 695. Italics are mine.

[2] This argument can be found in several widely-read modern works. See, for example, Friedrich Hayek, *The Road to Serfdom*, 1944.

Index

THE END